INSIDE CROWN COURT

Personal experiences and questions of legitimacy

Jessica Jacobson, Gillian Hunter and Amy Kirby

First published in Great Britain in 2015 by

Policy Press
University of Bristol
1-9 Old Park Hill
Bristol BS2 8BB
UK
t: +44 (0)117 954 5940
e: pp-info@bristol.ac.uk
www.policypress.co.uk

North American office:
Policy Press
c/o The University of Chicago Press
1427 East 60th Street
Chicago, IL 60637, USA
t: +1 773 702 7700
f: +1 773-702-9756
e:sales@press.uchicago.edu
www.press.uchicago.edu

British Library Cataloguing in Publication Data
A catalogue record for this book is available from the British Library

Library of Congress Cataloging-in-Publication Data
A catalog record for this book has been requested

ISBN 978 1 44731 705 0 hardcover

Cover design by Policy Press
Front cover: illustrations kindly supplied by Christopher
Tomlinson
Printed and bound in Great Britain by CPI Group (UK) Ltd,
Croydon, CR0 4YY
Policy Press uses environmentally responsible print partners

MIX
Paper from
responsible sources
FSC® C013604

Epigraph

When Gregory says, 'Are they guilty?' he means, 'Did they do it?' But when he [Cromwell] says, 'Are they guilty?' he means, 'Did the court find them so?' The lawyer's world is entire unto itself, the human pared away. It was a triumph, in a small way, to unknot the entanglement of thighs and tongues, to take that mass of heaving flesh and smooth it on to white paper: as the body, after climax, lies back on white linen.

Thomas Cromwell reflecting on the process of having Anne Boleyn's alleged lovers convicted of treason; from Hilary Mantel's *Bring Up the Bodies* (Fourth Estate, 2012).

****

Most nights her dad left the house again after dinner to meet with poor people he was defending in court for little or no money … In tenth grade, for a school project, Patty sat in on two trials that her dad was part of. One was a case against an unemployed Yonkers man who drank too much on Puerto Rican Day, went looking for his wife's brother, intending to cut him with a knife, but couldn't find him and instead cut up a stranger in a bar. Not just her dad but the judge and even the prosecutor seemed amused by the defendant's haplessness and stupidity. They kept exchanging little not-quite-winks. As if misery and disfigurement and jail time were all just a lower-class side-show designed to perk up their otherwise boring day.

On the train ride home, Patty asked her dad whose side he was on.

'Ha, good question,' he answered. 'You have to understand, my client is a liar. The victim is a liar. And the bar owner is a liar. They're all liars. Of course, my client is entitled to a vigorous defense. But you have to try to serve justice, too. Sometimes the PA and the judge and I are working together as much as the PA is working with the victim or I'm working with the defendant. You've heard of our adversarial system of justice?'

'Yes.'

'Well. Sometimes the PA and the judge and I all have the same adversary. We try to sort out the facts and avoid a miscarriage. Although don't, uh. Don't put that in your paper.'

Teenager Patty's view of the work of her defence attorney father; from Jonathan Franzen's *Freedom* (Harper Collins, 2010).

Contents

List of figures and tables

Figures

Tables

Acknowledgements

There are many people who helped us with this work. We must thank Her Majesty's Courts and Tribunals Service for granting permission to conduct research in the Crown Court and the Lord Chief Justice, Lord Thomas (then President of the Queen's Bench Division), for his support for the study. Thanks are due also to the resident judges of the two Crown Courts featured in this book, the national charity Victim Support, the National Offender Management Service and the Crown Prosecution Service for helping us gain access to victims, witnesses, defendants and legal professionals to interview for this study. We are especially indebted to the 'court users' – the victims, witnesses and defendants – who agreed to talk to us, in great detail, about their often upsetting and stressful experiences of Crown Court and the circumstances which occasioned their visits there. We would also like to thank all the professionals and practitioners who participated in research interviews.

We are grateful to Professor Mike Hough and Dr Tim McSweeney at the Institute for Criminal Policy Research for their contribution to the development of this study. We wish to thank a number of people who assisted us with the preparation of this manuscript; they include Professor Penny Darbyshire, Gemma Davies, Dr Deborah Golden, and Victoria Pittman, our editor at Policy Press – all of whom offered their expertise and helpful comments on earlier drafts. Thanks are also due to Christopher Tomlinson for producing the colour illustrations for the book cover and Sufi Gaffar for the graphics in Chapter 2.

We gratefully acknowledge the support of the Economic and Social Research Council, who funded the study on which this book is based.

ONE

Introduction

The Crown Court deals with under 10% of criminal cases that come before the courts in England and Wales: the vast majority of cases both begin and end in magistrates' courts. Nevertheless, the centrality of the Crown Court to the criminal justice system is clear: its daily business is the prosecution and sentencing of the most serious forms of criminality.

The Crown Court also occupies a significant place in the public imagination. The 'courtroom drama' is a staple of popular entertainment, reflecting the fact that the real-life happenings in court are indeed a drama. They are dramatic because they are focused on extreme, and often harrowing and tragic, events in otherwise ordinary lives. But the drama of the courtroom inheres also in its very structures and processes: in the adversarial system which pits alleged offender against alleged victim; in the ritual and formality of the wigs, the gowns and the archaic modes of speech and interaction; and in the performances of barristers seeking to impress judges and juries with their eloquence, passion and sophisticated understanding of the intricacies of the law.

The study

This book presents the findings of a 20-month qualitative study of the Crown Court, funded by the Economic and Social Research Council.[1] Through extensive interviews with victims, witnesses and defendants; interviews with professionals and practitioners who work in or around court; and many hours of observation of court hearings, the study set out to address three broad questions:

- What are the essential features of the Crown Court process, as it is experienced by victims, witnesses and defendants?
- What is the nature of the interplay between the different players – including legal professionals and members of the public – in the courtroom?
- To what extent do victims, witnesses and defendants regard court processes and outcomes as fair and legitimate?

1

The study emerged out of our interest in a number of overlapping themes. These include the factors that support or undermine access to justice for members of the public, both those accused of committing crime and those who are victims or witnesses of crime. Related to this theme is the question of whether individuals who come to court in any capacity feel that they are actively engaged in the process, and the extent to which any barriers to defendants' 'effective participation' in court proceedings compromise their right to a fair trial. Whether and how experiences of court contribute to a sense of the legitimacy of the court process and, more broadly, to trust in the justice system is another key theme. We were also interested in what is common to, as well as what differentiates, the experiences of victims, witnesses and defendants; and whether evidence of commonalities has any bearing on policy debate about the 'rights' of different groups of court users.

By providing some answers to the three questions listed above, this book is intended to advance academic knowledge and understanding of court processes – in relation to the Crown Court in particular, but also, beyond this, to the criminal courts more generally. The issues addressed by the book also have many implications for criminal justice policy development, and for practice within the courts. And while the focus is on the experiences of adult victims, witnesses and defendants, many of our findings and conclusions will be of interest also to those concerned with the treatment of children in court. Further, given that crime, punishment and the criminal courts are matters of abiding concern to the general public, we hope that this book will stimulate wider public interest and debate. The subject of the book is the Crown Court of England and Wales; nevertheless, the issues dealt with here are by no means parochial: our analysis is certainly applicable to other common law jurisdictions, and can also help to inform comparisons between common and civil law systems.

Before we proceed with a brief account of the background to the study and its methods, a short note on definitions is required. The main focus of the study is on three sub-groups of the public in the Crown Court, described as 'victims', 'witnesses' and 'defendants'. These three terms can all be defined in a variety of ways, but in the specific context of this research are used as follows:

- 'Victims' refers to individuals who have attended the Crown Court to give evidence in relation to alleged offences of which they, according to their own accounts, are the victims. We avoid use of the technical term 'complainant' in referring to this group of court users as it does not accord with how the individuals define themselves.

- 'Witnesses' refers to members of the public who have attended the Crown Court to give evidence for the prosecution in relation to alleged offences which they claim to have witnessed; this use of the term thus excludes victims who are also witnesses (for whom, as above, we use the term 'victim'), witnesses for the defence, and professional or expert witnesses who have been required to give evidence in a professional capacity.
- 'Defendants' refers to individuals who have attended the Crown Court for trial (in cases where they have pleaded not guilty) and/ or for sentencing (following a guilty verdict or guilty plea).

The generic term 'court user' is used here to refer to members of all three of the above groups, and individuals closely related to them who have attended court in a supportive role.

Background

Despite their centrality to the justice process, the criminal courts in England and Wales have been relatively under-researched – by both academic and policy researchers – compared to other parts of the criminal justice system such as the police service and prisons. In particular, little is known about how members of the public who attend court as victims, witnesses and defendants make sense of their courtroom experiences. Nevertheless, there is a substantial quantity of prior empirical and theoretical research that has helped to shape this study and to inform the conclusions drawn. It is not our intention here to provide a thorough overview of relevant prior research (much of which will be cited over the pages that follow); but we will briefly outline the four main strands of work on which we have drawn. These are: government research on court user experiences; prior ethnographic studies of the criminal courts of England and Wales; research and commentary relating to the 'victims' rights' movement in Britain and elsewhere; and the growing body of academic and policy-related research on 'procedural justice'.

Government surveys of court user experiences

The years 2005–10 saw some limited government research into the experiences of court users; research that has since fallen victim to cuts in public sector spending. The Ministry of Justice commissioned the Witness and Victim Experience Survey (WAVES): a nationally representative survey conducted annually from 2005/6 until it was discontinued in 2010. The survey explored victims' and witnesses' experiences of all aspects of the criminal justice system, the services they received, and their satisfaction with different aspects of the system. The headline finding of the survey was a high level of satisfaction (84% according to the most recent survey) with overall contact with the criminal justice system among victims and witnesses (Franklyn, 2012). Unsurprisingly, victims and witnesses were more likely to be satisfied where their case had resulted in a conviction. The strongest influences on victims' and witnesses' willingness to engage again with the criminal justice system were satisfaction with their contact with the system and the outcome of the case. When those who had attended court were asked if they had had concerns or worries about doing so, the issues most frequently raised by respondents were: coming into contact with the defendant and his or her family; being cross-examined; taking time off work; and the expenses incurred.

A small-scale piece of qualitative research involving a sub-sample of crime victims drawn from the large WAVES sample (Commissioner for Victims and Witnesses, 2011) explored in greater depth victims' relationships with the criminal justice process and their views on sentencing. Reflecting the wider WAVES survey findings, most victims reported being satisfied with how they were treated at court and the support they were offered. For some, however, this general satisfaction coexisted with a dissatisfaction with the outcome of the court case – for example, where the sentence was not perceived as proportionate to the harm suffered by the victim, or where the sentence was believed to be poorly enforced. Some also felt that financial compensation from the offender potentially had both a symbolic and practical role to play in terms of restitution for the harm caused by the offending.

For four years from 2007, HM Courts Service (now HM Courts and Tribunals Service) conducted a survey of court users in both civil and criminal jurisdictions. The survey was administered both to professionals (such as lawyers and police officers) and to lay court users (including victims, witness, defendants, family members, and those appearing as parties in civil cases) as they exited court buildings. It monitored the satisfaction of the whole range of court users and sought to identify areas for improvement. This survey again paints a broad brush picture of general satisfaction with court experiences, although professional court users were more likely to be satisfied than public users, and while civil courts recorded the highest levels of satisfaction, magistrates' courts recorded the lowest. The strongest drivers of overall satisfaction were the time spent waiting for the case to be dealt with, being treated fairly and sensitively by court staff, staff being able to respond promptly to queries, and staff keeping users informed of reasons for delays (Ministry of Justice, 2010).

Ethnographic studies of the criminal courts

This study has been influenced by several prior ethnographic studies of the criminal courts in England and Wales, both in terms of its design and in the elaboration of its findings. Two of these were carried out in the early 1970s: Bottoms and McClean's *Defendants in the criminal process* (1976) and Carlen's *Magistrates' justice* (1976a; see also Carlen, 1976b). Bottoms and McClean conducted observations and interviews in Sheffield Magistrates' and Crown Courts, through which they examined defendants' experiences and decision-making in relation to plea, trial venue, legal representation, bail and appeal. Their work combines attention to the detail of interactions within the courtroom and defendants' responses to prosecution, with a higher-level analysis of the key components of the criminal justice process. They characterise this process as 'liberal bureaucratic' in form, and argue that, in the interests of ensuring that the administration of justice on a day-to-day basis is relatively smooth, it imposes significant constraints on defendants' capacity to exercise their legal rights. Carlen's focus was on the 'production of justice' in magistrates' courts, in several of which she carried out observational research and interviews with practitioners. Her resultant book details how the 'appearance of legitimated social control' is belied by the realities of courtroom interactions and social relations, through which 'mechanisms of repressive social control ... lurk behind, and render absurd, the judicial rhetoric of the possibility of an absolute social justice' (1976a, p 128).

While much has changed since the 1970s in terms of the social, economic and political worlds within which the criminal courts operate, and even in terms of certain legal processes and structures (as just one example of this, the Crown Prosecution Service (CPS) was not established as the principal prosecuting authority for England and Wales until 1986), much of what Bottoms and McClean and Carlen describe as the patterns of social interaction and surrounding ritual of the courtroom is highly recognisable today.

Paul Rock's 1993 volume on *The social world of an English Crown Court* presents the results of a study conducted in 1989 to 1990 in a single court: Wood Green Crown Court in north London. Rock sought to obtain a detailed understanding of the court 'as a complex social world' (1993, p 2); and his work focused in particular on how this world was experienced by victims and other prosecution witnesses, and the ways in which these experiences were structured by time, space and conflict. As with the works of Bottoms and McClean and Carlen, many aspects of his account of Crown Court structures and processes remain highly resonant today and are reflected in our own findings. The ceremonial and highly stylised features of the adversarial trial, described in the pages of Rock's volume, have hardly changed; and nor have the essential features of the relationship of the 'insiders' (the professionals) with the 'outsiders' (the public) at court – the social divide between whom, Rock states, is built into the very physical structure of the courthouse. What has changed markedly since the time of Rock's fieldwork is that a demonstration witness support project which he observed being introduced at Wood Green Crown Court is now established, as the Witness Service run by Victim Support, in every Crown and magistrates' court across the country.[2] This is one important manifestation of a broader policy shift away from the situation observed by Rock whereby '[w]itnesses were little considered: they were unproblematic and taken for granted, the "fodder of the criminal courts"'; a situation which prevailed as late as the mid-1980s (1993, p 288). This is not to suggest, however, that witnesses' *feelings* of marginalisation, which are vividly described by Rock – 'They are confused and confusing, often distressed, a threat to the insiders who will not and cannot comfort them' (1993, p 283) – are necessarily a thing of the past.

Nigel Fielding's book, *Courting violence: Offences against the person cases in court* (2006) reports on the handling of cases of physical violence by the Crown Court. Fielding was interested in how violence is depicted and defined within the criminal courts, against the backdrop of broader social and cultural conceptions of violence and its harms. In addressing this theme, Fielding recognised that the role of the courts in dealing with violence – a commonplace phenomenon in day-to-day life, which only in certain exceptional circumstances becomes the subject of a criminal trial – is 'as much about the symbolic as the instrumental' (2006, p 1). On the basis of observations and interviews conducted at three Crown Courts, Fielding provides detailed and vivid descriptions of how cases unfold in the courtroom, with a particular focus on the interactions between the various participants. The book conveys, for example, the 'rawness' of exchanges between lay witnesses and lawyers about events that have caused considerable trauma but can only be discussed according to the strict 'conventions for giving evidence' and within the restrictions of the witness role; the anxiety and upset that this potentially causes victims and the limited scope that professionals have to allay victims' distress; the exclusion of lay participants from much of what is said in court because of the distinctiveness of the 'language of law'; and the artificiality and ritual aspects of the court proceedings which help to sustain their sense of separateness from the 'messy conflictual realities' of ordinary life. Another theme in Fielding's work, which has become central to our own study, is the very large extent to which lay court users appear to accept that court proceedings are legitimate; albeit this sense of legitimacy is 'implicit' in the sense that it 'goes unremarked', and is essentially a matter of court users' acceptance that this is 'the way society does this kind of business' (2006, p 7).

Darbyshire's *Sitting in judgment: The working lives of judges* (2011) provides an account – based on observational research and interviews – of the backgrounds, attitudes, approach and work of the modern judiciary, and also describes the courts, of all kinds, in which they sit. Her aim was to provide an account of 'real judges ... in their working world' that could be contrasted with the (highly negative, for the most part) images of the judiciary which prevail in the media (2011, p 43). Darbyshire's work provides insight into the 'working personality' projected by judges at court which, she argues, prioritises the qualities of 'patience, fairness, sympathy, good listening skills, decisiveness and courtesy' and is far at odds with the image of judges as 'out of touch' (2011, p 448). Her account of the work of the judiciary in the Crown Court stresses the practical difficulties and complexities associated with getting criminal cases to court and ensuring that the cases progress once they get there; the resultant 'fragility' of the judicial process and associated 'massive waste of public money' is something that she regards as likely to worsen over the years to come as increasingly under-resourced agencies continue to struggle to cope with their workloads (2011, p 210).[3]

Victims' rights

The latter half of the twentieth century and, particularly in England and Wales, the early part of this century have seen the development of a broad movement focused on the 'rights' of crime victims, alongside an increased political focus on victims, in efforts to counter concerns that they have traditionally been marginalised by a criminal justice system perceived as placing more weight on the defendants' rights. At the same time, a substantial research literature has evolved on the subject of victims and victims' rights.

It is widely acknowledged within the literature that victims of crime have traditionally been 'bit players' (Shapland and Hall, 2010, p 163) and 'normative outsiders' (Doak, 2008, p 138) in the criminal justice process. The place for victims within the court setting is said to be particularly restricted, and there are concerns that they are merely 'reincarnated' as witnesses rather than being given a more complete role throughout proceedings (Shapland and Hall, 2010, p 166). The victims' rights movement emerged in the United States in the mid-twentieth century before spreading across the Atlantic to the United Kingdom, where a notable development was the creation of the national charity Victim Support in 1972. A political emphasis on the victim and calls to 'rebalance' the criminal justice system in favour of victims became more evident during the Blair administration (see, for example, Home Office, 2002) at the turn of the twenty-first century (Shapland and Hall, 2010; Tonry, 2010, Hoyle, 2012; Walklate, 2012). Thereafter, government continued to stress its commitment to ending what was described as the 'poor relation' status of victims in the criminal justice system (Commissioner for Victims and Witnesses, 2010, p 2).

The past 20 years have seen the introduction of various provisions aimed at supporting victims and witnesses within the court process in England and Wales; including the establishment of the Witness Service in the criminal courts – the piloting of which was documented by Rock (1993), as noted earlier – and the introduction of 'special measures' to help vulnerable and intimidated victims and witnesses to give evidence in trials. (Some of the details of this provision, and research findings on its impact, will be discussed in Chapter Two.) However, debate has emerged around whether providing victims with increased access to *services* such as these is enough when the victims' (and other witnesses') rights relating to *procedure* remain unchanged (Doak, 2008; Manikis, 2012). There are several examples of 'procedural rights' that victims do not have, such as the power to influence sentencing and parole decisions (Manikis, 2012). Perhaps the key procedural right that is lacking for victims and witnesses called to give evidence is access to their own legal representation, which reflects the fact that offences are prosecuted on behalf of the Crown, rather than the victim. Within the Crown Court this creates a 'minimalist cast' of the judge, prosecution and defendant, whereby the victim only has a limited form of expression (Shapland and Hall, 2010, p 63). Walklate (2012, p 115) notes that the policy emphasis on 'victims' rights' belies the fact that victims 'do not have a general legal claim to rights except in very particular circumstances', reflecting the 'deeply-embedded conceptual failure' at the heart of the aim of 'rebalancing' the criminal justice system in favour of the victim.

Doak (2008, p 1) has pointed to the lack of clarity of public discourse about 'victims' rights':

The phrase 'victims' rights' has now entered into widespread usage among politicians, academics and the media. Unfortunately, the terminology tends to be deployed in an imprecise manner, and is often resorted to as a form of emotive polemic. Consequently, discussions round the idea of 'victims' rights' frequently produce more heat than light, and rarely succeed in eliciting the precise scope or legal nature of such 'rights' or the extent to which construction of such rights can be realised within the normative and structural framework of the existing criminal justice system.

Commentators have observed that the difficulty of delineating the nature and scope of 'victims' rights' can be clearly illustrated with reference to the functions of Victim Personal Statements, which were introduced (by Home Office Circular 35/2001) in 2001. These statements give victims the opportunity to describe the physical, emotional and financial consequences of the offence committed against them. The police are responsible for obtaining the Victim Personal Statement, which usually occurs at the same time that the witness statement is taken. Victims are entitled to request that, if there is a conviction, they read out the statement at the sentencing hearing, or that the prosecutor reads it out, or that a recording of the statement is played to the court. Whether or not the statement is read out or played to the court, it helps to clarify the extent of harm caused by the offence, and hence is likely to be taken into account by the judge as sentence is passed. However, the Victim Personal Statement does *not* allow the victim directly to influence the judge's decision on sentence: it is explicitly stated among the relevant provisions in the *Code of Practice for Victims of Crime* that 'you may not express your opinion on the sentence or punishment the suspect should receive as this is for the court to decide' (Ministry of Justice, 2013a, p 16).

The intention behind the introduction of Victim Personal Statements was to provide a service to victims, at the heart of which is the idea of their being given 'a *voice* in the criminal justice process' (Ministry of Justice, 2013a, p 16); but confusion about this function rapidly emerged. Some victims came to believe that Victim Personal Statements did in fact give them the opportunity to say what sentence should be passed; and inconsistent guidance from the government and misleading media coverage added to these misunderstandings (Reeves and Dunn, 2010). It would thus appear that the critical distinction between, on the one hand, victims' accounts of the full impact of the offence on them (which *should* be taken into account in sentencing) and, on the other hand, victims' opinions on sentence (which should *not* be taken into account by the sentencer) has not always been made clear to victims or, indeed, has not necessarily been entirely appreciated by the professionals. Lack of clarity about the purpose of Victim Personal Statements and related provisions is present among victims in various jurisdictions, and Roberts and Manikis (2011) noted that, a decade after their inception in England and Wales, some victims were still perceiving them as providing an opportunity to express their views on sentencing.

Another perennial issue in the debate surrounding victims' rights is whether the provision of enhanced rights and services to victims is automatically to the detriment of defendants. Government attempts to 'rebalance' the criminal justice system came with the implication that until this point victims' rights had been subservient to those of defendants (see Tonry, 2010 for a full overview). The opposing concern is that increased rights for victims could only come at the expense of the rights for the defendant within the adversarial process. This presumption of a 'zero-sum' relationship between victims' and defendants' rights has a populist edge, and some scholars (for example, Doak, 2008; Reeves and Dunn, 2010; Tonry, 2010) have argued that efforts to 'rebalance' the system in favour of the victim have been used as a cloak to disguise policies that are designed to treat offenders more punitively. From this perspective, it is claimed that – contrary to the rhetoric of some politicians and government documents – improved provision and the enhancement of rights for both victims and defendants can in fact be provided without resulting in a loss to either side, especially since the categories of 'victim' and 'defendant' are not mutually exclusive, but overlap in various respects:

> It does not necessarily follow that the interests of victims and offenders will always conflict. It is difficult to see how some rights, such as the provision of information, support at court, or the provision of good facilities, impact upon defendants at all. Indeed, the two groups share much in common, including similar socio-economic characteristics. It is well established that there are a number of scenarios in which the victim and the defendant will share mutual concerns, such as the desire for a prompt and efficient trial process and to be provided with information about procedure. (Doak, 2008, p 247)

Procedural justice

The extent to which court users regard the court process as legitimate, and what any such sense of legitimacy is based on, are questions that this study has sought to address, with help – in part – from the insights offered by the growing body of research on 'procedural justice'. This research has been largely associated with the work of Tom Tyler and colleagues in the United States,[4] but over the past few years has emerged as a prominent theme within criminal justice research in the United Kingdom and elsewhere in Europe.[5] Procedural justice theory is concerned with the factors which determine whether or not criminal justice institutions are perceived as legitimate and which, more widely, promote confidence in justice. The concept of legitimacy – which has long been a central concern to political philosophers, but 'has only recently re-emerged as a key [concept] in Anglophone criminology' (Hough et al, 2013b, p 246) – is thus central to the work of these scholars. While policing is the focus of much of the empirical research undertaken by procedural justice theorists, other elements of the criminal justice system, including the criminal courts, have also been widely explored.

In the broadest terms, legitimacy can be defined as the 'psychological property of an authority, institution, or social arrangement that leads those connected to it to believe that it is appropriate, proper, and just' (Tyler, 2006b, p 375). With respect to criminal justice, 'legitimacy resides most fundamentally in the recognition of the criminal justice system's right to exist, and in the justification of its authority in determining the law, governing through the use of coercive force, and punishing those who act illegally' (Jackson et al, 2011b, p 271). The critical importance of legitimacy to state authorities is that they can more easily influence the behaviour of people who 'feel obligated to defer to the decisions made by leaders with legitimacy and the policies and rules they create' than those whose obedience is achieved only through the use of coercion and/or incentives (Tyler, 2006b, p 393). From this perspective, the legitimacy of criminal justice institutions and processes can be understood in terms of the two public goods it yields: first, public compliance with the rule of law; secondly, public co-operation with the criminal justice agencies. Conversely, where legitimacy is eroded, the consequences include 'withdrawal of cooperation with authorities, and defiance and rejection of legal and social norms' (Fagan, 2008, p 136).

Moreover, as noted by Hough et al (2010, p 209), procedural justice theory provides insight into the means by which confidence in justice, and compliance and co-operation, can be promoted across the whole of a population – that is, not just among those individuals who would anyway seem to have a general inclination to follow the law, but also among those 'whose commitment to the rule of law is more tentative'. As noted in the above brief discussion of the victims' rights movements, much public and political debate on policing and criminal justice policy is based around simplistic notions of offenders' and victims' rights as existing in a 'zero sum' relationship whereby the one can be enhanced only at the expense of the other. A focus on the mechanisms for securing and sustaining legitimacy permits a more nuanced understanding of how individuals experience and react to the criminal justice system, and a recognition that fair procedure is meaningful and has positive implications for the range of overlapping and intersecting groups that make up any population.

Our own research project, as a relatively small-scale and qualitative study with a focus on the immediacies of the Crown Court experience, has not sought to examine the relationship between perceptions of legitimacy and confidence in justice, or the implications for subsequent compliance with the law.[6] Our focus, rather, has been on identifying which aspects of the court experience, and what kinds of prior experiences or expectations, help to confer legitimacy on the process, and how. In this, we have found it helpful to consider what procedural justice theorists have to say about the key drivers of legitimacy.

According to these scholars, perceptions of legitimacy tend to reflect individuals' personal interactions with the police, courts and other parts of the criminal justice system: 'legitimacy for most people is the aggregation of their experiences or the experiences of those around them, and the emotions they generate' (Fagan, 2008, p 139). Of course, it is hardly contentious to suggest that personal experiences of the criminal justice system inform evaluations of the system. But what is most distinctive about the procedural justice approach is that it asserts – 'counter to many people's views' (Tyler, 2001, p 216) – that the perceived fairness or otherwise of *outcomes* of interactions with the criminal justice system generally have less impact on overall views of the system and its legitimacy than the perceived fairness or otherwise of the *processes* in which individuals have been involved. In other words, the final result of police action, or a court case, or other criminal justice procedure, is often less significant than the nature and quality of the procedure itself. This privileging of process over outcome – albeit with differences in emphasis – is a consistent theme across the procedural justice research literature. However, separating out these two aspects of experience of the criminal justice system is not necessarily straightforward, as some observe: noting, for example, that 'both procedure and outcome are components of legitimacy, and deficits in either area can weaken popular legitimacy' (Fagan, 2008, p 136).

While procedural justice theory maintains – as its name indicates – a general focus on the procedural aspects of encounters with the criminal justice system, the empirical research conducted in this field has given rise to various conceptions of what exactly 'fair' or 'just' procedure entails. Much of the research on interactions between the public and the police concludes that, in broad terms, 'treating people with respect and in an unbiased fashion' are the key constituents of procedural fairness (Sunshine and Tyler, 2003, p 536). As noted by Bradford et al, the transparency of police processes – that is, 'visible performances of competency and proper decision making' – also emerges as a significant determinant of perceptions of fairness (2009, p 22). Research on the courts (both civil and criminal) has pointed to four key aspects to procedural justice for court users: voice (having the opportunity to tell their side of the story); neutrality (viewing the judge as neutral and having the rationale for rulings and decisions made clear to them); respect (respectful and courteous treatment from all officials within the criminal justice system); and trust (that their views are being listened to and considered) (Tyler, 2008). Benesh and Howell (2001, p 199) found that 'timeliness, courtesy, and equal treatment' all have an impact on the confidence in the court system of court users, but that also significant are the extent to which one has a *stake* in the outcome (which is negatively correlated with confidence), and the extent to which one has *control* over the outcome (which is positively correlated).[7]

Much of the research and the accompanying debate about what comprises procedural justice across the various parts of the criminal justice system focuses on two key dimensions: first, *fair decision-making* by the authorities; secondly, *respectful treatment* of members of the public by the authorities (Tyler, 2001, 2003, 2009; Fagan, 2008; Bottoms and Tankebe, 2012). In practice, it can be difficult to separate out these two aspects of procedure; but the first, in the words of Bottoms and Tankebe (2012, p 145), 'embraces a range of concerns that lawyers would place together under a general heading such as "the principles of natural justice"'. These include, for example, consistency in decision-making and the decision-maker's independence, neutrality and technical competence. Respectful treatment, on the other hand, concerns the quality of the interpersonal interaction between members of the public and the individuals who represent the authorities. For

Bottoms and Tankebe, the focus of this dimension of procedural justice is 'on whether the decision-maker treats the subject in a true sense as a human being, with needs for dignity, privacy, respect for his or her moments of weakness' (2012, p 145).[8]

Methods

The empirical research for this study was conducted in 2011–12. As appropriate to a study exploring the details and nuances of the court process and court experiences, the research was qualitative in form. There were three strands to the empirical work:

- semi-structured, in-depth interviews with a total of 57 professionals and practitioners working in or around the Crown Court;
- semi-structured, in-depth interviews with a total of 90 adult court users (45 from the prosecution side and 45 from the defence); and
- 200 hours of observations of a variety of Crown Court hearings.

The empirical work focused on two Crown Courts, selected to be contrasting in terms of the areas they served. One was a large court in an ethnically diverse urban area; the other was a medium-sized court in a small provincial city with a predominantly white British population. We conducted all the observations at these two courts; the large majority of court user respondents had attended either of the two; and almost all professional and practitioner respondents worked solely or partially in (or in services connected to) either one.

Interviews with criminal justice professionals and practitioners

The interviews with professionals and practitioners comprised the first component of the empirical work undertaken for this study. Respondents represented a range of criminal justice services and roles within the court; and all had extensive and direct contact with court users. They were recruited through opportunistic and snowball sampling, and with assistance from the resident judge and administrative office in each of the two Crown Courts and from the national headquarters of Victim Support and the CPS. The sample comprised Crown Court clerks and ushers (a total of 16); defence and prosecution advocates (13); full-time and part-time judges (11); staff and volunteers from Victim Support, including those working for its Witness Service in the Crown Court (9); police and CPS staff in Witness Care Units, which manage the care of victims and witnesses

(5); and registered intermediaries, who facilitate communication on behalf of vulnerable witnesses and defendants in court (3).

In the interviews, respondents were asked to give their views on which aspects of the court process pose the greatest practical and psychological difficulties for court users; the availability and effectiveness of measures to support court users' active engagement in court proceedings; and the factors which shape court users' perceptions of the fairness (or otherwise) of court processes and outcomes.

Interviews with court users

Background information on the 45 prosecution respondents and 45 defence respondents, and the cases in relation to which they appeared at the Crown Court, is provided in Tables A1 and A2, respectively, in the Appendix. To protect the anonymity of the respondents, all have been assigned pseudonyms – as applies also to the individuals who appeared in the observed cases. Some other minor details relating to certain individuals have also been changed to prevent inadvertent identification.

The 45 prosecution respondents interviewed for this study were largely recruited through the Witness Service at the two fieldwork Crown Courts, who sent an invitation to participate in the research to all witnesses who had attended court over the year prior to the research, and for whom they had an address. Some respondents were also contacted via snowballing from our initial contacts. Key features of the sample of 45 prosecution respondents are the following:

- The respondents ranged in age from 19 to 79; two-thirds were women; and the majority (36) were white, while four were Asian, three were black and two of mixed ethnicity.
- 14 prosecution respondents were victims, while 30 were witnesses (following the definitions provided above); the remaining prosecution respondent was the mother of a victim who had observed the trial in which her daughter gave evidence.
- 26 of the prosecution respondents were interviewed alongside (sometimes in joint interviews with) family members, friends or colleagues who were involved in the same case. In total, the 45 prosecution respondents had attended court in relation to 30 cases.
- The offences in relation to which the prosecution respondents had attended court included offences of serious violence, burglary, rape, sexual offences against a child, and theft.

- Two of the prosecution respondents' 30 cases were appeals, that is, the case had originally been heard in the magistrates' court, but the defendant had appealed against the conviction with the result that the case was re-heard in Crown Court.
- 24 of the 30 cases resulted in a conviction; in seven of these 24 cases, the defendant changed his or her plea to guilty on the first day of trial, or the first day of a retrial in two of these cases.
- In total, 38 of the prosecution respondents had given evidence at the Crown Court; the others had attended court but in the event were not required to give evidence, usually because the defendant had changed his or her plea to guilty.
- Four of the prosecution respondents had previous experience of the criminal courts as defendants, and eight as victims or witnesses.

In interview, the prosecution respondents were asked about the offence in relation to which they had attended court and its impact on them; their experiences and feelings during the run-up to the court case, while at court and immediately thereafter; their perceptions of their treatment by criminal justice professionals and practitioners; and their views on the fairness or otherwise of the court process as a whole and its outcome.

Of the 45 defence respondents interviewed for this study, 41 were themselves defendants. The remaining four respondents were close family members of individuals who had been tried and/or sentenced at the Crown Court and had attended court in a supportive role (one had also acted as a defence witness). Most of the defendants were recruited through probation offices local to the two fieldwork courts. Here, probation officers were asked to identify probationers among their caseload (including those serving community sentences and those on post-custody licence) who had been sentenced at Crown Court, and to invite them to participate in an interview. Additionally, a small number of the defendants were contacted through criminal lawyers and other personal contacts of the research team. The defendant family members were recruited for the study following their involvement in a resettlement initiative that was being evaluated by colleagues of the researchers.

The following are the key features of the sample of defence respondents:

- The 41 defendants ranged in age from 18 to 62; all but two were male; 21 of the defendants were white, while 14 were black, three were Asian and three of mixed ethnicity.

- At the defendants' most recent appearance at Crown Court, 18 faced charges of violent offending (including robbery, various levels of assault and offensive weapons charges); nine were charged with sexual offences; five with drug offences; and the remainder with a variety of other offences.
- Ten of the defendants pleaded not guilty, of whom six were subsequently found guilty (on at least some charges) and four were found not guilty on all charges or had the case against them dismissed. The remaining 31 defendants had appeared at court for sentencing only.
- Of the 37 defendants who were found or pleaded guilty, 22 received a custodial sentence, eight received a sentence of suspended custody, and seven received a community sentence.
- Thirty-one of the 41 defendants had prior experience of attending the criminal courts as a defendant; 24 had appeared at court multiple (at least four) times, including their most recent appearance. A little under half of all the defendants had had at least one experience of a Crown Court trial at some point in their lives. Two of the defendants had acted as jurors in the Crown Court.
- The four defendant family members interviewed for this study were all white and female, and aged between 29 and 44. Three were partners of a defendant and one was the mother of a defendant. The defendants to whom they were related had appeared at Crown Court in relation to drug offences (two of the cases), assault and robbery; three had appeared for trial and one for sentencing only; all had been convicted and sentenced to custody.

The interviews with the defence respondents followed a broadly similar format to those with the prosecution respondents, and focused on their experiences and feelings before, during and immediately after their most recent attendance at Crown Court; their perceptions of how they were treated by professionals and practitioners at court; and whether or not they regarded the court process as a whole and its outcome as fair. They were also asked about their past experiences (if any) of the Crown and magistrates' courts.

Observations

Observation was a core element of the research carried out for this study. It was undertaken on the basis that it would provide the most detailed insight into how the Crown Court operates on a day-to-day basis and, particularly, into the nature of the interactions between court users and the professionals in court. We recognise, like Baldwin (2008, p 246), that a significant limitation on the data collected through court observations is that 'open court proceedings present only the public face of justice' and that many of the most important decisions in criminal cases are made behind the scenes and 'often even before the case reaches the courtroom'. Nevertheless, we were of the view that our observation of the minutiae of proceedings within – and immediately outside – the courtroom could greatly help to inform our understanding of victims', witnesses' and defendants' experiences of the Crown Court. Certainly – and as will be reported over the course of this volume – the observational work enabled us to appreciate many aspects of the courtroom experience that interviews alone would not have adequately conveyed: such as the complex, chaotic and often confusing nature of court proceedings and the frequency with which they were interrupted for a wide array of reasons; and the juxtaposition of elaborate formality with informality, and of high drama with tedium.

We carried out a total of around 200 hours' observation across the two Crown Courts which were the focus of the study. We sat in the public gallery or, on occasions (where asked to do so by the court clerk or usher), in the seating reserved for probation officers and other officials. We observed seven trials in their entirety (with the qualification that one was halted after three days and listed for retrial). The seven cases were selected for observation from the range of cases being heard at the two courts during the fieldwork period on the basis that they represented several different offence types; all involved direct victims who were due to give evidence and a number of other non-professional witnesses; and the defendants were all adults. The offences and outcomes are listed below; and a brief outline of each case is provided in the Appendix.

Case 1: Assault occasioning bodily harm; outcome: not guilty verdict.

Case 2: Inflicting grievous bodily harm; outcome: guilty verdict.

Case 3: Perverting the course of justice (false allegation of rape); outcome: guilty verdict.

Case 4: Armed robbery; outcome: trial halted after three days (following alleged contact with witness by one defendant) and listed for retrial.

Case 5: Sexual assault and abduction of a child; outcome: guilty verdict on assault charge; not guilty on abduction charge.

Case 6: Robbery; outcome: guilty verdict.

Case 7: Dangerous driving; outcome: not guilty verdict.

In addition to observing the seven trials in full, we sat in on a number of other hearings where opportunities arose during adjournments of the fully observed trials, and when we were attending the courts to conduct the interviews with professionals. These additional observations encompassed eight sentencing hearings, five trials observed in part, and various other hearings including 'plea and case management hearings' (where the defendant is expected to enter a plea, and the necessary arrangements for the ensuing trial or sentencing are put in place) and cases listed 'for mention' before the judge (where a variety of outstanding administrative or other matters are dealt with).

Structure of the book

Following this introduction, Chapter Two of the volume will continue to set out the background to the empirical research with a description of the place of the Crown Court within the courts system of England and Wales, its structure and composition, and its day-to-day work.

Chapters Three to Seven will then present the empirical findings of the study. The subject of Chapter Three is *conflict management*: here, we will argue that court proceedings are not so much about establishing 'what really happened' in relation to an alleged offence, but are an arena for managing conflict between alleged wrongdoers and those allegedly wronged by them. This chapter will also consider the ritual and performative aspects of Crown Court proceedings, and will describe the ways in which various highly incongruous and contradictory elements are intermingled within the court process. Chapter Four will look at the inter-relationships between the different players in the courtroom and, particularly, at the *them and us* divide between the professionals in court, on the one hand and, on the other hand, the lay court users. This, it will be claimed, is a more fundamental divide than that between prosecution and defence.

In Chapter Five, we will turn our attention to the chaotic and confusing nature of the court process. Drawing on multiple examples from our observation and interviews, we will argue that a kind of *structured mayhem* characterises the court process: key players in a case fail to turn up; equipment does not work; paperwork goes missing or contains mistakes; and delays are commonplace – and yet an overarching order is maintained. Chapter Six will then look at many of the inherent, and often severe, stresses and strains of the court process for those who come to court as victims, witnesses or defendants. We will also make the case here that notwithstanding the difficulties and challenges they face, most court users display a *reluctant conformity* in court: they comply with the expectations and social rules of the process, and rarely do they actively disrupt it. In Chapter Seven, we will bring the discussion of the empirical findings to a close by arguing that court users' reluctant conformity is based on a belief in the *legitimacy* of the court process: that is, they obey the rules because they believe that they have an obligation to do so. The various dimensions of this perceived legitimacy of the court process are then outlined over the course of the chapter.

Chapter Eight will conclude the volume by considering how changes to professional practices in and around the courts, and to criminal justice policy, could help to reduce some of the social costs and limitations of the adversarial process.

Notes

[1] Grant title: 'The public's experiences of court: how victims, defendants and witnesses perceive and make sense of the criminal justice process.' Grant ref: ES/H0302981/1.

[2] In July 2012, the government announced its intention to open up the national Witness Service to competition (Ministry of Justice, 2012a). Current arrangements for provision of the Witness Service through Victim Support will conclude in March 2015.

[3] In addition to the research cited above, a number of other ethnographic studies of the criminal courts in England and Wales and in the United States also have a bearing on our research. Studies from this jurisdiction include Shute et al's investigation of minority ethnic witnesses' and defendants' perceptions of their treatment in Crown Courts and magistrates' courts (2005; see also Hood et al, 2003); Astor's work on magistrates' courts (1986); and Scheffer's ethnography of procedure in the Crown Court (2010; Scheffer et al, 2010). American studies include Blumberg's influential 1960s work on due process in the criminal courts of a large city (1967, 1969) and Feeley's (1992) research on the handling of cases in a lower court. Ethnographic research on the American juvenile court system has been conducted by Emerson (1969) and Kupchik (2006), among others.

[4] See, for example, Sunshine and Tyler (2003); Tyler (2001; 2006a); Tyler and Fagan (2008); Tyler and Huo (2002).

[5] For example, Hough (2012); Hough et al (2013a); Jackson et al (2011a; 2012); Crawford and Hucklesby (2013).

[6] Much of the empirical research undertaken by procedural justice scholars has involved the measurement, through large-scale social surveys, of public trust and the relationships between trust, legitimacy and compliance with the law. For example, Mike Hough and colleagues have developed and tested a range of hypotheses about the drivers of trust in justice and legitimacy across a large number of European jurisdictions, through the EU-funded Euro-Justis Project and the European Social Survey (Hough and Sato, 2011; Hough et al, 2013b; Jackson et al, 2011a and 2011b).

[7] Thus defendants, who have a lot of stake in the outcome but little influence over it, tend to have less confidence than jurors, who have little stake but a large amount of control.

[8] Although this is a theme that is beyond the scope of this study, it is worth noting that the approach to the law known as 'therapeutic jurisprudence' has drawn in a significant way on the work of procedural justice scholars. Therapeutic jurisprudence views the law 'as a potential therapeutic agent' (Wexler, 2007/8, p 78), although it has been described by McIvor as 'an approach or set of organizing principles rather than a theoretical perspective' which thus 'lacks explanatory power' (2009, p 42). Advocates of therapeutic jurisprudence are concerned with how specific types of interaction and other practices within the judicial process support (or, conversely, undermine) the well-being of participants, and potentially can contribute to positive psychological outcomes such as rehabilitation (for defendants) or recovery from the trauma of victimisation (for victims). Therapeutic jurisprudence is particularly associated with the work of Bruce Winick and David Wexler (see, for example, Wexler, 2008; Winick and Wexler, 2003; Stolle et al, 2000).

TWO

The system: what is the Crown Court and what are its functions?

In any jurisdiction, the system of criminal law defines certain acts as illegal, meaning that they are viewed as sufficiently damaging to society to merit intervention by the state when they are committed. It also sets out a structure by which the state determines whether illegal acts have been committed and administers punishments for these acts.

In England and Wales, the police have a duty to investigate any criminal offence that is reported to them; and, when a suspect has been apprehended, the police or the Crown Prosecution Service (CPS) will make a decision as to whether to charge him or her. If the suspect is charged, the case falls within the remit of the criminal courts: that is, a magistrates' court in the first instance and subsequently, in a minority of cases, the Crown Court. At court, it will be determined whether and what criminal offences were committed, and the punishment, if any, will be set out. The magistrates' courts and Crown Court operate within a wider structure of criminal and civil courts.

For the purpose of providing a broad context to the empirical research findings that are presented in the chapters that follow, this chapter will briefly outline the structure of the courts; the essential functions and composition of the Crown Court; and recent policy developments aimed at supporting victims, witnesses and defendants at court.

Courts structure

The courts system in England and Wales has a complex structure, as shown in Figure 2.1. At the top is the Supreme Court of the United Kingdom. The Supreme Court is the final court of appeal for civil cases from across the United Kingdom, and for criminal cases from England and Wales and Northern Ireland. Below the Supreme Court is the Court of Appeal, which has a civil and a criminal division. The High Court has both appellate and original jurisdiction, and consists of three divisions: Chancery, which deals with issues such as business disputes, fraud and insolvency, tax, copyright and patents; Family, which deals with matrimonial and family matters; and the Queen's Bench Division, which hears judicial reviews and oversees the decisions and actions of the lower courts. Below the High Court and Court of Appeal is the Crown Court, which hears relatively serious criminal cases, including appeals from the magistrates' courts, and undertakes a limited amount of civil work. Magistrates' courts comprise the lowest level of criminal court, and also deal with some civil matters. The County Court handles the majority of civil litigation, while family matters are dealt with by the Family Court – generally sitting in specialist magistrates' courts and at the County Court – and by the family division of the High Court. (The Family Court as a unified structure came into being in 2014 under the Crime and Courts Act 2013, which also created a unified County Court.)

Figure 2.1: Courts structure

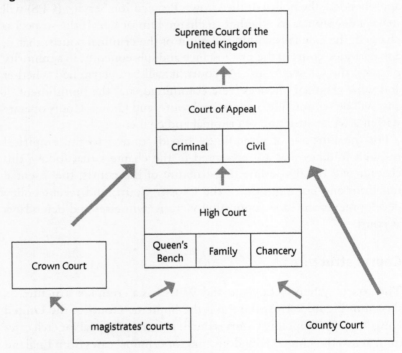

The Crown Court was established by the Courts Act 1971 and is administered by Her Majesty's Courts and Tribunals Service, which is an executive agency of the Ministry of Justice. There are 76 locations across England and Wales at which the Crown Court regularly sits.[1] Crown Court centres are assigned to three different tiers, in accordance with their level of input from High Court judges, which in turn reflects the seriousness of the cases they hear. First tier Crown Courts are visited by High Court Judges for criminal and civil cases; second tier for criminal cases only; and third tier usually have no input from the High Court.

Routes to the Crown Court

The core business of the Crown Court is the contested criminal trial before a jury, and sentencing. There are a number of routes by which a criminal case can come to the Crown Court. For the most part, cases heard at the Crown Court involve offences towards the more serious end of the spectrum. These include cases which can be dealt with *either* by magistrates' courts *or* at the Crown Court (including, for example, theft, burglary and assault occasioning actual bodily harm) and which are thus typically referred to as 'either-way offences'. 'Indictable only offences', on the other hand (including robbery, rape and murder), can only be dealt with by the Crown Court. As mentioned at the start of this book, less than 10% of all criminal cases come to the Crown Court for trial and/or sentencing: the remainder both start and end at magistrates' courts.

A case involving an 'either-way offence' is initially dealt with at a magistrates' court. If the defendant pleads guilty, or is found guilty in a trial at the magistrates' court, the case may subsequently be 'committed for sentence' to the Crown Court, if the offence is likely to merit a more severe sentence than can be imposed by the magistrates.[2] On the other hand, an either-way case can be 'sent for trial' to the Crown Court if the defendant pleads not guilty or does not enter a plea, and the magistrates decide that the case should be heard at the higher court on account of its seriousness or complexity; further, a defendant pleading guilty to an either-way offence can elect to be sent to the Crown Court for trial rather than be tried at the magistrates' court. If a defendant 'sent for trial' subsequently changes the plea to guilty or is found guilty at trial, the sentence is then passed at the Crown Court.

A defendant who is charged with an 'indictable only' offence makes an initial brief appearance at a magistrates' court but is then automatically 'sent for trial' to the Crown Court, even if he or she is intending to plead guilty (in which case there may be an indication of plea at the magistrates' court, but the plea cannot be formally heard at this stage). Following the preliminary hearing at the magistrates' court, the plea is then heard at the Crown Court. If the plea is guilty, the case will proceed to sentencing; where there is a plea of not guilty, a jury trial will follow unless the defendant subsequently changes the plea to guilty. The routes to a Crown Court trial and sentencing are depicted in Figure 2.2.

Figure 2.2: Routes to the Crown Court

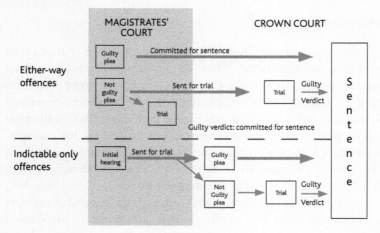

Criminal cases may also come to the Crown Court from magistrates' courts for appeal against either the conviction or the sentence handed down by the lower court.[3] The appeal takes the form of the re-hearing of the original trial or sentencing, ordinarily by a Crown Court judge sitting with two magistrates (who were not involved in the original case). The role of the Crown Court here is to consider whether the decision of the magistrates' court was correct, and the Crown Court has the power to confirm, reverse or vary the original decision on verdict or sentence, or to return the case to the magistrates' court. Other everyday business conducted at the Crown Court includes bail hearings, breach hearings (where the conditions of a sentence or of a post-sentence licence have been breached) and sentence reviews (where sentenced offenders appear before the court for a report on their progress under the sentence).

Only a very small proportion of cases involving defendants under 18 years are heard by the Crown Court: most defendants aged between 10 and 17 appear at youth courts, which are based in magistrates' courts and have jurisdiction to deal with most 'indictable only' as well as other offences. However, if the offence is exceptionally serious or where the defendant has been charged alongside an adult, a defendant aged under 18 may appear at the Crown Court for trial and/or sentencing.

The Crown Court: some facts and figures

There is no question that in many respects – and certainly in terms of its public profile – the contested criminal trial is the central event of the Crown Court; the trial is 'at the heart of the Court; its very reason for being' (Rock, 1993, p 27). However, the large majority of defendants who appear at the Crown Court do so for sentencing only, rather than for trial. In 2011, the Crown Court dealt with a total of around 106,000 defendants who had either been sent or committed for trial from magistrates' courts, of whom around 72,000 (about 68%) subsequently pleaded guilty to all counts, while just under 32,000 (30%) maintained a 'not guilty' plea (no plea was entered in the remaining small proportion of cases). A further 43,000 defendants were dealt with at the Crown Court having been committed for sentence by magistrates' courts. This means, therefore, that 32,000 of a total of 149,000 defendants dealt with at the Crown Court – or just over one-fifth – went through a trial.[4] Of those who were tried, 19,000 were subsequently acquitted,[5] while 12,000 were found guilty (Ministry of Justice, 2012b).

Four main types of sentence can be passed at the Crown Court: an absolute or conditional discharge; a fine; a community order; and imprisonment (which can be immediate or suspended). Imprisonment is the sentence passed most frequently: of the approximately 86,000 defendants sentenced in the Crown Court in 2013, 48,000 received an immediate custodial sentence; 21,000 were sentenced to suspended custody; 11,000 received a community sentence and 2,000 received a fine (Ministry of Justice, 2014). Findings of the 2012 Crown Court Sentencing Survey (Sentencing Council, 2013) reveal that the offence types most commonly sentenced at the Crown Court were assault and public order offences (23% of principal offences sentenced); theft, dishonesty and fraud offences (17%); drug offences (14%); burglary (12%); sexual offences (7%); robbery (7%); and driving offences (4%). Various other offences accounted for 16%.[6]

The cost of the Crown Court

The National Audit Office (2009) reported for the financial year 2007–08 that the cost to Her Majesty's Court Service of operating the Crown Court in England and Wales was around £382 million. Over one quarter of this budget (27%) was for the judiciary; 15% for court staff; and 15% for building maintenance and utilities. 10% of the annual budget covered jury costs, including travel, expenses and compensation for lost earnings. The remainder (33%) included the cost of services provided by the Ministry of Justice such as payroll, procurement and information technology and a cost to account for the depreciation of fixed assets.

The National Audit Office (2009) noted the requirement, in line with wider Government efficiencies, for HM Courts Service to reduce expenditure. In the three years to 2007–08, savings of £134 million were found, with a target of another £145 million of savings having been set for the period 2008–09 to 2010–11. Since 2011, the imperative to achieve efficiency savings has only increased, and the 2013–14 *Business Plan* for HM Courts and Tribunals Service reports that the service 'is on target to achieve more than £300m of savings required over the four years to 2014–15' (HMCTS, 2013, p 10).

The business and people of the Crown Court

Both the trial and the sentencing process are adversarial in nature, meaning that the prosecution (on behalf of the Crown) and the defence are required to present their cases to the Court. Decision-making is in the hands of a neutral third party: the jury in a trial, and the judge in a sentencing hearing.[7]

The Crown Court trial

A Crown Court trial follows a 'not guilty' plea by the accused. Over the course of the trial, the prosecution seeks to prove the defendant's guilt. The presumption of innocence of the accused is a fundamental principle of criminal law: there is no onus on the defendant to prove his or her innocence; rather, the burden of proof lies with the prosecution. Jurors are told that they must reach a guilty verdict only if they are sure 'beyond reasonable doubt' of the defendant's guilt; this point is usually reiterated to the jury throughout the trial by the judge and by the defence counsel.

The adversarial trial process has a clear structure and a number of essential constituent parts. Any single trial can range in length from a matter of hours to many weeks, months or longer; but Crown Court trials typically extend over several days. After the swearing-in of the 12 members of the jury, a trial begins with the prosecution's opening speech, which sets out the essence of the case. The prosecution counsel then calls witnesses (who may include the alleged victims of the offence) and presents any evidence additional to the witness testimony, including documentary evidence (such as written reports, photographs, maps, or video or audio recordings) and physical artefacts (such as clothing or weapons). Prosecution witnesses are questioned first by the prosecution counsel, to enable them to give their 'evidence-in-chief', and thereafter may be cross-examined by the defence. The defence will advance its case after the conclusion of the prosecution case, and likewise will call any witnesses and present any other evidence. The witnesses called may or may not include the defendant, depending on the defendant's own wishes and the defence counsel's view on whether oral testimony from the defendant will help his or her case. Defence witnesses are first questioned by the defence counsel and thereafter cross-examined by the prosecution. If there are several defendants, each is likely to have his or her own defence advocate, who may call his or her own witnesses.

Prior to the jury retiring to consider their verdict, first the prosecution and then the defence make their closing speeches to the jury. The judge then sums up the evidence and gives the jury any relevant directions on the law – for example, concerning the burden of proof; the definition of the offence; the status of certain types of evidence; and the need for separate consideration of different counts if the defendant faces more than one charge. The jury are initially asked to reach a unanimous verdict, but if none is forthcoming – and after a minimum period of two hours' deliberation – the jury may be directed that they can reach a majority verdict of 10 or 11.

Sentencing

Whether sentencing follows a guilty plea or a guilty verdict in a trial, the court frequently adjourns sentence in order to obtain reports – most often, a pre-sentence report prepared by the probation service,[8] but also sometimes a psychiatric or other report on the offender. A sentencing hearing usually opens with the presentation of the facts of the case by the prosecution counsel, including the impact and repercussions of the offence, although if sentencing follows immediately on a trial, the judge may deem this account unnecessary. (The prosecution may also alert the court to any statutory provisions relating to the offence or its sentencing, make requests for ancillary orders,[9] and set out the amount of prosecution costs to be claimed, but is not entitled to advise on what specific sentence should be passed.) This is followed by the defence counsel's plea in mitigation, which makes the case for the lowest possible sentence, usually on grounds of the particular circumstances of the offence and/or the background or situation of the offender.

The judge then passes sentence, imposes any ancillary orders and decides whether any costs should be awarded against the defendant.

The judge's 'sentencing remarks', in which the sentence is set out, should include the reasons for the decision reached. In determining the sentence, the judge has a statutory duty to have regard to relevant sentencing guidelines[10] and, in addition to court reports, may take into account any other material that has been submitted by the defence or prosecution (such as a Victim Personal Statement, references for the defendant, or letters from the defendant or his or her friends and family).

Key players in the Crown Court

All Crown Court hearings require the presence of certain key players: usually, at a minimum, the judge, defence and prosecution counsel, and at least one court clerk or usher. Depending on type of hearing, defendants are required to attend court in person or, increasingly, via video-link. Trials usually demand the assembly of a much larger cast of characters, including witnesses. Broadly, the key players in Crown Court proceedings can be grouped under the headings of 'professionals and practitioners' and 'lay participants'.

Professional and practitioner participants in court proceedings

The judiciary in the Crown Court comprises High Court judges, circuit judges and recorders; additionally, as noted above, magistrates may sit alongside a Crown Court judge in appellate cases from magistrates' courts.[11] High Court judges are members of the senior judiciary, and are appointed to one of the three divisions of Queen's Bench, Chancery and Family. The responsibilities of High Court judges who have been appointed to the Queen's Bench Division include hearing the most serious and complex criminal cases at the Crown Court. Circuit judges are full-time judges who are appointed to one of the seven regions of England and Wales. Some specialise in criminal cases, while others work in more than one jurisdiction. While High Court judges hear only around 2% of cases at Crown Court, these comprise over a quarter (27%) of the most serious (Ministry of Justice, 2012b). Circuit judges must have had at least seven years' experience as a lawyer with 'rights of audience' (that is, the right to appear as an advocate in court) and will usually have served as a part-time recorder prior to appointment. Recorders are practising barristers or solicitors who sit part-time as judges at the Crown Court, generally on less serious cases than circuit judges. In each Crown Court, a senior circuit judge – usually known as the resident judge – has overall responsibility for the court and its administration.

Judges in the Crown Court are responsible for interpreting and applying the criminal law. In a trial, the judge decides on matters of law – for example, relating to the admissibility of evidence – and makes directions about the progress of the case (Gibson and Cavadino, 2008). The judge is at the epicentre of the courtroom, both physically and metaphorically, sitting on a raised bench facing counsel and the defendant, with the witness box and jury box on either side (see Figure 2.3). Crown Court judges wear a wig and gown in court (except where it is determined that there should be a more informal atmosphere because of the vulnerability or young age of victims or witnesses); High Court judges sitting in the Crown Court wear a red robe, while the robe worn by circuit judges sitting on criminal matters is violet, with a red sash over the left shoulder.

Figure 2.3: Lay-out of typical courtroom in the Crown Court

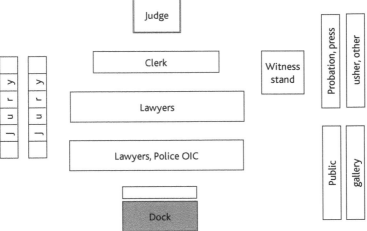

In a trial or sentencing hearing, or preparatory hearing, the prosecution and defence counsel are responsible for presenting the case on behalf of the Crown and the defendant respectively. Most counsel in the Crown Court are barristers – that is, lawyers who, by virtue of particular training and qualifications, have been accepted to 'plead at the Bar'. Traditionally, only barristers had 'rights of audience' in the Crown Court; however, under the Courts and Legal Services Act 1990, solicitors are able to qualify as higher court advocates, in which case they are known as solicitor-advocates. Prosecution advocates are either employed by the CPS or belong to independent law firms or chambers; some lawyers work variously as defence and prosecution advocates on different cases.

The defence case is generally prepared by a criminal solicitor, who then instructs a defence advocate to present the case at the Crown Court; this representation is publicly funded for defendants eligible for legal aid.[12] Defendants also have the freedom to represent themselves, although this rarely occurs at the Crown Court. In cases where there are multiple defendants, each normally has his or her own counsel. Under the 'cab-rank rule', which is intended to ensure that all defendants have access to counsel, barristers are obliged to accept instructions from a client, regardless of any personal preferences, provided they are available and have the necessary expertise to present the case.[13]

In a Crown Court hearing, advocates are positioned on benches at the centre of the courtroom, facing the judge, with the prosecution usually on the side nearer to the witness box and the defence nearer to the jury box. Junior lawyers or solicitors may sit with or behind them, and the police 'officer in the case' often sits behind the prosecution counsel. Counsel always stand when addressing the court. Barristers wear a wig and black gown in the Crown Court, while solicitor-advocates have the right to wear a wig with a solicitor's gown if they choose to do so.

Court clerks and ushers are responsible for ensuring that proceedings run smoothly within the courtroom. The clerk assists the judge and manages the courtroom; he or she sits at a desk just in front of the judge, takes the defendant's plea, keeps legal documentation in order, and may also swear in the jury and witnesses. The usher, who sits in any convenient place in the courtroom, has responsibility for ensuring that all the key players involved in a case are present and understand what they have to do during proceedings. The usher is the first point of contact for people in the courtroom, including barristers, witnesses and members of the public, and should keep the clerk informed if any problems occur. In addition to escorting witnesses, jurors and the judge in and out of the courtroom, the usher prepares the courtroom, passes evidence to the jury and judge as required, and operates any technical equipment being used; like the clerk, the usher may swear in the jury and witnesses. Court staff typically present during Crown Court hearings also include custody or dock officers, who are responsible for the safety and security of defendants; they sit in the dock with defendants, and escort defendants who are on remand to and from the courtroom.

The presence of a variety of other professionals and practitioners is also required to enable a hearing – particularly a trial, which has the largest cast of characters. This can include any combination of those listed in Table 2.1.

Table 2.1: Professionals and practitioners in the Crown Court

Participant	Description of role
Officer in the case	This is the police officer in charge of the police investigation into the case. In a trial, the officer in the case usually sits behind the prosecution advocate and provides assistance in relation to evidence and other aspects of the prosecution case. The officer in the case also usually acts as an important prosecution witness.
Professional/expert witnesses	These can include police officers involved in the case and those with specific knowledge on particular forms of evidence, such as doctors and other medical professionals, or experts on mobile phone or computer evidence.
Interpreters	Interpreters are appointed for hearings of all kinds where the defendant or witnesses have difficulties speaking and understanding English. Interpreters are arranged and paid for by the court.
Intermediaries	An intermediary may be appointed by the court to help a witness with communication difficulties to give evidence. More rarely, an intermediary may be appointed to support a vulnerable defendant. An intermediary sits next to the witness or defendant, and is allowed to explain questions or answers to facilitate understanding, but the substance of the evidence must remain unchanged. Intermediaries for victims and witnesses are required to be registered to ensure that they are professionally trained and accountable (see Talbot, 2012 for further details).
Probation officers	Court-based probation officers are often present in the courtroom when a verdict is being delivered or during a sentencing hearing. The judge may also ask the probation officer to provide clarification on sentencing options during the sentencing hearing.
Witness Service volunteers	Volunteers from the Witness Service often accompany witnesses to the courtroom and wait in the courtroom while the witness is giving evidence.
Journalists	In a case of general interest to the public, journalists may observe proceedings from the public gallery or an adjoining seating area.

Lay participants in court proceedings

A Crown Court trial often includes an array of lay participants: the defendant(s), non-expert witnesses for the prosecution (including, depending on the nature of the offence, the victim) and the defence, the 12 members of the jury, and members of the public observing proceedings from the public gallery. Other types of hearing are unlikely to have many lay participants, although the defendant is present at most, and a sentencing hearing may have some observers.

In a Crown Court trial, responsibility for deciding the verdict lies with the jury, made of up 12 members of the general public. These are individuals who have been summonsed for jury service following random selection from the electoral register. Prior to the start of each trial, a 'panel' of at least 15 potential jurors is brought into the courtroom, from amongst whom 12 are selected and directed to take their places in the jury box. All members of the jury are then required to swear under oath or affirm that they 'will faithfully try the defendant and give a true verdict according to the evidence'. At the conclusion of the prosecution and defence case, and following the judge's summing up, the jury retire to deliberate in private upon the verdict; when a verdict is reached, this is delivered by the foreman who will have been selected by his or her fellow-jurors.

During a court hearing, the defendant sits in the dock, which is a partitioned area situated at the back of the courtroom. A defendant who is on remand is brought to court from prison and then held in one of the cells within the court building before being taken to the courtroom when the hearing is about to start; the defendant will then be taken back to the cells during breaks in proceedings. A defendant who is on bail during court proceedings is responsible for making his or her own way to court, and may sit in the public gallery or outside the courtroom until the hearing starts and he or she is required to enter the dock. If a defendant gives evidence during a trial, the defendant will be told to leave the dock and enter the witness box, and then to swear under oath or affirm that the evidence to be given is truthful. During a sentencing hearing, the defendant remains in the dock throughout and is instructed to stand at the moment the sentence is delivered. If a custodial sentence is passed, the judge will pronounce "Take him down!" and the defendant will be taken directly to the cells.

During a trial, any number of lay witnesses may be called to give evidence. Witnesses for the prosecution may include any victim(s) of the alleged offence and others who have made statements to the police concerning their witnessing of it. Prosecution witnesses required to give evidence at court are contacted and provided with details of when to attend by the local Witness Care Unit, which is a joint police and Crown Prosecution Service team. Prosecution witnesses who are called to give evidence are legally obliged to attend court. If they refuse to do so they may be served with a witness summons; this is a formal and legally binding court order, and failure to attend court following a summons renders the witness liable to arrest for contempt of court. Once at court, prosecution witnesses usually wait in a designated waiting area provided by the Witness Service until the time comes for their evidence to be heard, at which point they are escorted into the courtroom by a Witness Service volunteer or an usher. Here, they enter the witness stand and swear or affirm they will tell the truth. When their evidence-in-chief and cross-examination is complete, they are formally released and may then leave the courtroom or, if preferred, stay on to watch the remainder of proceedings from the public gallery.

Witnesses may also be called on behalf of the defence, although typically there are fewer (if any) defence than prosecution witnesses in any given trial. Defence witnesses may be individuals whose evidence concerning the alleged offence supports the defence case, or they may act as character witnesses for the defendant. Defence witnesses receive instructions regarding their attendance at court from the defendant's lawyer and, when at court, are entitled to support from the Witness Service.

The final group of lay participants within the courtroom comprises the spectators who view proceedings from the public gallery. The large majority of proceedings at the Crown Court are open to the public and to the media; hearings that *can* be closed include, for example, those involving defendants aged under 18 if this is ordered under Section 30 of the Children and Young Persons Act 1933. Spectators are likely to include family or friends of the defendant or (perhaps less commonly) the victim, but may also include members of the general public with no specific connection to the case, and students or schoolchildren observing cases as part of their studies. Spectators are expected to remain quiet during proceedings, are asked to switch off their mobile phones, and are not permitted to bring any recording devices or cameras into the courtroom. They may be asked to leave the court under certain circumstances, for example in cases where there are reporting restrictions because children are involved, or when a witness who is giving evidence from behind a screen is brought into or out of the courtroom.

Access to justice

A significant feature of recent criminal justice policy has been the effort to enhance the 'access to justice' of those who come into contact with any or all aspects of the criminal justice system. Particular focus has been paid to vulnerable and socially excluded groups, such as those with mental health problems and/or learning disabilities (KM

Research and Consultancy, 2009; McLeod et al, 2010) and those from minority ethnic groups (Mason et al, 2009). Some of these policy developments demonstrate a recognition that, in particular, victims from certain socially excluded groups – including, for example, those with learning disabilities (Mencap, 2010) – have often seen offences against them go unprosecuted because of assumptions that they lacked the ability to give evidence. Thus a major strand of policy work aimed at facilitating access to justice has been the development of support within the courtroom for vulnerable and/or intimidated victims and witnesses. A separate, albeit less prominent, strand relates to support for vulnerable defendants at court (McEwan, 2013).

Provision for victims and witnesses at court

As discussed in the preceding chapter, the last few decades have seen an increased political and policy-driven focus in various jurisdictions on fostering a more inclusive approach to victims and witnesses in the criminal justice system. Over the past 20 years in England and Wales, for example, there have been several policy initiatives aiming to increase the standing of victims and witnesses within the court process.

The launch of the Witness Service at the Crown Court in 1994 was one of the first significant developments designed to help both victims and witnesses as they prepared to give evidence at court. Part of the national charity Victim Support, the Witness Service offers support to all witnesses before and during their attendance at court, and is staffed largely by volunteers.[14] This support includes the hosting of pre-trial visits, which enable witnesses to see a courtroom prior to the trial; the provision of quiet places for witnesses to wait before giving evidence; and accompaniment to the courtroom. The use of the Witness Service across the court system expanded rapidly, and by 2003 it had a presence across all criminal courts – magistrates' and Crown – in England and Wales.

Perhaps the first key legislative development aimed at supporting victims and witnesses at court, part of the impetus for which was the need to achieve best evidence in criminal trials (see Ministry of Justice, 2011), was the passing of the Youth Justice and Criminal Evidence Act (YJCEA) 1999. Sections 19 to 30 of the Act introduced 'special measures' for *vulnerable* and *intimidated* witnesses (both prosecution and defence) to improve the quality of the evidence they are able to provide, and to relieve some of the stresses associated with giving evidence. Vulnerable witnesses are defined as all those under the age of 18[15] and those whose quality of evidence – in terms of its 'completeness, coherence and accuracy' – is likely to be impacted by a mental disorder, physical disability or 'significant impairment of intelligence and social function'. Intimidated witnesses are those whose quality of evidence is likely to be impacted by fear or distress – including fear relating to potential intimidation by the accused.

'Special measures' allow for a number of adaptations to the normal court process, and have a particular focus on easing the process of giving evidence (Brammer and Cooper, 2011). Under 'special measures', witnesses may be permitted to give evidence from behind a screen so that they cannot be seen by, and cannot see, the accused; to use a pre-recorded video statement as their evidence-in-chief to the court; to give evidence at the time of the trial through a live TV-link to the courtroom (from another room within the court building); and to be helped to give evidence by a registered witness intermediary, who facilitates communication (Plotnikoff and Woolfson, 2014). Other 'special measures' include the clearing of members of the public and press from the public gallery; and the removal of wigs and gowns by the judge and lawyers. Complementing the statutory provision for 'special measures', recently developed guidance and training materials for advocates have focused upon how to formulate questions for vulnerable witnesses to achieve best evidence (also discussed below), including through the use of age or developmentally appropriate vocabulary (Krahenbuhl, 2011; Keane, 2012; Henderson, 2014). Rules for criminal procedure[16] now provide for a 'ground rules hearing' to discuss how a vulnerable person should be questioned, or how a vulnerable defendant can participate more effectively in the trial. A ground rules hearing is required when an intermediary is to be used, but is also promoted as best practice in any case involving a vulnerable witness or defendant (Plotnikoff and Woolfson, 2014).

With respect to adult witnesses, the police and CPS are expected to assess at an early stage of case preparation whether any 'special measures' are required and to make the application to the court; only the judge can then decide whether or not the request is granted. (Those aged 17 and under are automatically eligible for 'special measures', but may opt out.) A similar application can also be submitted by the defence team on behalf of a defence witness.

Since their implementation, the use and effectiveness of 'special measures' has been subject to a number of evaluations. Hamlyn et al (2004), for example, found 'special measures' to be beneficial to the well-being of vulnerable and intimidated witnesses – those who received them were less likely to feel anxious or distressed – and also made it possible for these witnesses to give evidence; a third who used 'special measures' said that they would not have been willing or able to give evidence without them. Moreover, vulnerable and intimidated witnesses who received 'special measures' were significantly more likely to express overall satisfaction with the criminal justice system than those vulnerable and intimidated witnesses who had not. Burton et al (2006) found that provisions for giving evidence via live TV links and from behind screens were well regarded by the witnesses, and that the removal of wigs and gowns and clearing the court, whilst considered helpful, were rarely used. However, the identification of witnesses eligible for 'special measures' was problematic, with some categories of vulnerable or intimidated witness being more likely to be identified than others. A further problem noted by the research was delay in CPS applications for 'special measures', some of which were only made on the day of the witness's court appearance (see also Charles, 2012).

Plotnikoff and Woolfson (2009) evaluated the implementation of government commitments to young witnesses in criminal proceedings and found that 88% of the 172 young witnesses who had given evidence had used 'special measures'. Of these, 75% gave evidence via live-link and 13% gave evidence from behind a screen in the courtroom. Overall, 82% of the total sample were happy with the arrangements made for them to give evidence and of these, 39% said that they would have been unwilling to give evidence in any other way. However, many respondents said that they had no choice about the way in which they gave evidence[17] and 78% said that they had no choice about who accompanied them at court as their designated supporter.

Closely following the provisions enacted as a result of the YJCEA, 'Victim Personal Statements' were introduced in 2001 under the commitments made in the Victims' Charter (Home Office, 1996). This followed the introduction of Victim Impact Statements in the 1970s and 1980s in a number of other common law jurisdictions such as the United States, Canada and New Zealand (Roberts and Manikis, 2011). Victim Personal Statements provide a means by which victims can express how they have been impacted (physically, emotionally or in any other way) by the offence. While the content of a statement cannot be cited as evidence in a trial, it may be read out or referred to by the judge at the sentencing hearing, in which case it helps to provide clarification about the extent of harm caused by the offence. All victims should be given the opportunity to make a Victim Personal Statement when making their witness statement to the police – and should also be permitted to make a further statement at a later stage in the prosecution process if they so wish.

Other measures for victims and witnesses have been designed to increase levels of attendance at court as well as the quality of their experience once there. Prime amongst these was the *No Witness, No Justice* initiative (Criminal Justice System, 2004) which has been credited with helping reduce the number of ineffective trials resulting from the non-attendance of witnesses. This initiative saw the piloting followed by national roll-out of dedicated Witness Care Units, jointly staffed by the Crown Prosecution Service and the police, to support witnesses during the court process. Witness Care Units were established in 2005 as a single point of contact for victims and witnesses, to offer guidance about the criminal justice system, information about case progress and outcomes and to assess witnesses' support needs to give evidence. The establishment of these units, along with the introduction of the *Code of Practice for Victims of Crime* (initially produced by the Home Office in 2005; henceforth the 'Victims' Code') and *The Witness Charter* (initially produced by the Ministry of Justice in 2008, and covering both prosecution and defence witnesses), helped to establish some minimum service standards for victims and witnesses as their cases progress through the criminal justice system. Notwithstanding this range of initiatives, a recent study by Victim Support (2011) found that victims were only being kept updated to a satisfactory level in approximately half of all reported incidents, which resulted in some feeling as though their cases were being neglected.

Developments since the beginning of the current decade have included the appointment of a Victims' Commissioner[18] to promote the interests of victims and witnesses and to encourage good practice in their treatment. Most recently, revised versions of both the Victims' Code (Ministry of Justice, 2013a) and Witness Charter (Ministry of Justice, 2013d) have been published. The new version of the Victims' Code, published in December 2013 under Section 33 of the Domestic Violence, Crime and Victims Act 2004, has been redesigned to make it more victim-focused and less process-oriented. It aims to ensure that resources are targeted at those groups of victims who are most in need: that is, victims of the most serious crimes, and victims who are persistently targeted or are vulnerable or intimidated. The Victim Personal Statement scheme has been included for the first time in the revised Victims' Code, in an effort to strengthen the voice of victims in the criminal justice system (Ministry of Justice, 2013c).

At the time of writing, Section 28 of the YJCEA, which provides for the pre-recording of cross-examination of vulnerable witnesses, is being piloted for child victims and witnesses, initially in three Crown Court areas; this provision was not originally implemented with the other 'special measures'. The potential benefits of pre-recorded cross-examination are that it allows the child to give evidence away from the pressured environment of the court and also reduces the stress associated with long periods of waiting for a case to come to trial. Lord Judge (2013) argued that the successful implementation of Section 28 for children could provide strong grounds for extending the provision to adult victims of sexual offences. Another recent development is the introduction by the CPS of the Victims' Right to Review Scheme[19] which gives victims the opportunity to seek a review of a CPS decision not to bring charges or to terminate proceedings against a suspect. The CPS has also produced new guidelines on prosecuting cases of child sexual abuse which, among other things, set out a new approach to assessing 'credibility'.[20] This focuses on the credibility of the overall allegation, rather than just on the credibility of the victim.

Despite the range of initiatives focused on supporting victims and witnesses throughout the prosecution process, there remain public and political concerns that change has not gone far enough – particularly on account of what has been described as poor treatment of victims in recent high profile trials concerning alleged sexual abuse (including historic abuse) of children and sexual offences against adults.[21] In a recent Victim Support (2013) report into the victimisation of people with mental health problems, only 10 of the 81 victims interviewed had been involved in cases which reached court. Several found their experience of cross-examination very difficult and felt unable to express their version of events. Moreover, few had heard of 'special measures' or had been granted them when they gave evidence. These findings correspond with those of McLeod et al (2010), who found that victims and witnesses with mental health conditions, learning disabilities and limited mental capacity often felt excluded from proceedings and frustrated in their interactions with legal representatives.

Provision for defendants at court

It is a long-standing principle in criminal law that defendants must be able to understand and participate effectively in the criminal proceedings of which they are a part (Jacobson and Talbot, 2009). This is reflected in the right to a fair trial enshrined in Article 6 of the European Convention on Human Rights, and the case law that supports it. The requirement for effective participation is reflected also in the criteria generally used to determine 'fitness to plead': namely, that the defendant can plead with understanding, can follow the proceedings, knows a juror can be challenged, can question the evidence, and can instruct counsel.[22]

Notwithstanding the fundamental importance, in terms of legal and human rights, of effective participation of defendants at court, the developing policy interest in supporting vulnerable victims and witnesses at court was not reflected – at least initially – in measures for vulnerable defendants. Most notably, Section 16(1) of the YJCEA explicitly excludes defendants from the 'special measures' provisions; it is stated that 'For the purposes of this Chapter a witness in criminal proceedings (other than the accused) is eligible for assistance by virtue of this section …' This relative neglect of vulnerable defendants' needs at court has been the focus of some considerable criticism (Jacobson and Talbot, 2009; Bradley, 2009; Tonry, 2010; Talbot, 2012). Talbot (2012), for example, has argued that statutory provisions for vulnerable witnesses and defendants should be equal and that the 'special measures' afforded to vulnerable witnesses, such as the provision of registered intermediaries as an aid to communication, should also be available to defendants. A recognition of the problems of understanding faced by vulnerable defendants, and the lack of specialist provision for these individuals, has also led to calls for further training and development for all court professionals (Talbot, 2008; Bradley, 2009; Jacobson and Talbot, 2009).

In light of concerns of these kinds, the statutory authorities, as well as legal professionals and practitioners, have increasingly recognised the need for support for vulnerable defendants to ensure that they are able to participate effectively in the court process and thereby exercise their right to a fair trial. Such support is further required if the courts service and other criminal justice agencies are to comply with their duty under the Equality Act 2010 to eliminate discrimination. In 2006, it was made permissible for a 'vulnerable accused' to give evidence to the court by a live television link, where certain conditions are met;[23] and in 2009 the right to support from an intermediary in court was extended to vulnerable defendants.[24] This latter provision has not yet been implemented; however, judges have the discretion to direct the court to appoint an intermediary for a vulnerable defendant (see Talbot, 2012 and Advocate's Gateway, 2013a).

While it does not have statutory force, Practice Direction III.30 within the *Consolidated Criminal Practice Direction* (Ministry of Justice, 2013b) outlines a range of measures for vulnerable defendants at both the Crown and magistrates' courts, most of which are aimed at supporting defendants' comprehension of the court process and their capacity to communicate, and making the court environment less intimidating:

> The court should ensure that what is to take place has been explained to a vulnerable defendant in terms he or she can understand and, at trial in the Crown Court, it should ensure in particular that the role of the jury has been explained. ... Throughout the trial the court should continue to ensure, by any appropriate means, that the defendant understands what is happening and what has been said by those on the bench, the advocates and witnesses. ... A trial should be conducted according to a timetable which takes full account of a vulnerable defendant's ability to concentrate. Frequent and regular breaks will often be appropriate. The court should ensure, so far as practicable, that the whole trial is conducted in clear language that the defendant can understand and that evidence in chief and cross-examination are conducted using questions that are short and clear.

In addition, the Practice Direction states that the judge should consider ordering the removal of wigs and gowns, permitting the defendant to sit with members of his or her family and restricting observation of proceedings from the public gallery. Many of these themes are also echoed in a toolkit recently produced by the Advocate's Gateway (2013a) which is designed to increase effective participation by young defendants at court. The toolkit recognises that defendants who are under the age of 18 need 'special consideration' at court and recommends several ways in which proceedings could be modified, including through the use of clear language, the provision of an explanation of proceedings at the beginning of the hearing in a way in which the defendant can understand, and seating the defendant outside the dock.

Access to justice for all?

The growing concern with the means by which defendants' vulnerabilities in the courtroom can best be addressed begs two important questions. The first is whether it is useful to maintain the distinction between, on the one hand, measures for vulnerable victims and witnesses and, on the other hand, those for vulnerable defendants. Relatively unusually, a report by the Advocacy Training

Council, *Raising the Bar*, published in 2011, looks at how the courts, and particularly advocates, should best address the vulnerabilities of *all* groups of court users: victims, witnesses and defendants. One of the major conclusions of the report is that the handling and questioning of vulnerable court users 'is a specialist skill, and should be recognised as such by practitioners, judges, training providers and regulators' (Advocacy Training Council, 2011, p 4). The report also calls for a 'change of culture' whereby advocates should develop the necessary awareness and knowledge both to identify and thereafter to respond appropriately to vulnerabilities, and in so doing to adopt a more individualised approach to the handling of court users. Since publication of *Raising the Bar*, the Advocacy Training Council has established a dedicated website, *The Advocate's Gateway*,[25] which provides a number of toolkits aimed at improving advocates' practice with respect to vulnerable court users. While some are specifically concerned with defendants *or* witnesses (such as the *Effective participation of young defendants* toolkit (2013a), referred to above), others maintain the broader 'court user' focus. These include, for example, a toolkit on the planning of questions to be put to vulnerable people or those with communication needs (Advocate's Gateway, 2013b).

The second question raised by recent policy and practice developments relating to vulnerable court users (of all kinds) concerns the rationale and criteria for defining 'vulnerability'. Some individuals who come to court have obvious mental health, comprehension or communication problems which may make it impossible for them to give evidence, or otherwise participate in the court process, without help. But – as we will demonstrate over the course of this book – the difficulties faced by victims, witnesses and defendants at court extend far beyond these readily definable vulnerabilities. Hence the task of helping all court users genuinely to engage with the court process entails much more than putting practical support in place for the most obviously vulnerable.

Notes

[1] www.judiciary.gov.uk/you-and-the-judiciary/going-to-court/crown-court (accessed 29 January 2014).

[2] The maximum sentence that can be imposed by magistrates is six months' custody for a single offence (12 months' for two or more either-way offences) or a fine of £5,000. (The £5,000 limit on fines will be removed when Section 85 of the Legal Aid, Sentencing and Punishment of Offenders Act 2012 comes into force.)

[3] Defendants dealt with at magistrates' courts have an automatic right of appeal to the Crown Court.

[4] These figures exclude 13,000 defendants who appeared at the Crown Court in 2011 in appeals against magistrates' decisions.

[5] This number is made up of around 12,000 who were discharged by the judge, 2,000 whose acquittal was ordered by the judge, and 6,000 who were found not guilty by the jury.

[6] The Crown Court Sentencing Survey is conducted by the Sentencing Council. The 2012 data are based on returns for April to December of that year, over which period information was collated on 58% of 63,357 sentences passed in the Crown Court (Sentencing Council, 2013).

[7] Various legal texts provide detailed descriptions of this process; see, for example, Gibson and Cavadino (2008); Padfield (2008).

[8] A pre-sentence report usually sets out the circumstances of the offence and the offender's background and current situation. It also presents what the probation officer considers to be the most appropriate sentencing option of those available to the court.

[9] For example a compensation order, restraining order or Anti-Social Behaviour Order.

[10] The main sources of guidance for sentencers are sentencing guidelines produced by the Sentencing Council (formerly the Sentencing Guidelines Council) and guideline judgments issued by the Court of Appeal. Further, sentencers are also bound by legislation which sets out maximum sentences and, in some circumstances, mandatory sentences.

[11] For more detail on judicial roles see www.judiciary.gov.uk/about-the-judiciary/who-are-the-judiciary/judicial-roles (accessed 16 January 2014); also Darbyshire (2011) provides an in-depth account of judicial roles, appointments and practices.

[12] At the time of writing, criminal lawyers are voicing much concern about the implications of proposed government reforms to criminal legal aid, aimed at reducing expenditure – but said by critics to run the risk of reducing defendants' access to representation and the quality of advocacy. On 6 January 2014, barristers effectively went on strike for the first time in their history, in protest at the proposed reforms (see 'Crime Doesn't Pay', *The Economist*, 11 January 2014).

[13] The rule has recently come under criticism from the Legal Services Board on the grounds that it does not serve a 'clear purpose' (Flood and Hviid, 2013, p 2).

[14] At the time of writing, a new, national court-based Witness Service is being commissioned by the Ministry of Justice. The existing arrangements for provision through Victim Support will conclude in March 2015.

[15] In the original Act, vulnerable witnesses included all children under 17 years of age, but this was amended to those aged under 18 by the Coroners and Justice Act 2009.

[16] New rule 3.8(4)(d) of the Criminal Procedure Rules 2013.

[17] It has since become possible for young witnesses to opt out of 'special measures' provisions, subject to the agreement of the court (www.cps.gov.uk/legal/s_to_u/special_measures/#a03 (accessed 29 May 2014)).

[18] The first Victims' Commissioner, Louise Casey, stepped down from the role in late 2011 and has since been replaced by Baroness Helen Newlove.

[19] www.cps.gov.uk/victims_witnesses/victims_right_to_review/index.html (accessed 23 January 2014).

[20] www.cps.gov.uk/legal/a_to_c/child_sexual_abuse (accessed 27 January 2014).

[21] See 'Stop "offensive" questioning of rape victims in court', *The Evening Standard*, 26 November 2013 (www.standard.co.uk/news/uk/stop-offensive-questioning-of-rape-victims-in-court-8964342.html (accessed 23 January 2014)).

[22] The legal test for 'fitness to plead', which dates from 1836, is widely criticised. The Law Commission, for example, argues that the test 'needs to be reformed so that it is fair and suitable for the criminal justice system of the 21st century' (http://lawcommission.justice.gov.uk/areas/unfitness-to-plead.htm (accessed 30 January 2014)).

[23] Under Section 33A of the YJCEA, inserted by the Police and Justice Act 2006.

[24] Under Section 33BA of the YJCEA, inserted by the Coroners and Justice Act 2009.

[25] www.theadvocatesgateway.org/toolkits (accessed 24 January 2014).

THREE

Court process and performance: constructing versions of 'the truth'

We tend to think of the Crown Court as a place where 'the truth' of an alleged wrongdoing is established – whether by way of jury verdict or a defendant's guilty plea – in order that, where the wrongdoing is proven, an appropriate punishment can be meted out. However, the findings of this study suggest that the reality is more complicated than this. Very often, court proceedings seem to be not so much about establishing 'what really happened' but, rather, are an arena for *managing conflict* between alleged wrongdoers and those allegedly wronged by them, and between their wildly different accounts of the same event. In the process, different black-and-white versions of what is often a shades-of-grey reality are aired and debated, while 'the truth' of it all remains unknown and unknowable. This process of conflict management, moreover, is undertaken through the medium of a highly ritualised public performance, which helps to maintain the court environment's 'delicate separateness to normal reality' (Fielding, 2006, p 53).

Drawing on the findings of our empirical research, this chapter will look at how and why 'the truth' often remains elusive in the Crown Court, both in cases which go to trial, and in cases where the defendant has pleaded guilty. This will be followed by discussion of courtroom 'performance' and ritual, and of the incongruities contained within these proceedings.

Crown Court trials and the elusive truth

'It's who told the best story won, I suppose.'

With the above comment, one of this study's respondents, Steve, summed up his most recent experience of the Crown Court. Steve was a middle-aged man who had appeared in court as a defendant many times; on the last occasion, he was on trial for arson. He was found guilty of the offence and received a six-year prison sentence.

Notwithstanding the taken-for-grantedness of 'the notion that trial is a truth finding exercise' (Sanchirico, 2001, p 1306),[1] arguably it is in the very nature of the adversarial system that 'the truth' is likely to remain at least partially elusive or hidden during a trial. The essential features of a Crown Court trial are that the parties in the case give voice to their opposing accounts of 'what really happened', while the role of the judge is effectively to act as referee, and the jury must decide whom to believe – albeit the principle of the presumption of innocence means that a 'not guilty' verdict, in theory, reflects the jury's *lack of belief* in the prosecution account rather than their necessary *belief* in the defence account. This contrasts with inquisitorial systems of justice (as present in civil law jurisdictions including France, Germany and Italy) in which judges, far from being neutral arbiters, have responsibility for investigating and uncovering the facts of the cases before them. It is thus a commonly voiced criticism of the adversarial system that outcomes tend to be shaped by the fluency and persuasiveness of the advocates – "who told the best story" in Steve's words – rather than the strength of the case.[2]

But if we are talking about the elusive truth in a Crown Court trial, there are two other considerations beyond the essential nature of the adversarial process. First, it is notable that a great many cases dealt with by the Crown Court concern messy and complicated occurrences or patterns of behaviour, in relation to which there exists no single, or conceivably accessible, 'true' version of events. Secondly, while there is an emphasis on *objectivity* in the presentation of evidence and juror decision-making, this is constantly undermined by explicit or implicit recourse to *subjectivity*.

Black-and-white accounts of shades-of-grey realities

When the case for the prosecution is presented in a Crown Court trial, the jury is usually given a clear-cut account of the event or series of events that allegedly made up the criminal offence. The defence, in turn, may counter the prosecution account by presenting an equally clear-cut alternate version of events, although sometimes the defence proceeds by undermining the prosecution version rather than developing its own alternative, given that its essential task is to introduce a 'reasonable' level of doubt in the jurors' minds about what the prosecution has told them.

Often, little of what the jury is told – from either the prosecution or defence standpoint – does justice to the complex and convoluted realities of the events with which the case is concerned. The court hears a 'deliberate simplification' of events, which tends 'to strip away volumes of context and history', and has the effect of 'amplifying the differences between protagonists, focusing on the circumstantial and situational, and offering a stark argument for fault-finding and judgment' (Rock, 1993, pp 31, 32). Pre-trial, the process of charging an individual with an offence involves redefining the alleged criminal actions in carefully circumscribed legal terms. During the trial, the rules of evidence determine what elements of the 'story' of those actions can and cannot be told.

Gaps and flaws in memory further limit the comprehensiveness of witness accounts of the events under scrutiny in a trial; although lawyers examine and cross-examine witnesses as if a perfect memory is the norm – asking them about the tiniest details of past events, and vigorously challenging them as soon as any inconsistencies emerge.[3]

A prosecution witness in one of our observed cases (Case 3) unwisely remarked, when pressed on what she had meant by a particular Facebook entry she had made some 20 months before, that she could not remember because "I have an awful memory, to be fair." The defence counsel leapt on this and repeated gleefully: "*You have an awful memory!* ..." Also serving to obscure the 'reality' that counsel seek to elucidate is the fact that many cases do not only revolve around purported actions, but also around the purported states of mind of the main players. For example, the defendant's intention is an underlying consideration in most cases, since it is a key principle of criminal law that a crime must have a psychological element (*mens rea* or criminal intent); and, in some cases, the extent or nature of intent may be the central consideration for a jury. Sometimes a victim's state of mind may also be a key issue, for example, where a defendant claims to have acted in self-defence against an attack by the alleged victim, or where an allegation of rape turns on the question of consent.

The highly chaotic circumstances of many offences, and alleged offences, is such that distilling the essence of 'what really happened' may seem a near impossible task – sometimes even for the protagonists themselves, let alone counsel, judge and jury. A barrister interviewed for this study told us that the "uncertainty" is the most difficult thing for defendants attending court: that is, uncertainty not only in the sense that they do not know what is going to happen to them at the conclusion of the case, but also

> '... because it may well be that, honestly reflecting on what happened themselves, they can't be sure [what happened] ... "I was drunk. I can't remember." "I'm sure I wouldn't have done it *if* ..." "That doesn't sound like me. I wouldn't do a thing like that – at least, not sober."'

In observed Case 2, a 21-year-old defendant, Emmanuel, was charged with inflicting grievous bodily harm on a fellow player at a Sunday morning football match. The assault had occurred in the course of what was variously referred to (by both prosecution and defence counsel and by the judge) as a "mass brawl", "mass confrontation", "melee" or "general hubbub", which broke out among a large number of the players after one had been sent off. There was no dispute that the victim had been severely assaulted – a punch to the side of the face had fractured his cheekbone – or that Emmanuel had been involved in the brawl; the question for the jury was whether Emmanuel had been the man who had thrown the damaging punch. Over two-and-a-half days, eight prosecution witnesses (the victim, five other players, the match referee, and one of the team managers) gave evidence about what they had perceived to be the ethnicity, height, build, hairstyle and clothing of the attacker. There was enough inconsistency between these accounts from witnesses – several of whom had apparently been reluctant to come to court, including the referee who had been threatened with a summons to compel his attendance[4] – for the prosecution counsel to feel he had to acknowledge it. He told the jury: "[A case doesn't come] in a neat and tidy package with a legal bow on top if it … That is not life … You'll make sensible allowances to reflect that reality." Nevertheless, the jury found Emmanuel guilty after more than a day of deliberation. (Meanwhile, during a break in proceedings, the court clerk and usher chatted about the case in somewhat disapproving terms: "I'm more concerned with the money wasted on a Sunday morning punch-up," the clerk remarked.)

Many offences, and particularly those that are violent or sexual in nature, occur – or are alleged to occur – in the context of difficult and complex human relationships. The messiness of human interactions is such that, as we have said, there may be a multitude of shades of grey to events that are presented to the court in largely black and white terms. In Case 1, Mark was tried for committing actual bodily assault against his (then) girlfriend's two-year-old daughter, Millie. Although Mark was found not guilty, it had not been disputed by the defence that Millie had received non-accidental injuries (in the form of bruising) and that the circumstance in which these occurred was the rapidly deteriorating relationship between her mother and Mark. Exactly how Millie's injuries had been inflicted remained unclear, and would doubtless always remain so. What did emerge with some clarity was the unhappy picture of the relationship breakdown, although prosecution and defence argued over some of the details, both significant and mundane: Which of the two of them made the final decision to end things? Did they or did they not have sex on their last night together? And why exactly did Mark take a bag of washing with him – and what items did this washing include – when he left the house for good the next morning?

Sometimes, the more extreme the case, the more multi-layered and tangled is the network of human relationships which forms the background story. We observed part of a trial of a father accused of having repeatedly raped his very young daughter, who was now in her early twenties. The daughter gave a detailed account of being raped by her father on the bathroom floor, while her mother watched television downstairs. Having not seen the verdict, we do not know if the rape allegations were ultimately proven; but there was no dispute in court about the generally dysfunctional nature of the family, and the chaos of the family home (the mother was said to be a compulsive hoarder). Nevertheless, while graphically describing the alleged abuse by her father, the daughter also spoke of how he had cared for her: "I enjoyed my childhood ... I wouldn't've changed it for the world ... He provided for us, he cared for us ... He was a loving father."

The jury and objectivity or subjectivity

The elusive nature of 'the truth' in a Crown Court trial is manifest also in the manner in which an emphasis on objectivity coincides with an emphasis on subjectivity throughout the process. A jury is told to return a guilty verdict only where the case against the defendant has been proven beyond reasonable doubt. In order to 'prove' its case, the prosecution usually takes the greatest care to demonstrate the objectivity of the evidence (of all kinds) it is placing before the jury; and often the defence case depends on refuting these claims to objectivity. Meanwhile, the judge frequently reiterates to the jury that they must make their decision only on the basis of the 'facts' that are presented to them. The *Crown Court Bench Book,* which provides guidance to judges on how to instruct juries, suggests that judges say, in explaining the respective functions of judge and jury: 'The directions I give you as to the law you must accept and apply. However, whenever I refer to the evidence the position is quite different: All questions of *evidence and fact are for you and you alone to decide*' (Judicial Studies Board, 2010, p 28; emphasis added). Accordingly, the judge at the outset of a robbery trial (Case 6) told the jury: "As in all criminal cases we will try the case together ... The law is my responsibility; the facts are a matter for you."

But at the same time as the jury are told to focus on the objective facts of the case, so too they are told time and again to exercise their 'judgement'; to draw, collectively, on their 'life experiences' in their deliberations; to use their 'common sense'. (Appeals to 'common sense' are particularly common in the courtroom, but are, as has been noted by Fielding (2006, p 133), 'a malleable tool'. In the name of common sense, 'jurors are asked both to tolerate contradiction and to punish it, to accept denials of the obvious, and to impute the most contrary motives or to look for no motive at all'.) How else, after all, can the necessary decisions be made about whom to believe among witnesses who present diametrically opposed versions of the same event, or about whose interpretation of physical or other evidence to accept? Thus jurors receive starkly contradictory messages about the precise nature of their decision-making role:

> 'The factual findings are for you and you alone ... The facts are subject to your own judgement.'
> [Prosecution counsel; Case 1 – assault]

> 'Ladies and gentlemen, this is a perfect jury trial – [it's about] credibility: your assessment of the witnesses ... Avoid any feeling of sympathy; avoid any feeling of prejudice. Please – just return a verdict of guilty.'
> [Prosecution counsel; Case 6 – robbery]

> '[We have 12 jurors because] it allows you to pool your common sense and your experience of the world ... You go into the jury room, and ask what does your common sense tell you about what went on; you judge if the witnesses are credible, reliable, as you judge people in everyday life – not just by what they say, but by demeanour, facial expressions ... But sympathy or emotion has no place [here] ... leave emotion or sympathy outside ... [You need to ask:] "What do the facts tell me?"'
> [Judge, summing up; Case 2 – assault]

We also see the juxtaposition of objectivity and subjectivity when counsel present conflicting interpretations of evidence that appears to be of a scientific nature or takes a seemingly immutable, physical form. Like almost any other piece of evidence, physical artefacts are 'open to interpretation', although nothing might seem to be 'more authoritative than physical objects, particularly those that can be exhibited and handled in court'; while, with respect to expert (for example, expert medical) evidence, 'the border between fact and opinion is crossed more often ... than we may think' (Fielding, 2006, p 76–9).

In our observed Case 1, as noted above, Mark was on trial for assaulting two-year-old Millie, the daughter of his then girlfriend. Among the prosecution witnesses who appeared in this trial was a consultant paediatrician, Dr Shah, who had examined Millie after the alleged assault, and had arranged for the bruising he observed on her body and legs to be photographed. In court, Dr Shah described the bruises, while the photographs were distributed to the jury. He stated that, based on their colouring, the bruises had been recent when he examined the child, and that they appeared to have been the result of non-accidental injuries caused, for the most part, by a rounded, hard instrument such as a knee, fist or elbow. In the face of this seemingly powerful evidence, the defence counsel approached the cross-examination of Dr Shah by challenging both the 'science' of the evidence – citing an academic article which disputed the normal medical practice of dating bruises by colour – and the witness's general credibility and professionalism – querying his failure to measure the bruises and to have some of the bruises photographed, disputing the accuracy of some of his notes, and asking if he was 'under pressure' at his hospital and had a large workload.

Three days later, when summing up the defence case, counsel recalled these apparent inadequacies of Dr Shah's evidence (declared as 'objective evidence' by her prosecuting counterpart) on the bruising. She undermined the claims to material, scientific status by referring to the 'mystery' of the absence of photographs of some bruises, and noted that "it's unfortunate, isn't it, that the busy Dr Shah had not made a comprehensive record of the injuries". She referred to the indistinct colours of the bruises in the available photographs, and observed that while the jury were being asked "to use science" in making their assessment of the evidence, "the science is incomplete". (We do not know how "the busy Dr Shah" himself viewed the experience of giving evidence; but we can guess that he may have found it somewhat frustrating, not least because he was told to attend court at 9 am but was not called to take the witness stand until 3.15 pm, and this was the third occasion on which he had attended court for this particular case, following two prior adjournments.)

While they are required to weigh up the conflicting pieces of evidence presented to them and, as we have seen, may be exhorted to draw on 'common sense' or 'life experiences' in so doing, jurors are frequently told that they must not 'speculate' about what they hear or see in court. "Don't be drawn into speculation – we do not decide criminal cases on guess work," said a judge when summing up in a case involving dangerous driving (Case 7). The issue of juror speculation came to the fore in a high profile case that, at the time of writing, was recently before the Crown Court. Vicky Pryce, an economist and ex-wife of former cabinet minister Chris Huhne, was tried for perverting the course of justice, after it was established that she had accepted speeding points on her driving licence on behalf of her (then) husband. The first jury to hear the case were discharged after telling the judge they were unlikely to reach a verdict, but prior to this had submitted 10 questions to the judge about how they should make their decision. One of the questions was the following:

> 'If there is debatable evidence supporting the prosecution's case, can inferences be drawn to arrive at a verdict? If so, inferences/speculation on the full evidence or only where you have directed us to do so, e.g. circumstantial evidence, lies, failure by Vicky Pryce to mention facts to the police.'

The judge replied in the negative, and added:

> 'The drawing of inferences is a permissible process, speculation is not. You must not speculate and you could not draw safe inferences from debatable evidence because you need to be sure that your inference, your reasonable common sense conclusion, is correct. In this case, the evidence on which the prosecution relies is largely undisputed.'

The distinction between 'speculation' and the 'drawing of inferences' is a fine one, and would seem to rest on the completeness of the facts or evidence from which a conclusion is being drawn.[5] Since much of the evidence before a jury is typically disputed, by the very nature of the adversarial court process – remember that the defence lawyer in the actual bodily harm case discussed above argued that "the science is incomplete" with respect to the evidence on bruising – a jury that pauses to consider the decision-making process might find it difficult to know when they are (impermissibly) speculating as opposed to (permissibly) inferring.

Another of the questions from the jury in the first Pryce trial also appeared to go to the very heart of the process of decision-making: the judge was asked to define 'reasonable doubt'. The judge's reply was:

'A reasonable doubt is a doubt which is reasonable. These are ordinary English words that the law doesn't allow me to help you with beyond the written directions that I have already given.'[6]

Although it has been noted by legal academics and judges that juries can find it difficult to understand the concept of 'beyond reasonable doubt',[7] judges are indeed explicitly discouraged from attempting to explain it. In the 400-page *Crown Court Bench Book – Directing the jury*, discussion of the concept is limited to the following: 'The prosecution proves its case if the jury, having considered all the evidence relevant to the charge they are considering, are sure that the defendant is guilty. Further explanation is unwise'; with an added note that 'Being sure is the same as entertaining no reasonable doubt' (Judicial Studies Board, 2010, p 16).[8] The Vicky Pryce jury, when being dismissed by the judge, were admonished for their "fundamental deficit in understanding of [their] role"; a criticism that was echoed in much of the reporting of the case.[9]

A final point worth noting on the theme of the intersection of subjectivity and objectivity in the court process is that once a guilty verdict has been reached and the case moves to sentencing, judges are often ready to stress the intuitive, subjective dimension of their own decision-making on sentence (Jacobson and Hough, 2007). Hence, for example, in sentencing a young woman for perverting the course of justice (Case 3), a judge commented that the defendant had been convicted on "clear and compelling evidence", and then provided her own assessment of the individual's personality: "I have seen and watched you give evidence and I conclude that you are a manipulative young woman."

Guilty pleas and the elusive truth

It is noted in Chapter Two that the bulk of defendants who are sentenced at the Crown Court have pleaded guilty to their offence or offences. On the surface, it might seem that the court's acceptance of a guilty plea means that a relatively straightforward or unambiguous account of 'what really happened' has been established. In fact, guilty pleas often reflect a contingent and highly contested version of events: in other words, 'the truth' can be just as elusive in cases in which there has been a guilty plea as in cases that have gone to trial. This is because guilty pleas are frequently the product of a process of negotiation between prosecution and defence – a process that is broadly termed 'plea-bargaining'.

Negotiated pleas

There are three main forms of plea-bargaining, all of which may occur simultaneously. First, defendants may plead guilty on the understanding that they will receive a lesser sentence as a result (the sentence discount for a guilty plea will be further discussed below). Secondly, the defence may engage in 'charge-bargaining' whereby a guilty plea is offered in return for a change in the *number* or *type* of charges faced. For example, a defendant might agree to plead guilty to a less serious assault charge than that with which he or she was originally charged, or to a single count of robbery rather than a robbery plus an offensive weapon count. Thirdly, 'fact-bargaining' involves negotiation between defence and prosecution about the 'basis of plea': that is, the specific details of the crime to which the charge relates. For example, a defendant could agree to plead guilty to a robbery on the basis that the victim fell to the ground in a struggle, but was not deliberately pushed or punched. (If the prosecution rejects the defendant's account, the court may opt to hold a 'Newton hearing': that is, a kind of mini-trial at which the judge, sitting alone, hears evidence and determines the basis on which the sentence should be passed.[10]) Both charge- and fact-bargaining entail a process of negotiation and compromise over 'what really happened'. As noted by Feeley with respect to plea-bargaining in the United States, 'much of what passes for plea bargaining is really negotiation over the meaning of facts ... Facts are malleable. They must be mobilized, and often they are manufactured' (1992, p 197).

Defendants are offered considerable incentives to plead guilty – the sentence discount, as well as the opportunity to plead to lesser charges and/or a more favourable version of events – because of the many benefits to the criminal justice system which flow from a high rate of guilty pleas. The benefits include the higher conviction rate than would otherwise be achieved, and the reduced number of resource-intensive criminal trials (and associated reduced emotional and other costs to victims and witnesses who are not required to give evidence in trials). Thus the fact that the large majority of defendants in the criminal courts plead guilty is 'in no sense ... a "natural" or "unavoidable" phenomenon: the system is structured so as to produce it' (Ashworth and Redmayne, 2010, p 418). More bluntly, Bottoms and McClean noted in 1976 that 'it is recognised that the whole system of criminal justice would collapse administratively if defendants exercised their right to plead not guilty in any significantly greater numbers' (1976, p 104).

Plea-bargaining is, then, a significant and pervasive part of the criminal justice process in England and Wales, although not to the extent that it is in some other common law jurisdictions. In the United States, it has been claimed in a widely cited observation, plea-bargaining is 'not some adjunct to the criminal justice system; *it is the criminal justice system*' (Scott and Stuntz, 1992, p 1912).[11] Traditionally in England and Wales, plea-bargaining has operated as an informal rather than formal system, and therefore has generally been 'low-visibility', such that 'all the interesting exchanges take place off the record often in hurried and furtive encounters at the doors of the courts' (Baldwin, 2008, p 247). The very informality of most plea-bargaining in this jurisdiction lends itself to criticisms on grounds of presumed inconsistency and the evident lack of transparency. With little empirical research into this issue having been conducted,[12] the extent of the practice, and its implications for the legal process, for defendants and for justice more broadly, are difficult to quantify. However, there have been relatively recent moves towards formalisation and greater openness of plea-bargaining in England and Wales: notable developments include the introduction of a structured system of sentence discounts for guilty pleas (see below), and a Court of Appeal decision which, since 2005, has permitted the court to provide advance indications of sentence, known as 'Goodyear indications'.[13]

Victim, witness and defendant perspectives on guilty pleas

One repercussion of a system in which guilty pleas are strongly encouraged (including through mechanisms for plea-bargaining) is that defendants frequently change their plea from not guilty to guilty at a late stage in the prosecution process. Guilty pleas as a trial is about to start or is already in progress are not uncommon, which can provoke mixed feelings for the victims and witnesses who are expecting to give evidence in court. On the one hand they may be happy to hear of the conviction and relieved that they no longer face the possibly very daunting prospect of giving evidence and being cross-examined. On the other hand, they may be frustrated that they have been denied the opportunity to 'have their day in court' and to provide their own account of events. If a late guilty plea follows a charge- or fact-bargain and, as a result, is perceived by the victim as reflecting a very incomplete or minimised version of 'what really happened', this can add considerably to a victim's frustration. So, too, can perceptions that the defendant has been 'game-playing' – for example, by waiting to see whether key witnesses turn up at court before deciding to plead guilty.[14]

A late guilty plea was certainly a cause of frustration for one of our respondents: Stella, who had witnessed a woman threaten a man with a large knife. Stella described arriving at court and being "sort of left to stew for a couple of hours while they all went off and negotiated what they were going to do". She was all the more frustrated because she could otherwise have used the time to visit her seriously ill son in hospital. She was then told, to her great surprise, that the defendant had pleaded guilty, and was angered to learn subsequently that the defendant had received a suspended sentence. In Stella's eyes, this was a highly inadequate sentence which reflected the defendant's effective manipulation of the system and the system's lack of interest in uncovering the real 'facts' of the case:

> 'I think had I got onto the witness stand she wouldn't have got away as lightly. ... What the police told me afterwards, and the barristers or whoever they are, said that she was claiming she was provoked and everything. She certainly wasn't provoked from what I saw. ... Even if she'd pleaded guilty to it, the judge should have still come and asked me what I saw. ... So she's got away on a much lighter sentence and she's probably laughing: "I've given them all this aggro, the police."'

Another of our witness respondents, Debbie, was left disconcerted by a late guilty plea. She had witnessed two men making their escape from a burglary, both of whom were subsequently arrested but only one of whom pleaded guilty. Debbie was willing to give evidence against the defendant who was pleading not guilty, but described being discourteously treated by the police and Witness Care Unit in the run-up to the court case, and facing some considerable inconvenience because of repeated rescheduling. She finally attended court and spent the day in the Witness Service waiting room. In the late afternoon she was told that the defendant had changed his plea to guilty. Debbie was left disillusioned with the court process, and particularly with what she saw as defendants' capacity to play the 'game' to their advantage through their pleas:

> 'What I've taken away from it is, it's all like a big game, really. And what shocked me at the time was that ... I was very surprised that one person had pleaded guilty and

somebody had pleaded not guilty. I assumed: well, clearly they're together. And they make separate [pleas] ... Then it was explained to me how sometimes people come to court because they kind of hedge their bets, because they know how difficult it is to get witnesses to court and they know how difficult it is to make everything work.'

One of our defendant respondents, Patrice, gave his own account of the process of charge-bargaining in which he had been involved:

Interviewer: At what point did you change your plea [to guilty]?
Patrice: Originally they charged with me with GBH section 18 [causing grievous bodily harm with intent] and the section 20 [inflicting grievous bodily harm]... and then they dropped the charges down to ABH [actual bodily harm], and then I wanted to drop it down to common assault, but my barrister said to me to leave it at ABH − don't go further − cause then they'll try to nick me for ... an offensive weapon [as well] ... It would've been common assault then, [and] it would've been an offensive weapon too.

The offence itself was an assault by Patrice on his former girlfriend. His description of the incident − according to which he had accidentally injured his ex-girlfriend (with a broken glass) in the course of an attack on his brother − reminds us of just how messy and unfathomable is much court business:

'Then [after I ended the relationship] it was like a woman scorned, and she kept phoning me up and threatening to kill my new partner's child and all this kind of crap was going on. And then she phoned us up ... said she was coming to my local pub to take my brother home and have sex with him − but she didn't put it that way, she put it another way! Know what I mean? And I went to the pub, and she come in there all gloating, and my brother was there, so I beat my brother up, and in the process she got injured − in the process.'

Patrice complained of the sentencing judge that he had failed to understand the anger that had caused him to attack his brother:

> '[The judge said] that [my ex-girlfriend] can go out with whoever she wants. But that weren't – that wasn't the issue ... The issue was my brother shouldn't be going out with her. That's why me and my brother had what we had. So he missed the issue! [*Laughs*] So he must've thought that I wanted to get back with her. And I want nothing to do with her – you know what I mean? She's free to go out with whoever she wants. It's my brother – he's *not* free to go with my ex-partner of 15 years.'

The sentencing of defendants who have pleaded guilty

In England and Wales, sentencing decisions are guided by the principle of proportionality: that is, the assumption that the severity of the sentence should match the seriousness of the offence. For this purpose, offence seriousness is defined by statute (Section 143(1) of the Criminal Justice Act 2003) in terms of two dimensions: the *harm* that the offence caused, was intended to cause or might foreseeably have caused; and the offender's *culpability* or blameworthiness in committing the offence (Ashworth, 2010; Ashworth and Roberts, 2012).

Again, however, we see here the slipperiness of representations of 'reality' in court: the relationship between offence seriousness, on the one hand, and severity of punishment, on the other, is more complicated and contingent than might be supposed. Factors other than offence harm and offender culpability can have a significant bearing on the sentence passed. Most notably, a defendant's guilty plea can have an enormous impact on sentencing. As discussed above, a defendant pleading guilty may have successfully negotiated a reduced charge, or may have admitted guilt in relation to a less serious version of events than had originally been alleged. Accordingly, the defendant is liable to face a less serious penalty than would have been the case had he or she been found guilty at trial of the original charge. Beyond that, as also noted above, the guilty plea *in itself* qualifies the defendant for a reduced sentence. Since the implementation of the Criminal Justice and Public Order Act 1994, the criminal courts have been required by law to take into account a defendant's guilty plea, and the circumstances in which the plea was submitted, in passing sentence.[15] The current sentencing guideline on plea (Sentencing Guidelines Council, 2007) identifies specific levels of reduction for various stages at which the plea is entered, ranging from a one-third reduction when the defendant pleads guilty at the earliest reasonable opportunity, to one-tenth where the plea is entered just as or after the trial begins. Moreover, a guilty plea can have a significant bearing on the *personal mitigation* that is taken into account in sentencing: that is, those factors relating to the defendant's attitudes or circumstances which may persuade a judge to pass a lesser sentence than would otherwise be imposed, given the seriousness of the offence. In particular, a defendant who pleads guilty can claim to be remorseful, and remorse is commonly treated as a mitigating factor. Logically, it is difficult for defendants who have pleaded not guilty subsequently to claim, at the point of sentence, that they deeply regret having committed to the offence, feel grief for the pain suffered by the victim, and will do their best never to repeat it (Jacobson and Hough, 2007).

The extent to which a plea can be intrinsically bound up with mitigation was amply demonstrated in the sentencing of defendant Emmanuel in Case 2, described above. Here, the defence counsel pointed to various mitigating aspects of Emmanuel's character and circumstances: he pointed out that this was a young man with no previous convictions, who was working hard as a plumber, having recently completed his training, and was both supportive of and supported by his family. (We had observed first-hand the support that the defendant received from his family: he was accompanied at court by his mother, grandmother, aunt and two uncles.) The judge, however, was unimpressed with these efforts at mitigation. He observed that "All of these points would have been good points if he'd pleaded guilty" and told the court that the defendant had "shown no remorse, no empathy" – although he also, in somewhat contradictory fashion, stated that Emmanuel would not be punished for fighting his case. In passing sentence, the judge commented that "If ever there was a case where credit for plea was so important, this is it" and said that a guilty plea would have given the court a wider range of options. The not guilty plea, however, meant that the defendant had lost mitigation other than his 'good character' (that is, his entirely clean record). The judge passed a nine-month custodial sentence, reiterating that Emmanuel was being sentenced as a man of "impeccable good character", which made his decision to plead not guilty "all the more distressing".

Having heard the sentence, Emmanuel spoke from the dock: "Judge – can I say something?" The judge ignored him, and he then waved to his family – "Bye, Mum ... Uncle" – as he was taken out by the security officer.

Ritualised, theatrical management of conflict

So far, we have argued in this chapter that many Crown Court proceedings leave undetermined, to a greater or lesser extent, 'what really happened' in relation to the alleged offence. These proceedings are a means by which the authorities seek to manage conflict between different parties, without necessarily providing for a definitive resolution of the conflict or uncovering of how it came about.[16] The process of conflict management entails, moreover, the translation of the messy realities of human misdeeds, intrigue and violence into a form of theatre. Indeed it has been argued that it is precisely this 'theatrical character of lawsuits' which enables them to 'redirect aggression', in the sense that '[a]ggression, the need to fight and have revenge, is acted out and is thereby ritually expressed and controlled' (Ball, 1975, p 107). Similarly, the 'performances' of the courtroom can be seen as having the capacity to 'represent and replay social conflict and violence, turning history into dramatic narrative, fictionalizing social trauma, transforming it into the system of social representations, exchanges, surrogacies that make up the law' (Peters, 2008, p 185).

The parallels between theatre and court proceedings – and particularly the adversarial trial – are many and have always been a subject of comment:

> Traditionally and situationally, judicial proceedings are dramatic. Aristotle noted the importance of forensic oratory as a special device of legal rhetoric; playwrights have always appreciated the dramatic value of a trial scene; lawyers have always been cognisant of rhetorical presentations. (Carlen, 1976a, p 19)

The theatre–court parallels include the fact that court cases are played out, or are potentially played out, in full public view. The content of many cases is in itself dramatic: they deal with extremes of behaviour and emotion, or at the very least with difficult, disturbing, unusual and occasionally blackly humorous circumstances and situations. The structure of the criminal trial could hardly be more theatrical: the entire process takes shape around the competing performances of prosecution and defence counsel and culminates in the moment of high drama when the foreman of the jury announces 'guilty' or 'not guilty' to the tense and silent court. The individual components of a trial are 'choreographed precisely and unambiguously', with the participants ready to 'come forward at their proper times to perform stylized parts' (Rock, 1993, p 27).

Many sentencing hearings, too, have their elements of theatre, such as when a defence lawyer makes an impassioned plea in mitigation, or when a judge hesitates before announcing the sentence, having built up to this point with a stern and vivid account of the seriousness of the offence. (Sometimes, for example, a judge might tell a defendant that he or she is facing custody, and certainly deserves custody, but will then pause before telling the court that on this occasion the defendant is to be spared a prison sentence.) The rituals and formalities of the Crown Court add further layers of theatricality, or more of a sense of a detachment from whatever we might consider real life. It is hardly surprising, therefore, that the criminal courts have long featured so centrally in books, plays, films and television dramas.

This is not to say, however, that the relationship between the courts and theatre is straightforward. Peters observes that while 'theatricality is essential to the production of law', there is also an opposition between the two, to the extent that we perceive the law as being about seeking out truths and theatre as being about the presentation of lies. Hence 'law must always be wary of the theatre that lies in its heart ... Theatre is law's twisted mirror, its funhouse double: ever-present, substantiating, mocking, reinforcing, undermining.' According to Peters, the law's 'oscillation between theatricality and antitheatricality' is manifest in our understanding of due process, such that, for example:

> ... criminal trials must be public, but not too public; show trials are bad, but secret trials are bad as well; evidence must be relevant, but not so dramatic as to be *too* relevant (no mutilated bodies on the legal stage); testimony must be live, but not be too lively (witnesses must stay in the box); what witnesses say and show should move juries, but it shouldn't move them too much (2008, p 198–9).

Public spectacle

One of the theatrical aspects of court proceedings is their public nature. This can be a source of concern or distress to those involved, regardless of whether the only people who view the process are a few individuals connected to the case, or whether media attention propels the case onto a much larger stage. The public dimension of the administration of the law is central to many conceptions of justice and, indeed, democracy. 'When cases proceed in public, courts institutionalize democracy's claim to impose constraints on state power' notes Resnik (2008, p 807), who also cites Bentham's well-known statement that 'Publicity is the very soul of justice ... It keeps the judge himself, while trying, under trial.' Open justice is a central requirement of Article 6 of the European Convention on Human Rights – the right to a fair trial, according to which 'Everyone is entitled to a fair and public hearing'.

The vast majority of Crown Court hearings are held in public: all courtrooms have a public gallery from which members of the public can observe proceedings. The media, likewise, have a right to attend and report on cases heard in the Crown Court, other than in certain specific circumstances where reporting restrictions are applied by the court (for example, in relation to most cases where defendants are under the age of 18). Criminal justice policy in England and Wales continues to assert that 'open justice' is a principle which is 'central to the rule of law' (Judicial Studies Board, 2009, p 6).[17] With the stated purpose of enhancing the transparency and openness of justice, the current government has introduced legislation, in the Crime and Courts Act 2013, to overturn the ban on the filming of court proceedings.

Some of the defendants and defendant family members we interviewed for this study had evidently been unprepared for the public nature of court proceedings, and found it objectionable that the serious business of their lives could seemingly be treated as a source of entertainment or casual interest by others.

> 'We had a nosey neighbour from the estate, which was just so horrible ... Horrible because it is like, this is my life, it is not something on TV. She has come to do a nosey bother about it you know; I don't like that.'
> [Trish; defendant's partner]

> 'It's not right that people can just come in to court because they feel like it ... to listen to people's stories.'
> [Danny; defendant]

> 'Yes, there were a few people in the public gallery. I think there was the victim's people, and press, I think – some journalists or something. You had some students – I think they may have been doing some law courses or something. And they came to it to see how it is in the courts of law, I'd say ... I was thinking: Wow, wow, these people, going

to know about what's happening here … Why? What's it got to do with them? That's what I thought.'
[Kwame; defendant]

Some of our defendant respondents had been convicted of sex offences and were particularly sensitive to being under public scrutiny both inside the courtroom and outside it, through media coverage of their cases. One such individual, Kevin, said that a "garbled version of events" had been presented in newspapers and discussed on the radio, and spoke of his fears that "I'd get a brick through the window or something". Another, William, described ringing his mother after the court case and being told by her: "By the way, you're in the *L– Reporter* and the *Messenger.*" Maurice told us that his case had been reported in *The Sun*, and that he had been aware that he "could have had six bells kicked out of me". In contrast, Ali, who had been convicted of a serious drugs offence, appeared to take pride in his notoriety:

'They had police guards there innit, because it was a high profile case. You can Google it, "Ali Shazad drug bust", innit. If you put my name in and put "drug bust 2008, 24-hour drugs operation" and all that, it will come up. It came up in *The Times* and the *Advertiser*: named and shamed.'

As he spoke, Ali pulled out his smartphone and showed the interviewer that his case could be found through a simple Google search.

Ritual and formality

In any courtroom, an array of rituals and formalities are expected to help create an aura of authority and a sense of detachment from the mundane world outside. As observed by Carlen with respect to magistrates' courts (1976a, p 25): 'Courtroom ceremony is maintained partly to facilitate physical control of defendants and any others who may step out of pace and partly to refurbish the historically sacred meanings attached to law.' If ritual and formality is a feature of most court processes, it is particularly pronounced within criminal proceedings of the Crown Court, in which the wigs and gowns worn by the judge and barristers set them apart from the lay participants in proceedings, and various archaic and highly formal modes of speech and interaction further underline the distinctiveness of the place and the activities within it. The authority of the judicial process can also be expressed through the very architecture of courtrooms and court buildings.[18] Courts create 'sacred' spaces of a kind, within which, as in cathedrals, people feel compelled to 'act in a ritualistic way: lower their voice, duck their heads, and tiptoe around once they enter' (Scheffer et al, 2010, p 141). But perhaps – to return to the theme elaborated above – it is a sense of theatre, more than a sense of sacred authority, that is most convincingly evoked by 'the design and appointment of the courtroom, enhanced by costuming and ceremony' (Ball, 1975, p 83).

The ritual and formality of the Crown Court left a profound impression on several of our defendant and witness interviewees. Defendant Jerome, for example, described the judges as "very powerful people, that's why they wear those wigs and stuff like that"; and said that they are "very old-fashioned and it comes from years and years ago from where people used to be beheaded". The old days of capital punishment were also in Sidney's mind when we spoke to him about his experiences of appearing in court as a defendant. He had recently been acquitted of assault in a trial in the Crown Court, but had a number of previous convictions from both magistrates' and Crown courts. He spoke about the "spooky" atmosphere of the old court building in which he was tried on the assault charge:

> 'I just felt very uneasy in there, very wary. Even though I knew I was innocent and I hadn't done anything, and I am being forced to stand in this dock that has been there for nearly 100 years now I think. It was a very old, weird place – it was built on the site of the old L– Prison and it was where they held public executions and stuff like that. Very very strange place.'

For some of our prosecution respondents as well, the ritual and formality of the courtroom added to their sense of apprehension about proceedings:

> 'It just seems very scary when you go in because of the way the setup is and everything. But it has to be that way I know. But it's just very frightening, very daunting when you walk in and you see all the chairs and the benches and everything set out and then you see all these people with their wigs on and the gowns. It's just very, very frightening.'
>
> [Julia; witness]

However, for Grace, a witness in a theft case, some of her anxiety about the Crown Court was subverted by an unexpected sight during her pre-trial familiarisation visit:

Grace: They took us round to two different sized courtrooms and these young blokes came in, laughing and joking, and I said, "Who's that?"... and [the Witness Service volunteers] said, "Oh that's the barristers." That made me feel better, because they looked like normal people. They don't, do they, in court.

Interviewer: So they didn't have their wigs on at this time?

Grace: No – they were throwing a couple around, and I thought: Well, who on earth's that, throwing their wigs around?

Dramatic games

A number of our respondents made explicit reference to the parallels between theatre and what goes on in court, or referred to court proceedings as a kind of 'game'. We spoke to Barbara about her experience of giving evidence in the trial of a care worker accused of stealing money from her 97-year-old mother. Barbara's mother also gave evidence during the trial and, according to Barbara, made the most of the opportunity:

'My mother actually got more and more excited about it once she'd settled down ... Well, I don't think she knew what giving evidence is like really. But she's a bit of an actress. So it was her last grand performance really. [*Laughs*] ... Yes – she thoroughly enjoyed herself once she got there! [*Laughs*]'

Some – such as Barbara's mother – might enjoy taking centre stage in court; more frequently, victims, witnesses and defendants appeared to be disillusioned or disturbed at the theatre-like aspects of court proceedings, or 'the multifaceted gamesmanship which constitutes judicial action' (Carlen, 1976a, p 40). Faris, for example, was a young man who had been the victim of a robbery committed by four men in an underpass near his home. He had felt very nervous about giving evidence, and even about entering the area in which the court was located. Once in court, he was perturbed by what he perceived to be play-acting by the defence lawyer:

> 'My barrister and the police officers told me that the defence barristers try to play these games with you and they will try and stare at you ... I noticed that every time [the defence lawyer] asked me a question, he'd have the stance of putting his elbow on the table and looking at the time, and so I felt it was as if to mock me. I didn't like him doing that. And he definitely kept the face of disbelief throughout the whole thing, in my opinion.'[19]

Michelle gave evidence in a rape case, an experience she described with the use of a sporting metaphor:

> 'After speaking to the prosecution I felt quite eased in and you are on a roll. Then when the defence comes, it is like you are playing tennis and it is going all right and then all of a sudden someone takes a massive shot at you and I was just: "No."'

Elaine had gone through the exceptionally difficult and painful experience of acting as a prosecution witness in the trial of her son who was charged with sexually assaulting her young daughter (the defendant's half-sister). One of very many upsetting aspects of the case – which resulted in a not guilty verdict – was that she felt that the entire judicial process was about "trickery" rather than seeking the truth:

> 'The justice is a law unto itself. It doesn't make any rhyme nor reason. You can't possibly know the facts that I know ... we *are* telling the truth ... Being a simple-minded person, I suppose, I don't understand. It's all trickery. If you say this, if you make up this lie then you can get off. It's not about telling the truth, it's not about being honest any more or perhaps it never has been. But perhaps that's what people think. If you tell the truth you're doing the right thing – but I don't think you are any more.'

From a defendant's perspective, Sidney articulated many of the themes addressed over the course of this chapter so far, in expressing the firm view that the theatrical character of a Crown Court trial means that the truth remains elusive throughout:

'I don't know if you have ever heard this, but I have heard this from barristers and solicitors that, in a court, a trial is like a play. The defence say a story, the prosecution tell a story and then the jury make up their own story – and the truth never comes out in court. That is exactly what I have been told by numerous solicitors and barristers. ... The prosecution always present their case first. So they present their story of what they believe happened, which is never actually the truth. Then you have got the defence that present their story – which we would *like* to believe was always the truth, but on a few occasions perhaps it wasn't. Then you have got the jury – the jury take the two stories and they take bits out of both of them to make up their own story. So the jury never actually know the truth. The truth never comes out in court: it is just simply they either believe you have done it or you didn't.'

The incongruities of the court process

The public performances which take place in the courtroom frequently involve an intermingling of highly incongruous and contradictory elements. High levels of formality are mixed with informality; the most intimate, personal and often sordid details of individuals' private lives are publicly recounted in elaborate fashion; matters of the greatest seriousness are discussed alongside multiple trivialities; and grief and (black) humour sometimes coincide.

Formality versus informality: attire

The formal elements of the courtroom inhere in the ceremony, court procedure and the language used during proceedings, but also in the style of dress worn by legal professionals and court staff. Court dress for circuit judges is: described as follows: 'bands worn over a violet robe with lilac facings and a short wig. As well as a girdle, the judge wears a tippet (sash) over the left shoulder – lilac when dealing with civil business and red when dealing with crime. Ordinary day dress is worn beneath the robe.' A barrister who is a QC wears a 'short barrister's wig and black gown worn over a court coat and ordinary trousers or skirt', and a junior barrister a 'short barrister's wig and black gown worn over a suit, with bands'.[20] Solicitor-advocates were initially not allowed to wear a wig in the Crown Court, but following complaints from some that this disadvantaged them in relation to barristers,[21] in

2008 the Lord Chief Justice handed down a Practice Direction which ruled that: 'Solicitors and other advocates with rights of audience have the option to wear wigs in circumstances where they would be worn by members of the Bar' (Practice Direction (Court Dress) No. 4). (Another symbol of the inequality between barristers and solicitors is that while barristers refer to each other in court as 'my learned friend', they refer to solicitors as 'my friend'.)

Court users interviewed for this study evidently perceived the wigs and gowns worn by the criminal justice professionals as symbolising the seriousness of the occasion and the legal power that could be brought to bear. Differences in dress between professionals in the Crown Court and lay magistrates in the lower courts were commented upon by one defendant, Kwame, as reflecting the different levels of authority of the two types of court:

> 'Oh, it's just more serious in Crown Court, because they're wearing the wigs and the gowns. Where, in the magistrates', it's just like it's a panel of three people, or something. And they're just wearing like suits, and their own clothes. And you just feel, like, it's not as serious.'

There is no formal dress code for witnesses or defendants, although a search of the internet throws up various web-based fact sheets for defendants attending Crown Court from firms of criminal defence solicitors – one suggesting, for example, that 'while there is no hard and fast rule, dress smartly. If you turn up in your ripped jeans the jury may think you are not taking your case very seriously and this won't impress them'.[22] Another site, Devon and Cornwall Police, responds to the frequently asked question from witnesses about what to wear to court by saying that 'most people choose to dress smart-casual'.[22] As in other areas of life, there has been some erosion over time of the social mores related to appearance and the necessity for wearing 'smart' clothes in certain social contexts. During observations, for example, we noted many witnesses and defendants dressed in casual clothing including jeans, shorts, t-shirts and training shoes.

However, that it is not to say that appearance was always deemed unimportant. For some defendants, making an effort to look smart served to demonstrate their respect for the court and their acknowledgement that the stakes were high. Jerome, for example, described coming to court "suited and booted", explaining that, unlike for the magistrates' court where he had been a frequent visitor, he made a special effort for his appearance at Crown Court, because of the potentially more serious outcome of the proceedings:

'Normally I'd just go in trackies, t-shirt or a vest into Magistrates. When you go to Crown Court it's the next judges up, so it's a lot higher. Also, there's a lot more risk of imprisonment. So, you look smart, you look the business. Smart appearance, you see. You kind of hope the judge will take that into account.'

While there is a perceived risk that a jury may respond negatively to a scruffily-dressed defendant, comments made by one witness suggest that the appearance and style of dress of the jurors themselves may be seen as signifying their seriousness and commitment to their role in proceedings. While jurors have no professional status, their power to decide upon guilt or innocence sets them apart from the other lay participants in court. Chloe, who was a witness in a trial and subsequent re-trial, made the following observation about the jury involved in each:

'In the first case, they looked like [*Laughter*] – this sounds really awful – but they looked really shabby. I would maybe look a bit smarter. [*Laughter*] And then in the second one they were smarter, more smartly dressed. In the second one I remember them staring at me, but that may have been because I felt like I was under the spotlight anyway from the barrister.'

Formality versus informality: mind your language

As with styles of dress, formality and informality often coexist within the language of the courtroom. Much of the language used by the professionals in court is formal and technical, to the evident bafflement of some court users (problems of understanding will be further discussed in Chapter Six). In Case 1 of our observations, the judge commented on this directly, saying to the jury at the start of the trial: "I must say, sometimes I feel sorry for you, because you're not used to speaking such antiquated language." He went on to tell them that he wished the oath could be modernised, but understood that "the antiquity of the language is supposed to make the occasion feel more serious; and it *is* very serious".

In contrast, everyday language can appear out of place or inappropriate in the solemn surroundings of the courtroom and this can inhibit witness and defendant accounts. One victim respondent, Nikki, said that when giving evidence she had not been sure if she should repeat verbatim things that had been said: "Sometimes you don't know whether to swear or not when you're relaying what's been said to you. But I did. [*Laughs*]." Indeed, witnesses often had to be cajoled to repeat expletives or obscenities as part of their evidence, or would seek permission from the judge to use this type of language when cross-examined. One 74-year-old man, Ernie, who had been violently assaulted when out walking his dog, reported being confident when giving his evidence and dealing with the cross-examination, but said he was very uncomfortable about having to repeat the language used by the defendant during this attack:

> 'I mean, some of the language he used was very profane and I had to say what he had said to me, which was something I didn't want to do. And I said to [the judge]: "I don't swear, I don't use that language." She said, "Well I'm afraid it's a court of law, you have to say what he said," so I had to say it.'

In observed Case 7, in which the defendant, Ahmed, was accused of dangerous driving and assault, the alleged victim, Athena, stated that the defendant had come out of his car and started swearing at her. "He was using 'F' words ... Do you want me to tell?" The judge told her not to be embarrassed and she continued her testimony. "He said, 'I fuck loads of girls like you.' I said, 'You hurt me and I'll fuck you up.' I thought he was going to attack me."

One of the more incongruous sights in court is that of well-spoken and articulate legal professionals engaged in efforts to decode colloquial expressions or analyse the precise meaning of a casual insult or an obscenity. The above exchange from Case 7 was followed by a lengthy discussion about the exact meaning of the phrase 'I'm going to fuck you up'. The defence counsel asked Athena, "What did you mean by saying, 'I'm going to fuck you up?'" Athena repeated that she had been scared, but the defence counsel insisted that she was the one who had caused fear: "The only threat actually came from you. Do you agree? ... There's no point shrugging. What does 'fuck you up' mean to you?" Athena responded by saying that she had just wanted to make Ahmed feel scared: "Nothing else; I've never hit anyone." At this point the judge interrupted, telling the defence counsel that

Athena actually said "If you touch me, I'll fuck you up", and that he needed to put the entire sentence to the witness.

Public versus private

Personal histories and the messy realities of family and intimate relationships are laid bare in court. What were once deeply private details of individuals' lives are pored over by barristers, assessed by juries and heard by all present in the public gallery of the courtroom – including, in some cases, by journalists who broaden the reach by reporting upon the case in the local and national press. The physical structure of the courtroom heightens this sense of a clash between the private and public, as the various parties sit or stand at much greater physical distances from one another 'than those usually, and voluntarily, chosen for the disclosure of intimate details of sexual habits, personal relationships and financial affairs' (Carlen, 1976a, p 23).

Tom, a witness, described the discomfort he felt at hearing 'everybody else's business' while waiting in the Witness Service room to give his evidence: "There was effing and blinding from other witnesses. You don't want to be hearing that. You're hearing the ins and outs of the dirty details of other court cases. I didn't like it; I didn't enjoy the environment."

Establishing or indeed undermining the credibility of a witness may involve delving into his or her background and character. Nikki, a victim of a sexual assault committed by an acquaintance after a party, vividly described what it is like to experience this. When asked whether any family members had attended court to support her during the trial, she responded:

> 'They dig up everything – all your medical records. I'm glad no one came [to court to support me] … They brought up all my history at home, my home life with my mum and dad, my teenage years, mental health, my physical health. I've had my right kidney removed, I've also had a hysterectomy, I've also had breast tissue removed under each arm. … And they brought a plain piece of A4 paper and an outline of a female body and marked off where all my scars were and they gave it all to the witnesses and him to say that's where all my operations were … I didn't realise they were going to hand a picture like that around the court for everyone to see my bodyline basically, like I'd been dissected.'

A case partially observed for this study was the trial of a college lecturer accused of sexual assault by one of his students. The student had reported in her statement to the police that the defendant's back was 'hairy', and that he had an 'unusually small' penis and was circumcised. This account was of much significance for the trial since the defendant denied having been naked in the presence of his student. The defence counsel thus sought to demonstrate the falsity of the student's claims by distributing to the jury a photograph of the defendant's back, purported to prove its almost entirely hairless condition. No photograph of the defendant's penis was produced, although the defence counsel asserted that by no means could it be described as small; he also pointed out that its circumcised state could be easily inferred from the defendant's obviously Muslim name.

Our observed Case 3 concerned a charge of perverting the course of justice, arising from what were said to be false allegations of rape by the defendant, Lola. This was a retrial, as the first jury to hear the case had failed to reach a verdict. As the prosecution counsel opened the case, he warned the jury that private lives would be discussed and beseeched them not to make moral judgements: "This is not a court of morals but a court of law. We are not here to make moral judgements." During the next few days, Lola was asked in great detail about her prior sexual relationships, including those with two of the key prosecution witnesses – Frankie (against whom one of the rape allegations had been made) and Max. In turn, Frankie and Max also faced close questioning about their prior relations with Lola.

One issue that proved to be of particular importance to both the prosecution and defence case was the nature of sexual contact between Lola and Max on the night that Lola made her allegations of rape. Both prosecution and defence agreed that the two of them, along with other friends, had been drinking in a pub that night, and that they had then gone together into a graveyard next to the pub. Here, the defence claimed, they had had full penetrative sex, while the prosecution argued that they had had oral sex. Both Lola and Max were questioned in court, in close detail, about whether penetration and ejaculation had taken place. In the course of this questioning, Max was asked by the defence counsel why he had not mentioned, when first interviewed by the police, that he and Lola had engaged in oral sex in the graveyard. In response, Max said that this was because of his embarrassment at having to talk about such a thing to a female police officer. In court, he described eventually admitting in the police interview that oral sex had taken place: "But I said it as uncrudely as I could ... in the most unrude words ... I wouldn't say this to my mum."

It is not just these very intimate or potentially salacious details that end up being scrutinised in court; also the private, petty squabbles and most mundane details of everyday life are discussed in this public forum and take on a far greater significance than anyone might have expected. In the course of our observations we saw, for example, discussions in court about the causes of spats and name-calling between a young woman and her ex-boyfriend's sister and friends; states of drunkenness and hangovers; the kind of underpants worn by a male taxi-driver accused of indecent exposure; and, quite literally, the contents of a dirty laundry bag.

The serious versus the trivial

The depiction of criminal trials in television and films focuses on their dramatic elements: the clashes between barristers and judge; the clever advocacy used to trip up and expose a guilty defendant or untrustworthy witness; the defendant, victim or witness who caves under the pressure of cross-examination; and, of course, the back story of conflict and tragedy that gave rise to the court case. There is no doubt that there are moments of high drama at court; but it is true also that even where this drama occurs it tends to be interspersed with 'lengthy periods of unrelenting tedium' (Baldwin, 2008, p 245) and that much court business is 'dull, commonplace, ordinary' (Bottoms and McClean, 1976, p 226). The tedium derives, in part, from the fact that seemingly trivial matters are discussed at immense length in the courtroom alongside issues of the greatest seriousness. The jurisdiction of the Crown Court is extremely wide, meaning that some of the cases which come before it are, arguably, trivial, such as certain cases involving small-scale shop thefts, low-level public order offences, or minor assaults. And in the course of hearings relating to serious offences, the building – and challenging – of the prosecution case is usually a slow-moving process which entails the painstaking critical examination and re-examination of a range of evidence (including physical artefacts, documentation and recordings and, often most importantly, oral testimony), much of which can turn on the minutest details of alleged events.

Both prosecution and defence often spend a great deal of time establishing or contesting matters such as 'the layout of settings, arrival and departure of participants and direction of movement' (Fielding, 2006, p 93). Hence, for example, in the course of a trial of a man accused of raping his teenage daughter and sexually assaulting his teenage niece, we observed the niece, as part of her evidence-in-chief, being asked to describe the exact location of each room in the large, five-storey house in which she lived, and in which she said she had been assaulted. Often, questioning of witnesses focuses on the precise timing of things they did or saw, which can bring to light their uncertainty or confusion – as explained by a witness, Barbara:

> '[Giving evidence] is very formal and it requires you to remember in such a specific way, and I think that that's very difficult for people. Especially a year on. They said something to me about, "Did this happen on such-a-such a day or before or after something?" And, really, I hadn't the slightest idea by that time. Because it was a matter of hours probably we were talking about. And it all merges into one big drama ... Trying to recollect the minutiae of it – it's difficult.'

Another witness, Julia, had struggled to remember the exact sequence of events immediately prior to the call she had made to the police to report the rape and sexual assault of her daughter:

> 'And he was asking me times. "How long did it take before she got home?" And things like that. Well it was like quite a while ago that this happened and you can't remember how long – the exact details. You know it happened but not the exact order of things.'

The questioning of witnesses about *line of sight* is also common, to help establish (or dispute) for the court what is was possible for a witness to have seen, given where he or she was positioned in relation to the action or event alleged to have taken place. In our observed Case 5 – the trial of Jamal for sexual assault and attempted abduction of a child – a witness claimed he had both seen and heard, from where he was fixing some machinery in his house, an altercation between the defendant and a young girl. He was asked by the prosecution about the size of the window in the hallway where he was working and to demonstrate this with his hands; if the window had clear glass (it did); if it had curtains or net curtains (it did not); and exactly how much of the path in front of the house he could see from this window.

A key tactic deployed by both prosecution and defence as they seek to undermine witness accounts is to highlight any discrepancies between oral testimony given in court and the original statements made by the witnesses to the police, often many months in advance of the trial. To this end, witnesses can be questioned in some depth about seemingly trivial details they mention in court that differ from those contained in the original statement – and which, given the natural fallibility of human memory (see note 2), they might hardly be expected to recall. As discussed above, we observed the retrial of Lola for perverting the course of justice (Case 3). During the retrial, some time was spent discussing the title and genre of the DVD that three of the prosecution witnesses said they had been watching in the early part of the night that Lola had made her accusations of rape. The defence counsel made much of the fact that there were discrepancies between what DVDs had been mentioned by the witnesses (variously, the films *Harry Brown* and *Dead Man Walking* and a DVD featuring comedian Lee Evans) in the retrial, in the original trial, and in their statements to the police. The focus on this relatively minor detail of the DVD viewed by the witnesses fully 19 months ago permitted the defence to cast doubts on the reliability of the witnesses' evidence concerning the events of later that night.

The black humour of the courtroom

It is often the very incongruities described above which give rise to flashes of humour within the sombre and formal atmosphere of the court. Amidst the tension or tedium of a trial or sentencing hearing, deliberate or unintended humour and laughter can help to ease the seriousness and formality of the occasion.

Humour was sometimes used as an intentional device by judge, counsel or even a witnesses to lighten the mood, reinforce a point or, perhaps, to 'play to the gallery' – the jury or any observing friends or family. In Case 5, the prosecution counsel had what might be described as a private joke with the jury at defendant Jamal's expense. Under cross-examination, Jamal said that he had found himself in the vicinity of the young girl he was accused of sexually assaulting because he had gone outside to get some fresh air. Counsel then asked Jamal if he habitually went outside for fresh air, and Jamal said that he did: he would sit on a bench near his flat for two or three minutes at a time, doing nothing. He was asked, "Are there windows in your flat?" to which Jamal answered "Yes", while looking somewhat confused by the obvious nature of the question. He then also answered in affirmative when counsel asked him if the windows opened. Counsel asked no further questions here, but shot a quick knowing glance at the jury, without humiliating the defendant further on the issue of the windows and their practical use.

In Case 3, as a pregnant witness took the stand, the prosecution barrister by way of introductory niceties said to her, "I see you may be pregnant," at which point the judge immediately interjected with, "It's hard to miss, Mr Greene!" to much laughter in the court. Later, when the court rose before the witness had completed her evidence, there was some informal chat between the witness and counsel about when her baby was due. The judge then turned to the barrister and told him with a smile that he had better not take too long over his questioning the next day. Max, a 19-year-old prosecution witness in this case, was sufficiently at ease when giving evidence to make a mild attempt at humour himself. In the course of giving his evidence-in-chief, he spoke of having gone to the local pub with friends for a beer, where he met "the usual crowd". When asked by counsel if he visited this pub on a regular basis, he replied "Yes", and then hesitated for a second before adding, with a smile, "Well, since I turned 18, yes", as members of the jury laughed. Later in the same trial, another witness talked of having picked up her daughter and son-in-law from the pub and admitted that she had parked her car illegally in doing so. As she said this, she turned to the judge and added "Sorry!", again to laughter from judge and jury.

The judge in this case was not averse to deploying humour herself, as the following exchange between prosecution counsel and the witness Max illustrates:

Counsel:	Anything stick in your mind about your conversation with her?
Max:	Yeah, we were playing on the fruit machine and she said – excuse my language – "If you asked me for a fuck, I wouldn't say no."
Counsel:	What did you take that to be a reference to?
Judge:	I think we can work that out for ourselves!

Another judge who undercut the seriousness of courtroom proceedings with humour was one whom we observed sentencing a young man for fraud. The defendant had pleaded guilty following his arrest for fraudulent use of prepaid gift cards, and was accompanied to court by four friends who sat in the public gallery. The judge provoked laughter among the defendant's friends throughout the brief hearing by making a variety of sarcastic comments about the offence itself; about the defendant's claims to have come into a significant amount of money through gambling ("You're a very clever man, Mr Thomas; I wish I had your secret!"); and the defendant's reputed skill at football, referred to in the plea in mitigation ("This is a good time for football – the January transfer window"). The judge brought proceedings to an end by sentencing the defendant to "a community order – whatever that means".

Sometimes humour emerges unintentionally through interactions between professionals and lay participants in court. Faris, a witness in a robbery trial, described how the jury laughed when he was describing what had happened in the immediate aftermath of the robbery:

> 'Straight after I was robbed, a car drove past with four people in it, and I wasn't sure if it was the four people who had robbed me or not. They shouted "bus stop wankers", which is from [the television series] *The In-Betweeners.* ... But they were all white in the car and the people who robbed me were like Middle Eastern or something so I knew it wasn't them. But the judge just asked me where that was from – the joke of "bus stop wankers" – but the jury all laughed ... when he said "bus stop wankers".'

Concluding remarks

This chapter has examined the nature of the court process. At the heart of this process, we have argued, is the tension between the purported aim of finding out 'what really happened' in relation to an alleged offence, and the practical impossibility, in many cases, of ever establishing a definitive version of events. In a criminal trial, defence and prosecution battle over their competing accounts of 'the truth', neither of which may be grounded in objective reality. Indeed, the complexities and messiness of much alleged offending is such that the very existence of an objective reality can, in some cases, be called into question. And even where a case is dealt with by way of a guilty plea rather than a trial – as applies to the large majority of cases that pass through the Crown Court – this does not imply that an uncontested and unambiguous version of 'the truth' of the offence has been established. Rather, a guilty plea is often reached through a process of negotiation and compromise between prosecution and defence over the nature and details of the offence.

We have, in short, defined the court process as focused on the *management of conflict*, and have also considered the highly ritualised nature of this process, and its many parallels with theatre. In the final part of the chapter, we have described some of the multiple and profound incongruities that characterise court proceedings: these are proceedings in which, for example, informality is mixed with high levels of formality; the most intimate and sordid details of personal lives are publicly and elaborately recounted; and grief and trauma coincide with (black) humour.

Notes

[1] As Sanchirico (2001) points out, the jury are expected to deliver the 'ver-dict', or 'truth statement'.

[2] There is a long history of academic debate regarding the scope for accurate fact-finding within adversarial vis-à-vis inquisitorial systems of criminal law. (For some recent texts which have addressed this broad and complex subject see, for example, Deffains and Demougin, 2008; Sklansky, 2009; Brants and Ringnalda, 2011; Findley, 2012). A related line of academic inquiry concerns the essential features of adversarial and inquisitorial systems and whether there is currently a degree of 'convergence' between the two within many European jurisdictions (for example, Jackson, 2005; Duff, 2007; Brants and Ringnalda, 2011).

[3] A very substantial body of psychological research, the earliest of which dates back to more than a hundred years ago, has examined the factors affecting the reliability of eyewitness testimony and the credibility of witnesses (for overviews of the research and many of the issues addressed see Fulero, 2009; Memon et al, 1998; Penrod et al, 1982; Miller and Burgoon, 1982). The research literature makes clear the inherent fallibility of human memory: the fact that 'the very act of forming a memory creates distortion' (Engelhardt, 1999, p 28) and that 'human perception and memory are not literal and objective recorders of "fact" ... [but] are personalised and subjective interpreters and recorders of information' (Ainsworth, 1998, pp 2–3).

[4] A summons can be served on a witness who is reluctant to attend court; if the witness then fails to attend, he or she can be prosecuted for contempt of court.

[5] Speculate has been defined as 'to conjecture without knowing the complete facts'; and infer as 'to conclude (a state of affairs, supposition, etc) by reasoning from evidence; deduce', www.collinsdictionary.com/dictionary/english (accessed 3 January 2014).

[6] Jury questions and answers cited on BBC news website, www.bbc.co.uk/news/uk-21521460.

[7] Darbyshire et al (2002); Mueller-Johnson et al (2013).

[8] The reader is also referred to the legal textbooks *Archbold* and *Blackstone* 'for a discussion of terms', while a footnote warns: 'Note the problems encountered in *Majid* [2009] EWCA Crim 2563 when the judge endeavoured to explain reasonable doubt to the jury.'

[9] See, for example, Harry Mount, 'Vicky Pryce trial: have juries had their day in court?' *The Telegraph*, 21 February 2013; Melanie Phillips, 'Do we need IQ TESTS for juries? Vicky Pryce trial has exposed a breathtaking level of ignorance and stupidity', *Mail Online*, 21 February 2013; Joshua Rozenburg, 'The Pryce of a jury's failure', *The Guardian*, 21 February 2013; Alex Wickham, '12 cretinous men (and women)' (www.thecommentator.com/article/2766/12_cretinous_men_and_women (accessed 3 January 2014)).

[10] If, however, the defendant's account is manifestly false or implausible, the judge may choose simply to reject the basis of plea without holding a Newton hearing.

[11] Plea-bargaining became increasingly common in the United States over the past two centuries (Fisher, 2003) and today it is widely reported that at least 90% of criminal cases are resolved in this manner (Devers, 2011). There is a very extensive research literature on the plea bargaining process in the American context; some of the more influential texts on this subject include Sudnow (1965), Blumberg (1967), Feeley (1992).

[12] Probably the most significant research on plea-bargaining in England and Wales is that of Baldwin and McConville, published in 1977, which found the practice, in explicit and implicit forms, to be quite widespread if by no means as common as in the United States. On the basis of existing research on charge-bargaining in England and Wales, Ashworth and Redmayne (2010) conclude that 'one or other form of charge bargain is a fairly frequent phenomenon' (2010, p 298). See also Bottoms and McClean (1976), McConville et al (1994), Rauxlho (2012) for descriptions of plea-bargaining practices, and their implications, in England and Wales.

[13] Further, since 2009 parties in serious fraud cases have been permitted to enter into formal plea negotiations (Lawrence et al, 2008; Alge, 2013).

[14] Similar mixed feelings about late guilty pleas were found among victim respondents in the qualitative WAVES research (Commissioner for Victims and Witnesses, 2011).

[15] These statutory provisions were subsequently reaffirmed by the Criminal Justice Act 2003.

[16] Relevant to our contention that court proceedings are more about conflict management than the definitive uncovering of 'the truth' is Duff et al's argument for a 'normative theory of criminal trial'. From this perspective, the trial is conceived as 'a communicative process that calls the defendant to answer', and the 'truth' that is sought through the process does not merely concern the facts of the offence but is a greater, 'normative truth' (2007, pp 3, 127). Duff et al's work contributes to a wider theoretical debate about the essential functions of the criminal trial (see Ashworth and Redmayne, 2010, for a brief overview).

[17] Albeit the Justice and Security Act 2013 has extended judicial powers to hold 'closed' civil proceedings relating to highly sensitive national security matters, provoking widespread criticism by civil liberties groups.

[18] For discussion of the relationship between architecture, justice and authority see, for example, Mulcahy (2011); Simon et al (2013).

[19] The underlying cynicism of courtroom performance that was perceived by Faris has been observed by many commentators. Writing in the 1960s about sentencing hearings in American criminal courts, Blumberg argued that the lawyer will:

> ... stage manage an impression of 'all out' performance for the accused in justification of his fee. The judge and other court personnel will serve as a backdrop for a scene charged with dramatic fire, in which the accused's lawyer makes a stirring appeal on his behalf. With a show of restrained passion, the lawyer will intone the virtues of the accused and recite the social deprivations which have reduced him to his present state. ... In the main ... the incongruity, superficiality, and ritualistic

character of the total performance is underscored by a visibly impassive, almost bored reaction on the part of the judge and other members of the court retinue. (1969, p 231)

[20] http://webarchive.nationalarchives.gov.uk/+/http:/www.dca.gov.uk/consult/courtdress/index.htm#anna3 (accessed 31 January 2014).

[21] See, for example, A. Lusher, 'Solicitor wants right to wear wig and gown at court', *The Telegraph*, 11 February 2001; and http://barristerbriefs.blogspot.co.uk/2008/04/wigs-off-for-uk-civil-judges-chief.html (accessed 31 January 2014).

[22] www.mulrooneycraghill.com/what-happens-at-a-crown-court-trial-an-introduction (accessed 3 January 2014).

[23] www.devon-cornwall.police.uk/SupportAdvice/VictimAdvice/Pages/Frequentlyaskedquestions.aspx (accessed 3 January 2014).

FOUR

Them and us: the divide between court users and professionals

In the preceding chapter we considered some of the respects in which court proceedings can be seen as a form of theatre. To continue with this theme: one might assume that within the theatre of the courtroom, victims, witnesses and defendants are the main players. In practice, however, these individuals play only minor, walk-on parts in proceedings, while the starring roles are played by the legal professionals – the judge and, particularly, the prosecution and defence counsel. Other professionals, such as the police, court staff and expert witnesses, often play supporting roles.

Victims and witnesses at court take centre stage only for the (usually relatively short) period of time when they give evidence in a trial. Even at this point, they are seldom granted the freedom to tell their story in full, in the manner they wish. This apparent marginalisation of victims within the court setting has been well-documented (see for example, Rock, 1993; Fielding, 2006; Doak, 2008; Shapland and Hall, 2010) and victims themselves often complain that their voices are silenced while defendants are placed at the heart of the court process. However, for their part, defendants often adopt an entirely passive role; they are the 'ever-present extras' in proceedings.

The clearest divide in the courtroom, therefore, is not between victim and defendant, or prosecution and defence, as might be expected; but between the legal professionals and the lay court users. Jurors, however, straddle this divide: on the one hand, they are members of the public, have no professional expertise, and are deliberately excluded from aspects of what goes on in court; on the other hand, in a trial, the responsibility for determining guilt lies with them alone.

The focus of this chapter is the 'them and us' relationship between the court users (victims, witnesses and defendants) and the legal professionals (judge and counsel). Particular attention will be paid to the ways in which court users are treated as 'them' by professionals at court. Court users are lay people, mere members of the public, who occupy an 'outsider' (Rock, 1993) or marginalised sphere. There is, undoubtedly, a need based on legal and security imperatives to keep a physical and metaphorical distance between 'them' and the

closeted sphere of 'us' occupied by the various professionals. This –
and its overlay of socio-economic or class distinctions – mirrors the
professional–client distance that is maintained in other settings, such
as hospitals, but there are various aspects of the world of the Crown
Court that serve to enhance it. These include the technical and legal
language used by the professionals and associated court ritual, the wigs
and gowns worn in court, the legal restrictions on contact, and even
the very architecture of the court building (see Carlen, 1976a; Rock,
1993). This chapter will examine the nuances of this professional vis-
à-vis lay court user divide in more detail; first, by looking at the role
and status of victims and witnesses in court, then at defendants' role and
status, and thereafter at the relationship between victims, witnesses and
defendants as a generic group of court users, and the professionals. The
final part of the chapter will consider the ambiguous status of the jury.

The role of victims and witnesses at court

Research by Paul Rock on the Crown Court, undertaken in 1989 to
1990, found that victims were traditionally seen as having a 'baneful'
presence at court:

> [Victims] threatened the conduct of cases. They threatened
> the appearance of neutrality so carefully cultivated by staff.
> They threatened the studied competence of counsel … In
> sum they were used in trials, indeed, they were indispensable
> to trials, but they were also kept somewhat at bay … they
> were thrust to a distance, never fully trusted, denied
> knowledge about much of what transpired, relegated to
> the safe, outer margins of the Court's social organization.
> Victims were outsiders. That was a most fundamental
> distinction. (1993, p 179)

Rock's research was undertaken prior to, or in the early stages of, various
pivotal developments aimed at improving the treatment and standing
of victims and witnesses within the criminal courts. As highlighted
in Chapters One and Two, recent decades have seen an increased
political and policy focus on victims' and witnesses' rights which has
aimed to counter their traditional 'bit player' (Shapland and Hall, 2010,
p 163) role in the criminal justice process. Key developments have
included: ensuring that each Crown Court has a designated Witness
Service office, the introduction of special measures procedures to help
vulnerable and intimidated witnesses give evidence, the development

and subsequent revision of the Victims' Code (Ministry of Justice, 2013a), and the introduction of Victim Personal Statements. However, as previously discussed, concerns about the victim and witness role in the court and wider criminal justice process remain – particularly, it has been argued that while recent policy and legislative developments have enhanced *service* rights for victims, these have not been matched with marked improvements in *procedural* rights (Doak, 2008; Manikis, 2012).

In short, it cannot be disputed that there is now an extensive policy framework for providing both practical and emotional support to victims and witnesses that was almost entirely lacking at the time Rock's fieldwork got under way. Nevertheless, it became evident from our own interviews with victims and witnesses that many continue to feel marginalised throughout the court process. One significant source of their sense of marginalisation is their lack of legal representation at court. Many struggle to understand why they should be denied representation, or mistakenly assume that the prosecution counsel is their own representative, and then feel disappointed when he or she does not make more of an effort to engage with them. Our respondents frequently referred in interviews to prosecution counsel as "my lawyer", "my barrister" or "my one" and were confused as to why they had not had more time with them:

> 'Yes, we just briefly spoke to [the prosecution counsel]. He didn't actually discuss the case with us, which I thought was a bit strange. I don't know what the procedure is. Maybe legally he's not allowed to; I don't know. But I didn't think it was very good. That's the one thing I wasn't happy with. I felt there should have been more interaction with him. … I would have thought I'd have been sitting down with him for maybe an hour, maybe 45 minutes, before the case … It didn't happen.'
> [Ron; victim]

Under the Crown Prosecution Service Prosecutor's Pledge,[1] prosecutors are formally obliged to introduce themselves to the victim or a family member of the victim, answer any questions they may have about the court process and procedures, and provide an indication of how long the victim is likely to be required to wait at court. We found that where prosecutors did introduce themselves, this was usually highly valued by the victims and witnesses. However because the Prosecutor's Pledge only covers victims and their family members, a wide variety of other prosecution witnesses, who may have their own anxieties and fears in relation to giving evidence, are excluded from this obligation. Furthermore, the lack of understanding among victims and witnesses about the role of the prosecutor in relation to themselves indicates that they have not received adequate explanations about legal concepts and processes, including – crucially – the fact that prosecution is undertaken on behalf of the state, rather than the victim.

Beyond the issue of lack of legal representation for victims and witnesses, another aspect of their marginalisation is that they are not included in many aspects of proceedings at the Crown Court. For example, research has highlighted that 'victims' may be relabelled as 'witnesses' within the court process, which can mean that their specific needs as victims of crime are not attended to (Shapland and Hall, 2010; Commissioner for Victims and Witnesses, 2010). For many, when they arrive to give evidence this will be the first time they have been to court. Fear of the unknown environment can add to any feelings of isolation they may have been experiencing before arriving at court.

Victims and witnesses are usually only present in the courtroom when they are on the witness stand. By law, they are allowed to observe the court proceedings only when they have finished giving evidence. This means that they miss out on the explanation of legal concepts that other lay participants in the court process are privy to at the outset of the trial, such as the burden of proof. Understanding of the burden of proof can be essential to victims' and witnesses' feelings about whether or not they have been believed, as some of the professionals interviewed for this study were aware:

> 'I will definitely before a trial go and speak to [a victim] and say, "And I want you to understand that just because [the defendant] doesn't get convicted it doesn't mean that people are saying this didn't happen." And I explain to them something about the burden of proof and the standard of proof; if you don't explain that to them they will think the process is unfair ... I do mention that I have a duty when opening a case to mention the burden of proof. So the jury hear it, the defendant hears it, but does the victim and the witness hear it? No.'
> [CPS advocate]

> 'I think if you explain to witnesses or it filters back, if a case goes against them, if it's explained why precisely then I think that sometimes helps as well. Often witnesses, as far

as we're concerned, just give their evidence and disappear from the process.'
[Judge]

Once victims and witnesses have given their evidence and are free to observe the remainder of the trial and, in cases where the defendant is found guilty, the sentencing hearing, they rarely do so. Very few victims and witnesses who participated in this study remained at court for the rest of the trial or attended the sentencing hearing. Several reasons emerged as to why they chose not to do this, including not wanting to spend longer at court and not having the time to do so. However, some did not attend court after giving evidence because they were not aware that they were allowed to do so, or because they were actively encouraged not to. Some were also concerned about the fact that, had they chosen to observe the rest of proceedings from the public gallery, they were likely to find themselves sitting with friends or family of the defendant; or were anxious about being seen by the defendant from the dock. One witness, Graham, who did choose to observe the remainder of the trial, spoke of his concern about seeing the defendant – his brother, who had been accused of sexually assaulting Graham's teenage daughter:

> '[Observing from the public gallery was] very hard, because I sat on the floor, because obviously if I sat in the seat I could see my [brother] in the other box. So I just sat on the floor because I didn't want to look at him; I didn't want him to see where I was.'

This evident lack of provision for victims and witnesses to remain at court after giving evidence supports claims made elsewhere that victims cease to be supported through the criminal justice process once they have given evidence (Shapland and Hall, 2010; Commissioner for Victims and Witnesses, 2010). Further, victims and witnesses are often not provided with adequate information about verdict and sentencing once they have left court. The absence of such information can leave them feeling that they are in a perilous situation, especially if the defendant is known to them:

> 'I got phone calls immediately after the case. We weren't even in court when he got the [verdict]. I got phone calls immediately after from one of the [defendant's friends] just reeling off abuse at me really ... When I phoned the police

officer involved in the case to report the abusive phone call he hadn't even heard the verdict.'
[Rhona; witness]

However, several ways in which victims' and witnesses' feelings of marginalisation can be alleviated also emerged from our interviews. The Witness Service proved to be an important source of support and information for those attending court, with many describing the staff and volunteers as "amazing", "brilliant", "approachable" and "reassuring". Additionally, many victims and witnesses were extremely positive about the support they received from the police throughout the investigation and often found the prosecution counsel to be supportive, despite the constraints of their role.

Constraints on the victim's and witness's 'voice' when giving evidence

Thus far, it has been demonstrated that as a case proceeds through court, victims and witnesses spend much time waiting to give evidence, and are quickly removed from the courtroom 'stage' once having done so. A further source of frustration for victims and witnesses attending court is that even at the very moment when they take centre stage to give evidence, they often feel that they are unable to tell their own, full story of the alleged offence as they might wish to. As noted in Chapter One, procedural justice theorists have emphasised the importance, to participants within criminal justice proceedings, of being given a 'voice': indeed, along with 'neutrality', 'respect' and 'trust', 'voice' is often described as 'one of the four procedural justice principles' (Tyler, 2008). From this perspective, it is not surprising that victims and witnesses were shocked or disappointed when they felt that they could not say what they wanted to at the point at which they finally took the stand in the court – as described, for example, in the following interview extracts:

'[Questions] sometimes are worded in such a way where there is only one answer you can give. But everything in life isn't just black and white. As soon as you start trying to give an explanation, the other guy stands up and says, "Is this relevant, Your Lord or Your Honour?" or whatever it was. And that's quite frustrating. Because *you* think it's relevant.'
[Tracey; witness]

'I did feel that I hadn't done my part. I'd not said what I needed to say. Yes, I felt that I'd let everybody down because I don't feel that I'd got my part of the story across.'
[Amanda; witness]

Fielding's research on Crown Court trials found, similarly, that witnesses were often frustrated at being unable to express themselves fully when giving evidence. Fielding explains that this is because a story-telling approach is not permitted in court: witnesses are only allowed to answer the questions asked of them. He notes that 'there is a balance to be struck against irrelevance and the possibility that lawyers' questioning misses important details' (2006, p 185). Further, there are various legal constraints to what can be admitted as evidence in court. For example, the hearsay rule[2] means that – other than in certain defined circumstances – witnesses are not allowed to relay information that has been told to them by another; also, witnesses are only able to talk about the offences that are being tried.[3] We found that limits to self-expression and the bafflement this may cause victims and witnesses was something that legal professionals were aware of and concerned about. For example, one judge commented that:

'The process of giving evidence is, many people might think, quite artificial: you are responding to questions and you are being restricted by those questions in terms of giving an account. The questions might restrict you from comment; you are being asked about matters of fact. Most of us, when we are giving an account of something, will sprinkle it with our impressions or what we thought about it or how we felt about it. [Giving evidence] is not a natural story-telling process.'

An example of restrictions imposed on witnesses' accounts arose during observed Case 3, in which Lola was on trial for perverting the course of justice, following her allegations of rape against her ex-boyfriend, Frankie, and one other. Frankie's sister, Zoe, gave evidence at the trial and was stopped by the prosecution advocate during her account of a telephone conversation she recounted having had with Lola on the evening the rape allegations were made. In the course of describing this conversation, she referred to an earlier telephone call between Lola and her mother, but was then stopped by the prosecution counsel who told her not to relay her mother's comments about this earlier call: this would have been inadmissible hearsay evidence. Zoe, however, again brought up the conversation between her mother and Lola when she was being cross-examined. The defence counsel accused Zoe of having "concocted" her own discussion with Lola, at which point she became agitated and retorted: "Does that mean my mum's lying as well?" She was cut off here by the judge, who sternly ordered her to "just answer the question!"

Another concern among some victims and witnesses, relating to the constraints on what they could say in giving evidence, was that they were not permitted to talk about the *impact* of the crime on them, but only about the 'facts' of the case as they saw them. But, as in the comment below from a witness, Donna, the question of what exactly constitutes a 'fact' is not easily resolved:

> 'It was weird that [the defence] would go in there and say all this stuff and we couldn't say what we wanted to say. And they asked you about the incident and things like that but I think it's strange that they don't ask you about what happened after, the effects that it had. But they want *facts*, don't they, about the night, but the fact of the matter is how it destroyed a family and me. I was signed off work and all sorts afterwards ... They don't ask you about how it's affected your life.'

Evidence on the impact of a crime on its victim will not be put before the court unless and until a guilty verdict has been delivered; at which point their Victim Personal Statement (if they have made one) will be considered by the judge. However, non-victim witnesses, such as Donna, are not permitted to make Victim Personal Statements, despite the impact that witnessing the crime may have had upon their life. It is also apparent that even victims who are entitled to make a statement were not always asked if they would like to do so or were not aware of having made one. This may, in part, be due to the fact that Victim Personal Statements are taken at the same time as evidential statements, and therefore victims and witnesses may not recognise the difference between the different kinds of statement:[4]

Interviewer:	Did you make a Victim Personal Statement at any point, do you know, to the police?
Denise:	What's that?
Interviewer:	Where you explain what kind of impact the offence has had on you.

Denise: [The police officer] took all these different statements, statements about the medicals. Statements about what happened to me. I don't remember one being named anything like that.

If having a 'voice' in criminal proceedings is of much importance to victims and witnesses, so also, perhaps even more important, is the sense that their voice is *heard* and *believed*.[5] Of course, the very process of giving evidence and, especially, being cross-examined is a process whereby what the victim or witness claims to have experienced is undermined and disputed; and this can be difficult to cope with, even when it is understood that this is what a fair trial entails:

> 'Yes, [the defence counsel] kept saying to me, "It didn't really happen. You really wanted it to happen, didn't you?" Trying to discredit your character; they're trying to prove that his person is innocent and I'm the guilty person. And I kept going back, "I did not ask him to do that. I did not invite him to my room. He assaulted me. He sexually assaulted me with his mouth and his hands."'
> [Nikki; victim]

And where a not guilty verdict is the outcome, the sense of 'not being believed' (even if, in fact, the verdict may reflect the jurors' inability to determine guilt 'beyond reasonable doubt' rather than a skepticism about any given part of the evidence) can be highly upsetting. As Natasha said of the verdict in the first trial of the man accused of armed robbery against her and two friends (a retrial resulted in a guilty verdict): "I was absolutely devastated about the [partial] not guilty because that makes you feel like someone doesn't believe you and it's horrendous. And I knew that this was the right guy and I was like, 'Oh, why don't they believe us?'" Elaine was deeply distressed by the not guilty verdict in the trial of her son who had been on trial for sexual assault against her daughter; but offered herself some comfort in saying: "The only thing that helps me is that as [my daughter] grows up she will know that *I* believed her 100%; that's the only thing that keeps me sane."

The role of defendants in court

> 'I would say that [defendants] probably feel ... as if they have no power in the situation. So everything is sort of going on

91

around them. And sometimes there's something that can be done about it – that they can do about it – but quite often there isn't ... And, you know, it all sort of passes them by really, with them occasionally chipping in.'

[Defence counsel]

If victims and witnesses occupy a walk-on role in proceedings, defendants could be said to take on the part of 'ever-present extras'.[6] Rather than being the focus of events, they often appear to be the least important character at court; almost incidental to the proceedings that, in fact, largely revolve around them. Defendants are present throughout the court process, albeit appearances for some hearings via video-link are becoming increasingly common. Trials and sentencing hearings would not go ahead without the presence of defendants, and they have the power to alter the course of proceedings entirely, for example by changing their plea from not guilty to guilty; however, they are rarely the focus of courtroom attention. The muted role of defendants at court led Carlen (1976a, p 81) to describe defendants as 'dummy players' within court proceedings: 'the defendant in magistrates' courts plays the ... game under a handicap. As a captive player he cannot physically (though he often does symbolically) withdraw from the game.' She also describes the defendant as a participant in court who is 'seen but not heard' (1976a, p 86).

One manifestation of this paradoxically central but marginal status of the defendant in court is that he or she tends to play a largely passive role in proceedings. This passivity, and a jaded attitude to the court process, were expressed in several ways by defendants during the interviews for this study. What we describe as defendants' 'passive acceptance' of the court process will be discussed in detail in Chapter Seven; however, in the context of this discussion of the relationships between the key players in court, some features are worth noting. First, this passivity often took the form of frequent references to legal professionals, such as the judge and counsel, as "doing their job", almost as if defendants are resigned to the fact that no one is on their side. Or it emerged through an evident lack of engagement with the court process, expressed through the use of phrases such as wanting to "get it over with" and "forget about it" and by references to not being able to remember details of the trial and/or sentencing hearing:

'I wasn't really taking much of it in, I was just worried about what I was going to get sentenced to ... My mitigation ... I can't remember to be honest, you know. As I said, I was in a bit of a daze. I was just wondering about what I was going to get sentenced to, I weren't listening to the talking. Actually when the judge sentenced me I still didn't hear what he said fully.'

[Charlie; defendant]

As the above quotation highlights, one aspect of defendants' jaded attitudes towards court proceedings is that they tend to regard themselves as small parts within a wider criminal justice process that buffets them this way and that, as they progress through the system from arrest and police interview, through various court hearings and eventual sentence. This is particularly true of 'professional defendants' or 'career criminals' who have appeared in court on multiple occasions. Damien, who had a number of convictions for various acquisitive and drugs offences, described a certain frustration about his apparent powerlessness within the process. He was not able to interject when legal professionals described his previous convictions incorrectly: "What I can't stand is that they get the dates wrong of your convictions ... or they even get the offences wrong." Conversely, for first-time defendants, feelings of uncertainty were often dominant, alongside fear or nervousness about what the court process would entail:

'The fact that even the criminal doesn't know what is happening and isn't told ... It was like justice was *done to me* rather than for me or even with me ... Not involved, no idea how serious it was going to be, what effect it was going to have on me and the rest of my life, family. No one really explained it, and still no one's really explained it.'

[Kevin; defendant]

Passivity can mask underlying difficulties of understanding what is going on in court, both among habitual and first time defendants: "If you are a bit common you are going to find it very hard to understand what they're saying", explained Jerome, a defendant who had been in court on several occasions. The very structure of proceedings and interactions between professionals can be detrimental to understanding among defendants – as when judge and counsel discuss, at length, technical matters of law, which can be difficult for any layperson to follow.

The passive demeanour of defendants in the courtroom may also stem from their lack of opportunity to express themselves. We have already discussed, above, the limited scope for victims and witnesses to exercise their 'voice' in the courtroom. Often, the voice of defendants is heard even less. The part that physical features of the court can play in isolating the defendant has been noted by both Mulcahy (2013) and Carlen (1976a) in relation to the structure and location of the dock. Mulcahy explains that positioning of the dock makes it difficult for defendants to consult their advocates (who sit with their backs to their clients), a problem which has been further compounded by the advent of 'secure' glass-screened docks. This means that 'rather than facilitating their participation in the trial, the use of the dock appears to signal the expectation that the defendant remains silent and passive' (2013, p 6).

The only real place for defendants to put their story across is when they give evidence at a trial. However, many do not take up this opportunity; and frequently they are not encouraged to do so by their defence counsel – or, indeed, are actively discouraged. "I don't want them expressing themselves ... It is our job to speak for them", remarked one defence lawyer unapologetically. Another defence lawyer spoke more generally about the difficulties of marshalling the testimony of both defendants and defence witnesses. He explained that he usually avoids calling defence witnesses because: "They generally don't say quite what the defendant has said. And every difference tends to be thought of as a lie. Better to focus on the prosecution case I feel." Where defendants do opt to give evidence, they often struggle to express themselves or – like victims and witnesses – are constrained in their attempts to give their own accounts by the structure of the adversarial trial process and legal constraints. This reflects King's earlier findings on the impact of court procedure and a defendant's reliance on legal professionals on his or her overall level of engagement:

> The general effect of the formal law and rules of procedure ... is to inhibit and often restrict altogether the defendant's active participation in the hearing. The less he speaks out for himself, the greater his dependence upon the courtroom professionals who will almost inevitably attempt to define him and his conduct in terms which will accentuate the difference between him and 'law-abiding citizens'. (King, 1981, p 114)[7]

As highlighted in Chapter Two, the large majority of defendants who appear in the Crown Court will have pleaded guilty at some point in the court process and therefore only attend court for sentencing (and any related pre-sentence hearings). This means that they are given no opportunity to address the court themselves. Gerry described the disappointment he felt at not being given the chance to speak when he was being sentenced (in his case, for sex offences against a child):

'It's very frightening and there's no human contact ... You don't feel like you can communicate if you've got something to say or an emotion that might be useful in their analysis of the situation; there is no way of portraying that. There's no way of getting across the whole story; they don't want to have the story, they don't want to know what happened, and they're not interested in mitigating circumstances. They're not interested in what's led up to this thing you've done that you are ashamed of, that you wouldn't have done ten years ago.'

Defendants' lack of 'voice' during the sentencing hearing may, arguably, contribute to their passivity or apathy in relation to the court process. In essence, the sentencing hearing is about them but they have no active role within it. Some defendants indicated that they would want to be more actively engaged in the process. Sam, for example, who had many burglary convictions, stressed his sense of exclusion from the sentencing process:

'The only thing I will say about when you get sentenced is that the moment you're sentenced you're taken straight away, and that's the one thing I've never liked about a court. "You're done now – go away. You've just ruined your life; we don't care. Off you go." That's a bit inhumane, the way it happens. For a judge to send you to prison, I would expect someone to try and give some advice ... It's like "Two years, you can go now." Like I'd come to buy something ... Take a few minutes out and speak to the guy, say: "You're too old for it now. You need to sort your life out." Don't just brush people off.'

The following account by Jerome of being sentenced clearly conveys his sense of simultaneously being at the centre of what was happening and yet disengaged from it:

'There's a lot of looks and a lot of judging by looks without actually speaking. As soon as you walk into Crown Court, everyone, it's eyes on you. There's a lot of eyes looking at you as well while the – *what's the person called, person who don't like me saying all the things about me?* – yes, the prosecution. When the prosecution barrister is actually saying all the convictions I've done, you get a lot of heads turning around looking at you. So, I don't know, I didn't really like that. Makes you feel quite bad and quite small. Those looks are quite intimidating.'

The professional-lay person divide

The marginal or passive role of court users that has been documented so far is in stark contrast with the active, central role of the legal professionals in the courtroom. Attention will now focus on the 'them and us' relationship between, on the one hand, lay court users and, on the other hand, the legal professionals. This is a relationship which is defined, in part, by the imperatives for professionals to keep a 'safe' distance from court users – that is, 'safe' both in terms of avoidance of physical danger, and in terms of protecting the integrity of the legal process. Rock describes this with particular clarity (1993, p 261):

> Everything that happened within the confines of the courthouse was affected by the insiders' abiding preoccupation with the conflict, danger, and threat to confidentiality represented by outsiders. The courthouse itself was constructed to work as a great engine of social control. Groupings were separated; knowledge was protected; compromising encounters were prevented; and vulnerable groups ... were shielded.

'Them'

It has been argued above that court users – victims, witnesses and defendants, alike – tend to feel marginalised during Crown Court proceedings. From what many said in interview, it would seem that their exclusion from the *relationships among the professionals* at court is an important part of this sense of marginalisation. For example, victims Ron and Faris both expressed a certain anger at what they perceived to be an inappropriately 'chummy' relationship between prosecution and defence counsel. Both Ron and Faris appeared to feel that the lawyers' main commitment was to each other and their lawyerly clique, rather than to the case at hand:

'It was just like the [prosecution counsel] came in, shook my hand and said, "Hello, you're the victim, blah blah." Which I wasn't happy with really; I didn't think it was good. The guys are overpaid barristers getting big money; they don't really care about the victim, the impact on the victim. But they should remember: it's not a game. They're playing with people's emotions and people's lives, and they're there to get a bloody prosecution. It's not a human rights exercise or a game. With some of these barristers, I think they see it as a game. They go out drinking champagne afterwards, all pals together, do you know what I mean?'
[Ron]

'I just felt like [the defence counsel] didn't look happy; he looked miserable: a face of disbelief at what I'm saying. But it's funny, because every time we were paused for a break that face would just go and he would laugh and talk to my barrister as if they were friends.'
[Faris]

Likewise, several defendants indicated feelings of being isolated within, or incidental to, a process that in many ways appears to be centred around the legal professionals. The passivity of defendants and marginalisation of victims and witnesses mirror each other and underpin the divide between the 'us' (professionals) and 'them'. Lack of understanding and difficulties in relation to self-expression are other aspects of the court experience that all three groups of court users share. Echoing the comments of victims Ron and Faris, cited above, some defendants expressed in interview their frustration at the sense that the lawyers in court are on the same side; that signs of combat are merely part and parcel of their performance or play-acting.

'They're all in cahoots ... they sit at the same Bar. They see each other every day. It's a joke. It's an absolute joke.'
[Steve; defendant]

'If you're a defence lawyer ... you should always fight as in, if your client is saying, "I'm not guilty," you should fight for him like he's not guilty ... [but] they're pally pally as well, with the prosecution. I see them coming in and they're laughing and joking. I'm thinking: What's

this? Like you're going for some drinks or something.'
[Kwame; defendant]

This would seem to support Fielding's (2006, p 109) argument that if court users were fully able to engage with the process, professionals would lose their power to 'manage and manipulate' proceedings in the chaos that could ensue; and the above quotations from court users strongly echo Blumberg's description of the professional interplay that follows a sentencing hearing:

> There is a hearty exchange of pleasantries between the lawyer and district attorney, wholly out of context in terms of the supposed adversary nature of the preceding events. The fiery passion in defense of his client is gone, and the lawyers for both sides resume their offstage relations, chatting amiably and perhaps including the judge in their restrained banter ... These seemingly innocuous actions are indicative of continuing organizational and informal relations, which, in their intricacy and depth, range far beyond any priorities or claims a particular defendant may have. (1969, p 231)

Our own observations of courtroom interactions sometimes provided a similar impression of court users on the periphery of a process focused on the legal professionals. Case 4 was the retrial of two men, Ike and Jayden, for armed robbery – at the original trial, the jury had failed to reach a verdict on some of the counts faced by the two defendants. On day two of the retrial, an important prosecution witness, Simon, was called to give evidence, which he did from behind a screen. After the court had broken for lunch, Simon re-entered the courtroom to resume his testimony. At this point, both prosecution and defence counsel and the judge embarked on a detailed discussion about the fact that what Simon had said before lunch about events immediately prior to the alleged robbery differed markedly from the evidence he had given at the original trial. There was thus a suspicion on the part of the prosecution counsel that Simon had been 'persuaded' to change his evidence by one of the defendants: namely, Ike, who unlike Jayden was out on bail. As the discussion about this possible turn of events continued, the judge sent out the jury but openly debated with counsel about how to proceed with the case, in front of both defendants as well as the witness who remained in his position behind the screen. The professionals did not offer a direct explanation to the defendants or witness of what exactly was under consideration; but the fact that something was amiss did not go unnoticed by Ike, who later left the courtroom muttering anxiously.

The following day, the retrial was stopped because, by now, Simon had alleged that he had indeed been contacted by Ike (by mobile phone, when he was in the court building) about his evidence. As a result, Ike was charged with perverting the course of justice in addition to the original charge he faced. A second retrial was therefore scheduled, and in the course of discussions – in open court – between counsel and judge about potential dates for this, the defence lawyer acting for Ike asked how he could ensure that he and the solicitors would receive payment (via legal aid fees) for their further work. The judge sought to reassure him on the matter, but the lawyer persisted in voicing his concerns, and described having appeared in similar circumstances elsewhere on which occasion the authorities "resolutely refused to pay". He was eventually reprimanded by the judge, who appeared more sensitive than the lawyer to what the defendant was likely to think of this discussion:

Judge: It is *unseemly* to talk about money in front of
                     your client, in view of his predicament.
Defence counsel: Quite so, quite so.

Another set of court users who occupy the outer periphery of proceedings are those who attend court as spectators to support friends or family members appearing as victims, witnesses or (more commonly) defendants. The interviews for this study included a small number with individuals who had observed court proceedings in a support role, and their sense of disengagement from the process emerged strongly from their accounts of this experience. Family members of defendants often felt very uncertain about aspects of court proceedings and even as though they were being viewed in the same light as the defendants:

'[The court was] a harsh place to go to. It is very cold, not welcoming, I mean obviously it is not supposed to be. But just because somebody is on a trial, doesn't mean everybody else is guilty of crimes you know? A lot of nice families, maybe the children have done something … maybe [they] shouldn't judge everyone with the same tar.'
[Trish; defendant's partner]

'They just treat you all as a criminal, that's how they treat you … They're just rude, you know, if you ask where you've got to go or how long you've got to wait, they just say "just wait", instead of telling you anything. And they look at you like you're rubbish.'

[Louise; family member of defendant]

The feeling of being surplus to proceedings that both defendants and those accompanying them to court may experience was, again, plain during Case 4. During the Crown's opening speech the prosecutor repeatedly got the first name of the defendant, Ike, wrong (and was not corrected by anyone, including Ike's own advocate). This did not go unnoticed by one of Ike's supporters, who outside the courtroom remarked, "They don't even know which defendant is which."

'Us'

The separation of legal professionals from court users is choreographed into Crown Court proceedings. This has been well documented in existing research (see, for example, Rock, 1993; Fielding, 2006). Rock (1993, p 181), in his ethnographic study of a London Crown Court, described this relationship between professionals and court users as an 'insider' versus 'outsider' relationship, with professionals alone occupying the inner circles of the court:

Barristers looked like the calmly reasonable, successful, and confident representatives of a rational order who were effortlessly superior to the ungainly and emotional creatures coming to be judged and give evidence. (Rock, 1993, p 62)

This 'insider' versus 'outsider' relationship was evident during our observations and was marked by the way professionals and court users presented themselves physically and in the personas they adopted within the court building; counsel walked briskly and purposefully through corridors into different parts of the court – heels clicking and gowns swishing – while court users sat restlessly or slouched on benches outside courtrooms waiting to be let in. The secondary status shared by court users during proceedings is fuelled, in part, by the perception on the part of professionals that the distinction between the victim role and the defendant role is not always clear-cut – particularly, for example, in cases of violence where both 'offender' and 'victim' have been exchanging blows:

> 'You're constantly having to remind yourself I guess, when you look at victims and defendants, to remember that they're not goodies and baddies. Very often they're baddies and baddies. Or sometimes they're goodies and goodies. There's an awful lot of crime up here where you toss a coin to decide who sits in the dock and who gives evidence against them in the witness box.'
> [Judge]

Throwaway remarks from counsel that we overheard during observations further illustrate the professionals' view of the court users as 'them'; for example, one lawyer referred to conflict arising in the Court's smoking area as a problem because the court users ("these people") all smoke. In interview, some professionals were inclined towards a thoughtful appraisal of the peripheral role of the court user within proceedings. As one lawyer commented:

> 'A trial gets a life of its own; it just does. Things come out, things are said and very often a trial looks a bit like an argument between two lawyers with another lawyer refereeing. And very often it's very easy to forget that the defendant's sitting at the back watching all of this.'

A defendant's own account of this was offered by Ali, who had many convictions for violent and drugs offences:

> 'Well, it's posh innit? The courts are posh. It's all posh to me, everyone in wigs; everyone talks in this funky language.'

This "funky language", and the difficulties court users may have in following it, is very evident during the banter that occurs between professionals in the courtroom. Our observational data highlight how there may be little thought given to whether or not court users are engaged with this repartee. The following barbed exchanges may have provided stimulation to the professionals engaged in them, however it is easy to see how court users may have felt alienated:

Prosecution counsel: That seems like a sensible suggestion.
Judge: Thank you, I shall treasure that.

Judge:	I'm just pausing for thought, which is sometimes wise.
Defence counsel:	I should pause for thought more often.
Judge:	It is quite a difficult case for your client to present.
Defence counsel:	Yes, but the Bar is known for its fearless advocacy.

Sub-divisions within 'Us'

> To the court administrator, to the judge or magistrate, to the professional lawyer, the court is a familiar place. Familiar rituals are re-enacted daily, often many times a day. [They] know with almost unfailing precision what will happen next – a prosecutor's speech, or the introduction of evidence, or whatever. They share also a common stock of experience which, despite their different roles in the courtroom drama, pulls them together. (Bottoms and McClean, 1976, p 55)

While, as we have argued above, the main division within the courtroom is between the court user 'them' and the professional 'us', there are also various nuances to the 'us' relationship among the legal professionals. First, and probably most evidently, divisions emerge between the judge and other professionals. While judges may engage in banter with counsel, they remain unequivocally at the top of the pyramid, or in the 'first circle' (Rock, 1993, p 181); some even assume what could be described as a severely paternalistic role towards counsel. Several examples emerged during observations of judges sharply chastising counsel, usually as a result of the latter not being as speedy or efficient as the judge may have liked:

Prosecution counsel:	A matter arises, your honour.
Judge:	No it doesn't! No it doesn't!
Defence counsel:	... do the injuries merit an ABH charge?
Judge:	Without a doubt.
Defence counsel	It's easy to say that.
Judge:	Because it's obvious.

Meanwhile counsel, whilst very careful to avoid the wrath of judges where possible, often deferred to them in a tongue-in-cheek manner:

Judge: Lead until you're told not to.
Prosecution counsel: Thank you, your honour; it's lovely to
                                     be told.

Despite playing a subordinate role to judges, counsel are still granted a central standing in court proceedings that is not afforded to other professionals. Other court staff such as clerks, ushers, loggers and dock officers adopted a subservient stance towards judges and counsel, but were nearly always treated very politely and respectfully by judges in our observations, and were privy to information that many other actors in court were not: ushers and clerks for example, are permitted to enter judicial chambers. During adjournments in court proceedings, counsel and court staff would tend to engage in friendly and even jovial conversation – sometimes discussing the case currently before the court, and giving their views on its peculiarities or likely outcome. These friendly relations were often mutually beneficial as they allowed for informal exchange of information which could help to move proceedings along. Once the court rose, there was often an abrupt change of tone as serious and distressing matters, along with much of the courtroom formality and ritual, were put to one side, and court staff and counsel chatted and joked about their private lives (a clerk regaled others about his forthcoming appointment with a "drop dead gorgeous" dentist); about the judge ("He's got the bladder of a camel; he never rises"); or about a missing witness ("He's certainly alive!" "Well, that's a start but he ain't here.").

In contrast to the court staff, other professionals and practitioners in the courtroom tended to have much more formal and at times solemn relationships with the key legal professionals. Witness Service volunteers, for example, only attended court when witnesses were giving evidence; they usually sat quietly, away from both the legal professionals and the court users, and maintained a reserved demeanour. Staff and volunteers from the Witness Service were highly sensitive to the need to keep a clear boundary around their support role, and to avoid accusations of coaching witnesses or any kind of over-involvement in cases. Intermediaries in court, who are employed to facilitate communication between vulnerable witnesses and the lawyers, told us in interview that legal professionals often lacked understanding of their role, which could result in their feeling that their presence in the courtroom was not properly accommodated.

Police officers occupy a precarious position in relation to other professionals. Officers in the case usually sit behind prosecutors at trials and are able to assist with factual points between counsel and the judge – reflecting the fact that their knowledge of the case and day-to-day involvement in the investigation is likely to exceed that of all other professionals and practitioners. In the cases that we observed, we noted that in some instances the police officers appeared to be allowed into the protected, central sphere occupied by counsel, especially to the extent to which they were sharing invaluable information or discussing the prosecutorial approach; in other cases, however, they seemed isolated from the formal and informal interaction among the other professional participants. In general, the police officers did not appear to share the relaxed camaraderie that could be seen among the lawyers and hence were not part of the inner circle of 'us' within the courtroom.

When police officers gave evidence as witnesses, counsel appeared to tread much less carefully with them than they did with civilian witnesses; and defence counsel would not spare their words or apparent scorn when reprimanding them for any seeming shortcomings in the investigation process – all the more so because these shortcomings were often central to the efforts of the defence to undermine the prosecution case. In Case 3, for example, the officer in the case was lambasted and accused of failing in her duty because potentially vital forensic evidence had been destroyed by the police at an early stage in the investigation. The defence counsel went as far as to read out to the court the official definition of the officer's role and to outline the various ways in which she had failed to fulfil it. In the course of our partial observation of a trial involving a university lecturer accused of sexually assaulting a student, the defence counsel was scathing in his criticisms of the officer in the case because the police had failed to investigate an email account from which an email – which was highly relevant to the prosecution case – had been sent. With a heavily sarcastic tone and much rolling of his eyes, the lawyer repeatedly utilised the phrase "You don't have to be *Sherlock Holmes*, do you?" when pointing out to the officer the simple investigative steps that he had apparently overlooked.

The ambiguous status of the jury

In the adversarial justice system of England and Wales, the jury occupies the status of the 'controlled audience' in the courtroom. Selected at random from the electoral register and sworn in at the beginning of every Crown Court trial, they observe proceedings as 'triers of fact'. Once all the evidence has been heard, the 12 members of the jury retire to deliberate behind closed doors, before returning a verdict, assuming they are able to reach one. They are controlled in the sense that they are present throughout proceedings but are not privy to the *whole* story; for example, they are shielded from hearing any evidence deemed inadmissible, and are required to leave the courtroom during certain legal arguments; they will also remain unaware of any negotiations taking place between lawyers and judge in the judge's chambers.

Throughout the cases that we observed, juries were repeatedly ushered out of the courtroom and then back in again. They were taken out while counsel and judge engaged in legal argument; while audio or video recordings were prepared for playing to the court; while the screens shielding witnesses were put up and taken down; and while witnesses giving evidence from behind screens entered or left the courtroom. During one such brief interlude in Case 4, the judge, aware that the jury had already been in and out of the court several times, asked for them to be taken to wait in the corridor just behind the courtroom rather than back to the jury waiting area which was further away. Jurors, in short, can be said to be both the most and least important characters at court. They are most important in the sense that they alone decide upon the verdict – a power that is often used in ways that neither the legal professionals nor court users can easily predict – yet least important because their voice is otherwise entirely unheard (other than on rare occasions when they submit written questions to the judge), and where they can go and what they can hear is highly circumscribed.

The unique status of jurors as representatives of 'ordinary people' who are given the ultimate decision-making responsibility can provoke mixed feelings among lay participants in court. Among the defendants we interviewed, a number voiced a profound mistrust of jurors, notwithstanding jurors' lay status and lack of insider connection to the courts. Some believed that jurors' supposed independence is in fact subverted by the judge or the structure of the court process:

> 'I think the judge speaks to the jury in the first place anyway ... The judge shouldn't speak to the jury; no one should speak to the jury. They should find people guilty or not guilty themselves. But to be honest, I think judges are bent. They say, find them guilty, or not guilty.'
> [Christian; defendant]

'I personally believe they work for the courts, because nobody knows what happens in that jury room other than the jurors.'

[Jonathan; defendant]

Some of the defendants' mistrust of jurors would seem to reflect concerns about their class or ethnic make-up and associated prejudices. Patrice, for example, said of the jury that "they're supposed to be your own people – but they don't know people from this neck of the woods … They're, like, in a rich area, or they don't know what it's like in your vicinity … they ain't the same class as me. Not in my circle sort of thing." A different kind of prejudice was perceived by another defendant, Christian, who thought that the jury in his case was biased against him "because of my name": his two brothers, he said, had been the first people in the county to have received Anti-Social Behaviour Orders, and the jurors would have been aware of this. Two defendants referred to the tabloid newspapers being read by members of the jury which, they argued, was a clear marker of bias:

'And also in that time period, there was a lot of knife crime going around. And this was a knife crime too. And on the front page of the newspaper I saw in one of the juror's pocket, there was someone got stabbed that day as well. And he had that paper in his back pocket. So I'm thinking – you know how *The Sun* is? And then *The Mirror* – lynch mob, yes? They all just want to just go and get somebody, yes? So, when I saw that as well, I was kind of thinking, "Ah, this is going to be difficult."'

[Kwame; defendant]

'As far as the jury goes – let me tell you something. I'm not discrediting anyone. But when you come into the courtroom with *The Sun* tucked under your arm – I'm in trouble! [*Laughs*] Do you understand? You're in big trouble.'

[Steve; defendant]

Some defendants also expressed concerns about jurors who appeared to be uninterested and inattentive; to be "bored or asleep" (Jonathan). Although the victims and witnesses we interviewed were largely positive about the concept of the jury, a few shared defendants' concerns about jurors' lack of attentiveness or broader cynicism. Tina, the mother of a sexual assault victim, observed the jury with a certain amount of anguish, trying to ascertain their reaction to her daughter's evidence:

> 'You kind of keep glancing over at them and I was thinking, "You're a mum," or, "You look like you might be a dad," or, "You might have a sister," or ... how would I be feeling if that was me sat there and I'm listening? Would I be believing what was said here? Some of them were sort of sitting there looking as if all they really want to be doing is going home and watching the Jeremy Kyle show, and they don't really want to be there at all.'

Court users' ambivalence and uncertainty about the juror role arguably reflects the ambiguous status of the jury, suspended as it is between the 'them' of the court users and the 'us' of the professionals. For the professionals themselves, jurors, whose decision-making is often unpredictable and can never be questioned or examined, exist in their own isolated and secret sphere:

> 'So it's always one of the things about the criminal justice system that amazes me, how random it all is, what your experience is going to be. And random as to the outcome, because the 12 people who end up being selected to judge you could be on your side, not on your side, half on your side. They could be persuaded, not persuaded by a speech in opening, by a speech in closing, by a particular tiny weenie piece of evidence that none of us even spot, that one person that notices and brings to the attention of the others ... We all do the things that we do, thinking that "If I do this, the jury will think this" ... But we have no idea whether that's right. We have no idea whether the things that we think they'll like or hate are actually the things they like or hate.'
> [Defence lawyer]

Concluding remarks

This chapter has argued that the main divide in the courtroom is not between prosecution and defence, or between defendant and victim, but between the lay court users and the legal professionals. This 'them and us' divide runs through all Crown Court proceedings in England and Wales and is manifest in various ways. In the drama of the courtroom, victims and witnesses play 'walk-on parts' and defendants are 'ever-present extras', while the legal professionals take on the starring roles. Despite a plethora of recent policy changes aimed at improving their standing, victims and witnesses are still often left feeling marginalised in the court process; without an adequate voice and unable fully to express themselves. Defendants, meanwhile, are in the paradoxical situation of being central yet marginal to proceedings, which renders them with a largely passive role in the process.

A key part of the marginalisation of lay court users is their exclusion from the inter-relationships among legal professionals which, whilst necessary to maintain the 'closed community' (Blumberg, 1969, p 224) required for adversarial justice, is often perceived as overly 'chummy' or 'pally' and can be alienating. Relations between different groups of professionals at the Crown Court are multi-faceted and have varying levels of formality and informality and inclusivity and exclusivity.

Finally, this chapter has also sought to highlight the ambiguous place of the jury – the 'controlled audience' – who are given the ultimate decision-making responsibility in a criminal trial. The standing of the jury generated mixed responses among court users and legal professionals alike and adds a further dimension to the complex 'them and us' relationship between lay court users and professionals in the Crown Court.

Notes

[1] www.cps.gov.uk/publications/prosecution/prosecutor_pledge.html (accessed 16 September 2013).

[2] Section 114 of the Criminal Justice Act 2003 defines hearsay as 'a statement not made in oral evidence in the proceedings'.

[3] Additionally, certain previous incidents involving the defendant may be defined as inadmissible bad character, although the witness may believe that evidence to be a vital part of his or her story.

[4] Further, having made a Victim Personal Statement does not guarantee a sense that one's voice has been heard. Roberts and Manikis (2013) found that roughly a third of victims participating in the Witness and Victim Experience Survey (WAVES) who had made a Victim Personal Statement either did not feel that their statement had been taken into account or could not remember whether or not it had been taken into account.

[5] The Stern Review (Home Office, 2010) which examined the handling of rape complaints found that feeling believed and listened to can be just as, if not more important, for victims than a conviction.

[6] Carlen (1976b, p 54) also deployed the imagery of the theatre when describing the role of defendants at court, arguing that radical reform would be necessary to promote defendants from 'marionette' to 'co-star' status.

[7] Conversely, other commentators, such as Duff et al have argued that a defendant's participation might be better secured *because* advocates communicate on behalf of defendants. This is because, as the above quotations from defence lawyers highlight, advocates are more able to make effective interventions using 'correct speech' and are less emotionally attached to the case than the individual defendant (2007, p 212).

FIVE

Structured mayhem: the organised yet chaotic nature of court proceedings

There are many chaotic aspects to the public performances played out in court: key participants in trials and other hearings do not turn up when they are supposed to; equipment fails to work; vital paperwork cannot be found or contains glaring mistakes. A casual observer might frequently sense that a case is unravelling, as defendants, witnesses and counsel are called with an increasing sense of urgency across the PA system of the courthouse; court staff hurry to find missing people or missing technical apparatus; police officers or junior lawyers are dispatched by an angry judge or frustrated counsel to retrieve or photocopy documents; and juries, witnesses and people in the public gallery are sent in and out of the courtroom on a variety of pretexts. The rhythm and momentum of a case frequently shifts, with delays and periods of tedium giving way to bursts of tense and even frantic action. And yet, despite the apparent disorganisation and disruption, cases progress through their various stages in an innately structured and logical manner. The court sits with the judge at the head, surrounded by court staff and counsel who perform their respective roles in the manner ascribed to them by law and tradition; defendants enter the dock from where they watch their fate unfold; other professional and lay participants are ushered in and out of the courtroom as required; and the case reaches its conclusion in accordance with the rules of the judicial process and the information put before the court.

The term 'structured mayhem' is used here to describe this juxtaposition of order and disorder in the business of the Crown Court. The theme of structured mayhem will be examined in detail over the course of this chapter, the first part of which will focus on the process of getting a case to court, and the second part on the stop-start progress of cases once they are at court. The chapter will conclude by looking at a single case to demonstrate structured mayhem in practice.

This discussion of structured mayhem should be set in the context of 'austerity Britain' and policies driven by a government 'with a tight financial settlement to work within and with considerable exasperation about how quickly and effectively our courts operate'

(Bowen and Whitehead, 2013, p 6). We were told by criminal justice professionals – and observed for ourselves – how recent funding cuts[1] have impacted on the efforts to maintain adequate levels of staffing and to ensure that cases progress as scheduled at court. During our period of observations at one court, loggers (those responsible for recording and transcribing proceedings) were made redundant: they were present on a Friday afternoon but gone by the beginning of the following week. Many courts operated with either a clerk or an usher per courtroom rather than, as had been normal practice until recently, both. This had ramifications for other services within the court; for example, Witness Service staff and volunteers were now required to be present in video-link rooms from which witnesses under 'special measures' gave evidence – a task that had hitherto been carried out by an usher. Bearing this level of responsibility was described as "terrifying" by one Witness Service volunteer we interviewed; "It's a tremendous responsibility if things go wrong", she added.

Court staff such as clerks and ushers sometimes appeared to be overworked and exasperated. One morning when assorted individuals in a busy courtroom were waiting to find out if a trial would go ahead, the designated clerk entered and exited the room repeatedly. He made an effort to ensure that the teacher of a noisy group of observing schoolchildren was as informed as possible and eventually clouted a (seemingly less conscientious) usher over the head with a folder in a jovial but overwrought fashion.

Other recent court-based research has found a similar state of flux. Darbyshire (2011) reports that a pair of clerks and ushers could be required to cover two or three courtrooms between them; the consequent delays were said by a judge she interviewed to waste a day per week of court time. It is, perhaps, inevitable that efforts to increase the speed and efficiency of court proceedings, allied with attempts to reduce their overall cost, will generate their own problems and may ultimately run the risk of being entirely counter-productive.

Getting to court

The investigation of a reported offence is usually a complicated process in itself. Once a defendant is charged, the complexities of bringing the case to court – especially where the defendant has pleaded not guilty and a trial is to be scheduled – can hardly be overstated, given the legal and administrative procedures that must be followed, the evidence of varying kinds that must be collated, prepared and disclosed, and the array of different characters who must be brought together for proceedings to commence.

We ourselves, as observers at court, were drawn into the atmosphere of uncertainty and waiting that pervades the Crown Court setting. We would often sit in dimly lit corridors or the sparse court café – sometimes alongside bored-looking defendants and their supporters, or distracted counsel leafing through papers – waiting to find out whether or not cases were going ahead as scheduled, during lengthy adjournments, or while juries were deliberating. We observed the contrasting scenes of anxiety and fear, tedium and reassurance among victims, witnesses and Witness Service staff and volunteers during our fleeting visits to the Witness Service offices in the court buildings. We were asked to exit courtrooms along with other observers in the public gallery while 'special measures' provisions were put in place for vulnerable or intimidated witnesses or as the court rose at the end of each session, and we often walked past court users waiting, smoking or chatting outside the court building at the beginning and end of each day.

Given the intricacies of executing proceedings in the Crown Court, they are bound to have their glitches; but the main reason we bring attention to them here is because of the significant *human costs* they bring to bear on the court users involved, whose anxiety, uncertainty or frustrations relating to attending court can be exacerbated by delays to, and confusion within, the proceedings.

Routine court data for England and Wales collated by the Ministry of Justice[2] shows that between April and June 2013 it took an average of 42 weeks (based on 22,961 cases which concluded in the Crown Court) from the time of the offence to case outcome; this included an average of two weeks between the charge and the first hearing in court, and a further 22 weeks between the first hearing and the outcome of the case. Among the cases in which our victim and witness respondents were involved, the period of time from when they first reported the offence to sentencing ranged from three months to nearly two years.

The scheduling or listing of trials in the Crown Court is a judicial responsibility and function; it is the resident judge at each Crown Court who is responsible for deciding listing practice at that court.[3] Listing of trials must take a number of factors into consideration, including the needs of victims and witnesses and their ages, the time required by prosecution and defence to prepare for trial, and more practical considerations such as the number of courtrooms in the court and the facilities available in each. Depending on the nature of the offence, a case might be given a fixed date or, alternatively, be placed on the

Crown Court's 'warned list', also known as the 'trial window'. In the latter scenario, the witness would be notified of a period of time (usually one week) within which the case would be called if space in court became available. If the case was called during this period, the witness would be telephoned by 5pm the day before and asked to attend court the next day. If, in contrast, none of the dates on the warned list became available for the trial, the case would be placed on a new warned list at some point in the future.

The period of waiting between being told that they will need to attend court and the eventual trial is something that court users find difficult. The HM Courts Service *Court User Survey* (Ministry of Justice, 2010), conducted over four years from 2007 to 2010, found that waiting times were one of the strongest factors affecting court users' overall satisfaction with the criminal justice system. Delay was consistently prioritised as the most important issue across the four rounds of the survey and by witnesses, defendants and professional users alike.

The problem of delays or of lengthy waiting times, both before a case comes to court and once it is under way, has been raised in a number of contexts. Current criminal justice reform, for example, is focusing on the securing of guilty pleas earlier in the process and improving efficiency through greater use of technology as opposed to paper-based systems of case and trial management (Ministry of Justice, 2012c). The Victims' Commissioner has also suggested system change to reduce waiting times for victims of serious crimes by, amongst others things, increasing magistrates' sentencing powers to reduce the number of cases committed for sentence to the Crown Court.[4]

The scheduling of trials caused considerable inconvenience to many of the victim and witness respondents in our study, especially those who found themselves placed on a warned list. Barbara's 97-year-old mother had been a victim of theft at the sheltered housing complex at which she lived. Barbara had urged the police and Crown Prosecution Service to speed up the progress of the case: "I kept saying, 'Your chief witness will be dead if you don't get a move on with this.'" Other respondents reported facing difficulties fitting court appearances around childcare, work and hospital appointments, particularly when they had been given no clear idea about when they might be called to give evidence. Ernie, an elderly victim of assault, was told to attend court at the end of a three-week warned list, just as his wife was about to go into hospital. Debbie, a witness to a burglary, was not called until the "eleventh hour" of a fourth warned list, meaning that she had spent a period of eight weeks in a state of limbo:

'I couldn't make appointments, I mean I'd just started university, and I felt like I was going to get taken out of lectures potentially to sit around for hours. And it caused me a lot of hassle, really. And I felt I couldn't make appointments, couldn't go to the dentist, couldn't get my hair done ... I almost felt like I shouldn't make plans to do anything.'

For some, problems associated with these delays were exacerbated by a lack of adequate information about the progress of the case. Tina, the mother of a victim of sexual assault, was angered by a recurring administrative problem that resulted in the police providing information to another witness (her daughter's friend) rather than directly to her daughter, the victim:

'We weren't really informed about anything really ... [the defendant] kept going backwards and forwards to court, but the other witness kept getting all the information and passing it on to my daughter. But my daughter didn't really get any information. I've got to be honest with you, I in the end phoned up the police officer and I actually had an argument with him, because I felt that my daughter – you know, being the victim – should have been getting the information before [the witness].'

Victims and witnesses also reported experiencing last-minute changes to scheduling. For example Natasha, a victim of an armed robbery (described as a 'car-jacking'), was informed just before the trial commenced that the court where the case was to be heard had changed and she would therefore be giving evidence in a different court to the one she had attended for a pre-trial visit. The same thing happened to a defendant, Sidney, who was told the day before that his trial had been moved to a different court.

First-time defendants who were unfamiliar with the court process also found it confusing and disconcerting that they were required to attend court for several different hearings. For example, Dominic, who had been charged with the possession of an offensive weapon in a public place, commented:

'Going through the magistrates' four or five times, each time [getting] another date to come back in there didn't really make sense really – why have I got to go back there for another date and another date before it actually went to the Crown? It was pointless, I think.'

In the end, Dominic's case was thrown out by the judge on the first morning of his trial in the Crown Court, before the jury had even been sworn in, because the judge deemed the evidence to be entirely inadequate. Meanwhile Andy, a lorry driver who was eventually acquitted of the importation of Class A drugs, described his anguish at discovering he would continue to be remanded over the festive period because his case, which he had earlier been told was to be dropped, was actually being scheduled for a retrial:

> 'There was a serious cock-up ... I rang [my solicitor] up and the secretary told me that they're not going to retrial. So, I said, "Why am I still stuck in prison then?" ... When I rang back Friday, she said, "Well, we've got in touch; we're trying to get [the remand] lifted." So, I sat in prison for that weekend ... Tuesday four o'clock, she turned around and she said, "There's been a mistake. They have decided now to go for retrial." Apparently, because nothing had come from the prosecution, she'd decided to type in "no trial". It was an administrative error, but a week before Christmas ... I was absolutely gutted. So were all my family.'

Start-stop

Even once a case reaches court for a trial, there is no guarantee that it will go ahead: only around half of Crown Court trials are 'effective', meaning that they proceed as planned. In contrast, what are known as 'cracked trials' are those in which the case is stopped without the need for the trial to be re-scheduled; for example because the defendant changes his or her plea to guilty to the original charges or to alternative charges that have been offered by the prosecution, or because the prosecution ends the case and the defendant is acquitted on the grounds of insufficient evidence, public interest or for other reasons. In these circumstances, victims and witnesses may be inconvenienced by being required to turn up at court and wait around, only to find that they are no longer required to give evidence. Finally, 'ineffective' trials are those which do not go ahead and require rescheduling. This could be for a wide variety of reasons, such as the failure of the defendant or witnesses to appear at court, lack of preparedness on behalf of the prosecution or the defence, unavailability of jurors, or missing paper work or exhibits that are crucial to the case.[5] In 2011, 46% of trials in the Crown Court were effective, 40% were cracked and 14% were ineffective (Ministry of Justice, 2012b).

Where a trial is 'effective', it frequently proceeds in a start–stop fashion when under way. Many aspects of the process still reflect the picture painted by Rock based on his research conducted in the Crown Court almost 25 years ago:

> Trials were precarious, prone to die stillborn, and an early bustle would characteristically dissipate into uncertainty and then inertia. Matters could be held in suspense as counsel went to the judge in chambers, seeking 'indications'. There could be protracted private deliberations between lawyers, *'voir dires'*, to ascertain the admissibility of evidence and witnesses, and periods of anxious quiescence as missing witnesses were sought. (1993, pp 141–2)

In the following part of this chapter, we will consider what the jolting nature of court proceedings means for the various lay participants in the process: victims and witnesses, defendants, jurors and observers from the public gallery. We will then consider some of the more specific reasons for hold–ups and disruption at court. These reasons range from the mundane and relatively predictable, such as the defendant arriving late for the hearing, to more critical matters, such as the discovery that a potentially vital piece of evidence cannot be retrieved. Reasons for delay and disruption will be discussed under two headings: 'missing players' and 'practical and technical hitches'. We will then briefly consider the issue of retrials.

Victims and witnesses waiting at court

> Indeed, the characteristic experience of *being* a witness was to wait. (Rock, 1993, p 280; emphasis in original)

During any trial, all parties involved are usually required to do a great deal of waiting around at various stages of proceedings. An evaluation conducted by the National Society for the Protection of Cruelty to Children of government commitments to young witnesses, recorded an average waiting time to give evidence at the Crown Court of 5.8 hours (Plotntikoff and Woolfson, 2009). Several of the victims and witnesses we interviewed had been required to wait at court for reasons including absent defendants, professionals or other witnesses;

negotiations over the defendant's plea; late decisions about whether or not 'special measures' would be instituted; missing documentation, equipment or exhibits; and delays due to legal argument between lawyers and judges. Even once a witness takes the stand, the process of giving evidence can itself be protracted, as illustrated by this quotation from Nikki, a victim of sexual assault:

> '[I] went in on the Monday; I had to say who I was, swear myself in ... Then they went over the evidence, and the evidence took the rest of that Monday, all day Tuesday, and then the Wednesday I was cross-examined ... all day, from 10.30 in the morning till 4 o'clock in the evening. I had two hours off, for break and lunch. And because [the defendant's supporters] kicked off in the court – they started slagging me off in court, his wife, laughing at me giving my evidence – they had to halt the case and the judge said, "If you don't stop it I'm going to remove you from my court."'

Nikki – whose alleged attacker was known to her – had been granted 'special measures' and thus gave evidence via a live video-link in a different part of the court building; this added to her sense of confusion when proceedings were disrupted as she could not immediately tell what was happening:

> 'You don't know what's going on in court. You can't hear ... Anything in the background is quite muffled, but you can hear something's going on.'

Court users can also be halted when giving evidence when points of law are raised and debated by counsel, which can make the process seem stilted and difficult. For instance, Karen gave evidence against her brother-in-law who had been accused of sexually assaulting her teenage daughter, and was upset and disconcerted when her evidence was interrupted several times by legal argument:

> 'I had to go in three times; I got dismissed three times in the first ten minutes, so that was really, really awful ... I think they were asking me about [my daughter's] education – she'd got all A's – you know, golden child basically. And [the defence] didn't obviously like [the report from the school]. So they were asking me questions to do with that and he was obviously saying it's got nothing to do with

the case ... So I was in and out, and that was really, really hard going, because you build yourself to go up in there. Nobody warned me about that and I was coming out and I was saying to [the Witness Service]: "What have I done wrong? What have I said?"'

For Karen, this was a confusing and even somewhat chaotic scenario; and yet the process of giving evidence followed its own internal logic and structure. Michelle was another witness who described a scene verging on chaos within which the judge played a pivotal role in ultimately maintaining order: "The judge was like the referee. When phones kept going off in the public gallery he told them to switch it off otherwise they were going out. When the barristers were arguing with each other he split them up." Darbyshire (2011, p 178) points to the considerable efforts made by judges to ensure that cases progress through to completion, despite administrative, staffing and other systemic problems:

> I have watched judges struggling to move business along in an underfunded system. The building is gloomy, overcrowded and decrepit and rain comes in. Electronic facilities often do not work; staff are overworked, underpaid and ill-trained; files are a mess ... and post takes eight days to get to him. The probation service cannot keep up with the demand for reports.

Several victims and witnesses interviewed for our study spent hours waiting to give evidence only to find out that the defendant had entered a last-minute guilty plea. As already detailed in Chapter Three, this evoked mixed feelings: while some were relieved at not having to give evidence, others felt angry at having been made to wait and being denied their opportunity to tell 'their story' to the court.

Many victims and witnesses often found the frequent delays and associated periods of waiting at court difficult to endure; this amplified their existing anxiety about giving evidence. They used phrases such as "nail-biting" and "horrendous" when asked to describe how they felt when waiting to be called into the courtroom. Ilan, a witness in a sexual assault case in which his sister was the victim and his mother was also a witness, described his own feelings of distress when he passed his "distraught" mother in the corridor as he was being led in to give evidence while she was coming out: "She was in tears and I wanted to make sure she was OK, but they wouldn't let me. They rushed me away from her."

Professionals interviewed as part of this study expressed their sympathy for victims and witnesses who are kept waiting. A member of staff from Victim Support, with responsibility for supporting vulnerable and intimidated witnesses, explained that victims and witnesses are often taken aback by how slowly a court case will proceed, and by the fact that even the interaction between counsel and witness can move at a very slow pace:

> 'People imagine it's all going to be a lot more exciting. It's going to be a lot more aggressive and it's going to be a lot faster. Whereas actually in reality, the whole thing tends to go really slowly. There's loads of waiting around ... That's another thing people aren't told about before they come; the long waiting ... And even the whole questioning; [advocates] will ask a question and then they'll pause – there's obviously people writing things down. And they'll ask another question and then there'll be a pause. And I think people aren't really expecting that.'

Court staff, lawyers and even judges are also often kept waiting at court, as are professional witnesses, including police officers who can be called to give evidence at short notice. During the first morning of Case 4 that we observed, a police officer walked into the courtroom and remarked in an exasperated manner, "Nobody's told me what I'm here for!" It later transpired that he was due to give evidence in a case being heard in a different courtroom.

After a trial has concluded with the closing arguments of both prosecution and defence and the judge's summing up, there will be a further period of waiting (during which victims and witnesses rarely remain at court) for the jury's verdict and then, if a guilty verdict has been delivered, for the sentencing hearing. Indeed, sentencing hearings – whether scheduled following a guilty plea, or after a trial – are frequently delayed. Several of our victim and witness respondents spoke of sentencing having been adjourned, sometimes on more than one occasion; in a small minority of cases, sentencing had not yet taken place. Delays in sentencing, as in other parts of the court process, can occur for various reasons, including where a report for the court has not been provided on time by probation or other services, if the defendant is not 'produced' from prison because of administrative error or a logistical problem, or if the necessary court paperwork is incomplete or contains mistakes.

Defendants waiting at court

Much waiting must also be endured by defendants, whether they are at home on bail or are appearing at court from prison where they are being held on remand. As their presence in the courtroom is usually required throughout a trial and for sentencing, they will usually spend much more time at court than victims and witnesses. They are also often required to attend court for various pre-trial and pre-sentence hearings, including hearings to consider bail applications and hearings at which they are required formally to enter a plea (known as plea and case management hearings, or PCMHs).[6]

On the basis of our courtroom observations, it would seem that the most visible chaos at court tends to occur during these shorter hearings, which often take place at the beginning of the day or just after lunch. In some courts, these hearings are scheduled one after the other on a single day, usually a Monday or a Friday. On such a day, there is a great deal of hustle and bustle at court, as the courtrooms typically fill up with professionals, defendants and defendants' supporters from the various cases waiting to be heard. Shorter hearings are often dealt with so quickly that huffing and puffing counsel and bored or anxious-looking defendants spend much more time waiting for their turn than in the ensuing hearing.

Towards the end of one busy Friday afternoon, during which a judge had been dealing with a large number of these hearings in quick succession, we observed more than 10 barristers gather in the courtroom to speak with the judge about a forthcoming trial involving 12 defendants. When there was a pause in proceedings at the end of a PCMH, one of the waiting advocates asked if she could have a moment of the judge's time before the next hearing to discuss the arrangements for the trial. The judge, who was renowned for dealing with counsel in a snippy fashion, remarked that they could speak, but only for a minute and that he would kick them out if they took longer – "the clock is ticking". All the advocates hurriedly crammed into position behind the benches, and one of them took the lead in explaining to the judge that the case in question was going to be spread over two trials (presumably because of the sheer number of defendants); she wanted to ask if it was possible to move her client from the second to the first trial. The prosecution made no objection to this and the judge speedily granted the application, pronouncing: "Well done ...

Right off you go, all of you!" While none of the defendants was present during this quick-fire exchange, the matter evidently required the attendance of defence counsel for each as well as at least one advocate for the prosecution.[7]

Earlier that day, we had seen another illustration of the frantic yet organised nature of proceedings when a defendant on remand had been brought to court from prison for the scheduling of a PCMH but had no counsel present in court to represent him. The defendant was able to provide the name of the solicitor's firm representing him before being taken down to the cells while court staff called the solicitors. The defendant was brought back into court less than half an hour later when the judge confirmed that the solicitors had acknowledged that they were representing him but were unable to attend the court that day. A decision was made to schedule a PCMH for a later date. Once this had been done, the defendant – expressing his evident lack of understanding of what was going on – asked if that was when he would be sentenced; the judge replied that this would depend on whether or not he pleaded guilty at the PCMH.

Several barristers voiced, in interview with us, their concerns about the frantic manner in which shorter hearings are conducted, and particularly about how this potentially impacts on defendants' understanding of and engagement with the process – and, more broadly than this, on how defendants' friends and family members may perceive the process of criminal justice:

> 'My concern is not so much with the trial, it's with all other hearings ... Because the vast majority of hearings are not trials, and trials feature very few individuals ... if you go to [the Resident Judge's] PCMH list tomorrow, you'll probably see about 50 cases involving 200 individuals, and those are the cases where people can take away their first and most impressionable impression of the justice system – that's the first cut.'
> [Barrister]

> 'Outside Court 4 on a Friday can be like Piccadilly Circus. And it's difficult sometimes to find your defendant, to find your opponent, all of that. And I think that must be quite intimidating for a lot of defendants.'
> [Barrister]

Jurors and the view from the gallery

Jury selection and issues with the jurors during a trial add further delays and pauses to the process; and jury members themselves are often required to wait and are moved frequently back and forth between court and their own waiting areas. In several trials observed for this study, delays occurred relating to jury canvassing and selection of the jury. For example, a Wednesday afternoon was lost – "fucking waste of a day", muttered the defence barrister – at what should have been the start of Case 7 as the judge and court staff tried to make decisions about how the jury should be selected. This was due to concerns that the trial could outlast the two days it was scheduled for, meaning that jurors would need to be selected on the basis that they could attend court the following Monday. Jurors were eventually selected the next morning, at which point seven of 19 potential jurors brought into the courtroom were ruled out due to work requirements the following week, including a doctor and a teacher. The majority of the panel finally selected were middle-aged to elderly men; and as it turned out the case was completed by the Friday afternoon.

Once jurors have been selected they are frequently required to leave the courtroom for periods of time of varying lengths during the trial, for example, during legal arguments about the admissibility of certain evidence, or while provision for 'special measures' for witnesses is put in place. "They're up and down like yo-yos!" exclaimed one witness. In the course of our observations, we saw several unforeseen problems arise in relation to juries. In Case 1, an assault trial, a short delay occurred while the judge investigated a complaint made by a juror who had been photographed leaving court by a member of the press; it emerged that the photographer had been trying to get a snap of a defendant in a different case.

In Case 5, concerning the alleged sexual assault and abduction of a child, the jurors were twice taken out of the courtroom, for less than one minute each time, in the course of their viewing of a video recording of a police interview with the nine-year-old victim, Leititia. Around 10 minutes into the recording, at which point Letitia was describing to the police officer having been touched by the defendant, the prosecution counsel stopped the video player and the judge informed the jury that there would now be 'a brief break for technical reasons'. Once the jury were out of the room, the prosecutor asked the judge if he could restart the video, and with the consent of the judge he did so. In the absence of the jury, the court now saw on screen the police officer asking Letitia what she had thought of the defendant;

Letitia replied, "I think he's trying to rape me." The lawyer then paused the recording, and restarted it once the jury had been brought back into the courtroom. A further few minutes into the recording, the tape was again stopped by the prosecutor; the judge said, "Same again?" and the procedure was repeated. With the jurors outside the courtroom, the court saw, on screen, the police officer asking Letitia what she had meant in saying she thought the defendant was going to rape her; she said, "I thought he was going to kill me."

A final set of lay participants who experience the sometimes discombobulating aspects of proceedings are members of the public who sit in the gallery as observers. They are often made up of family members and friends of the defendant but can also include victims, their families and friends, schoolchildren or students observing cases as part of their studies, or any other members of the public who have a general or specific interest in proceedings. Members of the public gallery occupy an uncertain terrain during court proceedings. On the one hand they are able to observe much of the process including the testimony from witnesses, legal argument and speeches from counsel. However they have no formal place in proceedings and can be asked to leave for a variety of reasons, including for short periods while screens are put in place for vulnerable victims or witnesses; or for longer periods, for example if their presence is causing a disruption.

Case 1 was the trial of Mark, accused of physically assaulting his ex-girlfriend's two-year-old daughter, Millie. Millie's father, paternal grandmother and another family member observed the first day of proceedings from the public gallery, and frequently muttered under their breath, or more loudly, angry comments about Mark and Millie's mother. Towards the end of the day, while the judge and counsel were discussing (in the absence of the jury) Millie's current living arrangements, the family intervened from where they were sitting in the public gallery, raising their hands, and seeking to explain that Millie was residing with her father. Commenting that "this is a bit unconventional", the judge, in a kindly manner, invited them to say more. He then told them that while they were entitled to be present at court they should not react to what was being said in case the jury perceived this as interference: "English juries are very independent ... It's far better for you to keep quiet ... Do you understand that? I do have the power to ask you to leave, but I don't want to do that." This direct exchange between judge and observers was relatively unusual; no one is responsible for providing members of the public gallery with information and it was not uncommon during our observations for spectators to exchange bewildered glances and whisperings with regard to what was happening in the court.

Missing players

A number of conditions need to be in place in order for trials, sentencing hearings and other matters to proceed at court; and, first and foremost, the presence of certain key players is required. Along with judge, counsel and court staff, other professionals and practitioners who need to be present may include – depending on the type and nature of the hearing – police officers, court-based probation officers, intermediaries, interpreters, expert witnesses and Witness Service staff and volunteers. The lay participants required at court are likely to include, at a minimum, the defendant(s); for a trial, lay witnesses will also be required at specific times in the process and, of course, the jurors. Like other court studies, for example Rock (1993) and Darbyshire (2011), during our observations we encountered many situations in which one or multiple participants were absent when they should have been in court.

Defendants were arguably the group most likely to be missing for some or all of proceedings. In the course of the cases we observed, we heard a wide array of reasons for the absence of both bailed and remanded defendants. Many who were on bail simply turned up late to court, with explanations cited for tardiness (some undoubtedly more genuine than others) including work commitments, transport delays, engagement in prayer and medical appointments or problems. For example, a defendant who was due to be sentenced had not turned up at the allotted date and time because, he said, he had not wanted to ask his new employer for time off work. At the rescheduled hearing one week later, both the defendant and his counsel were severely reprimanded by the judge:

> 'Are you telling me he made a deliberate decision not to come on Friday afternoon? ... I'm not running some health club or a gym ... I am not going to be put second to the defendant's employment ... If you are telling me he made a deliberate decision not to come on Friday afternoon then that is a very serious matter.'

While they might very frequently be late, however – or even miss a hearing altogether, as in the above example, and have to come to court on a new date – very rarely would defendants absent themselves from court indefinitely.

It was also common for defendants on remand to be missing from or late for proceedings. For example, one young defendant refused to leave the young offenders institute in which he was remanded to attend his trial for fear that he would be sent back to a different establishment, noted by the judge to have a particular stigma attached to it. In Case 3, the defendant, Lola, was not produced by the prison on the day of her sentencing hearing, much to the judge's anger.

There was a delay on the second day of Case 4, an armed robbery trial, while the advocate of one of the two defendants (Jayden) requested an adjournment because his client, who was on remand, had not been accommodated properly the night before. The advocate explained *at length* the circumstances in which the problem had arisen: Jayden had been returned to prison from court too late on the previous evening to be allowed back in and as a result had been driven to two different police stations in search of a custodial place at which he could spend the night. Having arrived at the first station at midnight, the defendant had asked to be moved because he was "alarmed and concerned" (in the lawyer's words) as this was the station at which he had originally been arrested and charged. He was subsequently driven to a different police station but did not arrive there until 4 am and therefore only had two hours sleep before being woken to attend court the next day. The defence advocate, coming to the end of his tale, emphatically concluded that "the appropriate course would be to adjourn today so he can rest *properly*, eat *properly*". The judge dismissed this request; however, he did allow time for the defendant to be given a short break for food and agreed to end the court day earlier than usual. A further short delay occurred when the defendant failed to reappear in court at the required time after his refreshment break, by which point the judge's patience was evidently running low.

Witnesses make up another group of court users who may be absent from proceedings and, in contrast to defendants, we found that if they were absent, they were more likely not to attend at all than to attend late. Some witnesses who failed to appear at court could not be contacted on the day of their appearance, and efforts made by the police to find them, which included going to their home addresses, were rarely fruitful. For example, when Billy, a witness in Case 3, did not attend court on the day he was called, the police officer in the case telephoned him and he claimed to be on the train on his way to court. When he failed to arrive, a summons was issued and police officers were sent to several addresses with which he was associated, and told to patrol the nearby areas in case he turned up. It transpired that Billy was wanted for offences unrelated to the case and a warrant was issued for his arrest. As this was a retrial, the prosecution and defence agreed to use his original evidence as an agreed statement to be read out to the jury. The absence of jurors could also delay proceedings; one case we observed, for example, was adjourned for a day because a juror was ill, and the following day there was a short delay because two of the jurors were stuck in traffic. For the most part, however, the absence of witnesses or jurors appeared to be relatively uncommon.

Delays could also be caused by professional and practitioner participants, such as the prosecution barrister who was let down by public transport or the six police officers who, because of a poor hand-over when there had been a change of prosecution counsel, had not received the necessary instructions to attend court to give evidence. The latter instance was not well received by the judge, particularly when it emerged that three of the officers were currently on night duty, and that taking them away from this in order that they could give evidence at short notice would incur an unnecessary cost to the public purse. We observed part of a trial of a minicab driver accused of having exposed himself to two female passengers which was delayed for several hours on its second day because the Kurdish interpreter required for the defendant, who had been present on the first day of the case, had not returned to court, much to the annoyance of counsel and court staff. Successive calls to court translation services eventually produced a new Kurdish interpreter.

Practical and technical hitches

Once the large and diverse cast required for a court hearing – and, particularly, a trial – has finally been assembled, progress may be disrupted by practical problems and technical hitches. During the cases we observed, we found that aspects that might have been expected to be both vital and routine for hearings to proceed often caused great difficulties, such as the quality of basic technical equipment like video-link devices, or the availability of maps to be referred to in the giving of evidence.

Discussions between judge and counsel regularly focused on practical problems relating to the presentation of evidence. Decisions often had to be made about how best to shorten transcripts or video recordings of police statements, or how long it would take to prepare other vital pieces of information for presentation to the jury. If these matters were not completed on schedule, delays could be incurred. In one case, for example, the judge dismissed the defence counsel's claim that he required one month to edit a police interview which was 24 pages in length: "That's more than a day a page!" Counsel hastily responded that if he had the availability he could do the work in a single afternoon.

During trials and other hearings, technical difficulties emerged frequently when equipment failed, was of poor quality, or was missing. In one example, counsel discovered that a Blackberry mobile phone that was to be used as evidence would need charging because it had been out of use, while stored at a police station, for several months. There followed a panicked realisation on the part of the lawyers that no one in the court had a charger suitable for a Blackberry phone. They agreed that a tannoy announcement should be put out across the courthouse to ask if anyone in the building had such a charger, but this failed to produce one. The usher volunteered to ask in the court administrative offices (within which the tannoy could not be heard), but came back empty-handed, and commented, "I've asked all the jurors as well – no one has a charger."

Practical and technical problems relating to the use of 'special measures' for vulnerable or intimidated witnesses were commonplace; this has a certain irony given that the intention behind 'special measures' – "Rolls Royce treatment" in the words of one barrister – is to ease the process of giving evidence for those who are most anxious about it. In one court building, the screens used to shield witnesses from being seen by the defendant and spectators bore a strong resemblance to hospital partitions, and the structure of the courtroom was such that the upper level public gallery had to be cleared if a witness was giving evidence from behind a screen, as they could otherwise be seen from above. A victim in a different court told us that he was required to sit down whilst giving evidence because he was too tall for the screen and his head could be seen over the top of it if he stood. There was a short delay to the start of Case 5, concerning the alleged sexual assault and abduction of a young child, due to concerns that the assigned courtroom was not equipped for the presentation of video-link evidence; these proved to be unfounded, however, and the case proceeded as scheduled.

Two witnesses described to us, in interview, an extreme example of problems with video-link technology. Karen and Graham's teenage daughter gave evidence over the live link against her uncle, Graham's brother, whom she alleged had sexually assaulted her. The first jury to hear the case failed to reach a verdict, and hence a retrial was scheduled. At the retrial, it emerged that the sound quality of the evidence over the live link was so poor that the jury could not hear it properly; as a result, a second retrial had to be arranged, meaning that the young victim ultimately gave evidence three times. Karen and Graham were stunned that equipment failure should have had such an impact: "Well, we couldn't believe that … We are thinking this is basic technology and they can't get it working: why is this happening? We couldn't get our heads around it." Technical hitches have been observed in other studies of this kind. Of 172 young witnesses interviewed by Plotnikoff and Woolfson (2009), for example, 40% described problems or delays because of practical and technical problems arising from 'special measures' procedures, such as faulty live-links, difficulties in playing pre-recorded evidence and a lack of screens. Darbyshire (2011, p 436) refers to court media and information systems as 'almost too painful to describe', recounting delays because of video-links not working, including a case where a judge requested that a fourth trial be ordered because of problems with the presentation of video footage in the preceding three.

A thoroughly modern dilemma that emerges for legal professionals, particularly in cases involving young people, relates to the use of evidence arising from defendants' and witnesses' use of social media such as Facebook, Twitter and Blackberry Messenger. In cases that we observed, evidence based on social media caused difficulties in terms of its availability to the court, its content and meaning, and the fact that legal professionals were evidently grappling with concepts with which they were unfamiliar, and which they would not even have been required to consider a few short years ago.

"You make me feel old!" said the defence counsel to a prosecution witness in Case 3, when the latter said that he, like most young people, used Facebook. In the course of this trial, there were several instances in which evidence based on social media was submitted to the court and closely examined. One witness, Rhiannon, was asked in great detail about the nature of her online, Facebook 'friendship' with the defendant, Lola. Rhiannon was required to explain what it means to be 'added as a friend' on Facebook; she explained that she had declined Lola's 'friend request' several times before eventually accepting. Lola was also grilled about this under cross-examination: "Rhiannon never asked you to be her friend, did she?" Another witness was questioned about the "heated discussion" she had had with Lola via Facebook about the allegations of rape which Lola had made, and which were the basis of the charge of perverting the course of justice that Lola now faced. When the judge asked when this discussion had taken place, the defence counsel explained that it is not always possible to ascertain the specific dates of entries made on Facebook. Facebook relations came under scrutiny again when the defence attempted to ground his theory of collusion between the prosecution witnesses by pointing out that the stepdaughter of the officer in the case was 'Facebook friends' with one of the witnesses.

In a pre-trial hearing for another case, there was discussion between counsel and the judge regarding the difficulties of accessing messages – which could potentially serve as evidence – sent via the Blackberry Messenger instant messaging service. One prosecutor explained that it would take two months for evidence from Facebook and Blackberry Messenger to be investigated, and that expert witnesses would be required to attend the eventual trial to respond to this evidence. In another trial, the content of a series of text messages sent between the defendant and his alleged victim was discussed at length. This was a rape trial in which the allegation turned on the question of whether or not there had been consent to sexual intercourse; and the text exchange between the two protagonists, which dated from shortly after their sexual encounter, was angry but non-specific and hence both prosecution and defence sought to marshal it as supporting evidence for their respective claims.

Missing evidence is a not uncommon source of difficulty in trials. In Case 5, a police incident report book was lost from the file between the time when the defendant first went on trial (which resulted in a hung jury) and the retrial. In the course of Case 3, there was much concern about and discussion of the implications of missing forensic evidence that was of critical importance to the case. As outlined earlier, Lola was on trial for perverting the course of justice, regarding allegations she had made of rape by her ex-boyfriend, Frankie, and his best friend, Jim, and which were said by the prosecution to be false. Forensic samples taken from Lola, Frankie and Jim in the immediate aftermath of Lola's report of rape to the police had been destroyed when the police made the rapid decision to discontinue the rape investigation, despite the obvious relevance of the samples to the case subsequently opened against Lola. Lola continued to maintain that she had been raped, and this was the basis of her defence. The destruction of the samples resulted from miscommunications of various kinds between the police officers involved, and was a matter of "the left hand not knowing what the right hand was doing", the prosecution counsel conceded during his closing speech.

While the collection and preservation of forensic samples relating to a rape allegation raises particular sensitivities, other forms of evidence might be assumed to be more straightforward to present to the court; and yet practical difficulties can still arise. In the trial of the minicab driver accused of having exposed himself to two female passengers, an issue which unexpectedly came to the fore was whether his minicab was a manual or automatic; the importance of this was that the defendant was said by the alleged victims to have masturbated prior to exposing himself, but he responded that he could not have done so as he needed both hands to drive his (manual) car. During a break in proceedings, there was a discussion between the defendant and both counsel, with assistance from the Kurdish interpreter, about how best to obtain evidence on the type of car. It emerged that the car was currently at a garage as it had recently been involved in an accident. The prosecution counsel telephoned the garage owner from a side room adjacent to the courtroom to request a description of the vehicle, but said that he was not satisfied with the account given over the phone as there appeared to be a personal relationship between the defendant and the garage owner. The defendant offered to have the car towed to the court the next day so that it could be examined. Eventually it was agreed that the officer in the case should visit the garage and take a series of photographs of the car (at the instruction of the prosecutor, this was to include both close-up and distant views); for further reassurance, a junior lawyer present in court offered to accompany the police officer.

Missing paperwork and errors in documentation are a common feature of court proceedings. This may, in part, reflect the slowness of progress towards digitisation of court records.[8] Legal professionals and court staff can frequently be seen carrying cumbersome paper files around the courts with them. Jenny, a defendant in a fraud trial, who had no prior experience of the criminal courts, was somewhat alarmed to see documentation being treated in this manner:

> 'When you're sat in the dock, just looking around there is so much unorganised paperwork everywhere. There's just bundles of paper, box files overflowing under desks. And it makes you think: well if there's all this unorganised stuff everywhere, how organised are people really? ... That's important paperwork – why is it just being thrown around?'

Examples of poor quality and shoddily presented documentary evidence also emerged during observations. For example in observed Case 5, when discussing the location of the offences in relation to the home of one of the witnesses, counsel relied extensively on a map that had been roughly hand-drawn by the prosecutor. Other researchers have reported similar findings; Fielding (2006) for example, found that the quality of photographic and CCTV evidence could depend on the proficiency of the individual responsible for taking or recording it. Darbyshire (2011, p 428) is very critical of the completeness and accuracy of files used at court:

> Documentation was incomplete in *most* case files, because of the Crown Prosecution Service (CPS) or the court office. Files were in no logical order. Post took eight days to get through, even when marked 'urgent'.

Retrials

It will have become apparent during the course of this chapter that retrials are relatively common: of the seven full trials we observed, for example, three were retrials, one of which (Case 4) resulted in a second retrial. A substantial minority of the court users we interviewed had been involved in retrials.

Case 4 provides an example of the convoluted circumstances in which retrials can come about. This case centred on an armed robbery which took place in August 2009. The victim of the robbery was Joe, who had met one of the defendants, Ike, expecting to purchase a quantity of cannabis from him for an agreed sum of £1,000. Joe alleged that the £1,000 had been stolen from him when he arrived at the pre-arranged venue for the deal and that, in the course of the robbery, Jayden had fired several shots at him. In the original trial, held in early 2011, five defendants (including Ike and Jayden) had faced charges of conspiracy to commit robbery and firearms charges. The trial concluded with the jury acquitting the three co-defendants, but jurors were unable to reach a verdict with respect to either Jayden or Ike. The latter two thus appeared for a retrial in September 2011; this was the trial which we observed. As outlined in the preceding chapter, this was stopped after three days because Ike was charged with perverting the course of justice following an accusation from a key prosecution witness that Ike had contacted him. The third trial was held four months later and concluded after several weeks with the jury convicting Jayden but, once again, failing to reach a verdict on Ike (who had, in the meantime, pleaded guilty to perverting the course of justice, for which he was sentenced to two years' custody). At this point, after two hung verdicts with respect to Ike, the Crown Prosecution Service determined not to pursue the robbery charge against him any further. In total, approximately two-and-a-half years elapsed between the committal of the original armed robbery and the eventual sentencing.

In interview, some victims and witnesses spoke of the added strain and uncertainty caused by having to participate in a retrial. Eva described her reluctance to give evidence a second time in an armed robbery case which, first time round, had resulted in a hung jury. She had concerns that her own evidence was not as strong as that provided by the other key prosecution witnesses; and her anxiety was exacerbated because the retrial was delayed for several months as the defendant, who was on bail, had gone missing. Samantha, a witness in an assault and criminal damage case, was also called to attend a retrial after the first trial was stopped because a juror had overheard a conversation about the offence between the defendants. Samantha described her feelings upon discovering that she was required to give evidence again:

> 'When we'd given all our evidence, we went home feeling all relieved that it was done, just for them to call up again and be like, "Look, no, you've got this all over again." Oh, I felt sick. Really, because I just thought it's one hour out of my life just to be in front of those people. And all I could think is I have to do it again. The court changed as well, we was in a different court [the second time] … So I was thinking, great, a whole new set out and everything.'

Retrials caused practical problems as well as anxiety for victims and witnesses who were hesitant about asking their employers for further time off to attend court; and some reported a dwindling level of understanding from their employers as a result.

Concluding remarks and structured mayhem in action

The aim of this chapter has been to convey the chaotic aspects of court business, but also to highlight its underlying structured and ordered character. The process of getting a case to Crown Court is often littered with delays, caused by a variety of factors ranging from administrative and legal issues – such as court listing arrangements and rules relating to the presentation of evidence – to problems associated with the task of assembling the cast of Crown Court players (who might include an inconvenienced witness, a restless defendant, a lawyer engaged in court business elsewhere, or a lost police officer). Even when a trial or hearing commences and begins to take shape, proceedings can easily, and perhaps inevitably, be fractured and jolted. Waiting and uncertainly are arguably intrinsic aspects of court proceedings and undoubtedly have a pervasive impact on all involved.

It may seem surprising that, despite the clamour and confusion, cases do progress and eventually reach some kind of logical outcome, thanks to the innately structured mechanics of the Crown Court process. We will conclude by using a single case to demonstrate how this happens in practice: Case 3, in which Lola was tried and eventually convicted of perverting the course of justice. The progress of the case is outlined below, with some details simplified to aid readability. Aspects of Lola's trial and sentencing have already been discussed in this chapter and in preceding chapters, but the aim here is to present the key features of this case in a single narrative.

Case 3 Summary: Trial and sentencing of Lola for perverting the course of justice

Background

Lola was charged with perverting the course of justice on the grounds of having made a false allegation to the police that she had been raped by her ex-boyfriend, Frankie, and his friend, Jim. She said she had been raped while walking home from a pub in the early hours of the morning, and that a third, unidentified, individual had also been present at the rape. Frankie and Jim were arrested and taken to the police station where they underwent forensic examination. They were released 12 hours later without being charged or bailed after the police had interviewed a number of witnesses. Lola was subsequently arrested for perverting the course of justice but denied the allegation, maintaining that her original story was the truth.

Lola first went on trial approximately nine months after she reported that she had been raped; this resulted in a hung jury. She appeared for a retrial 19 months after the rape allegations. A total of 12 civilian prosecution witnesses were called for the retrial – most, but not all, of whom had also appeared in the original trial; all of them (along with Lola) lived in the same small town and had various social and familial connections to each other. Two police officers also gave evidence as did three defence witnesses, including Lola herself. The retrial lasted for eight days. The evidence heard largely related to Frankie's and Lola's former relationship and its breakdown, and the whereabouts and activities of Lola, Frankie and Jim over the course of the evening and night on which Lola claimed she had been raped.

Progress of the retrial

On the first day of the retrial, the defence applied to have the trial stopped, arguing that the police's inadvertent disposal of forensic evidence gathered in relation to Lola's rape allegations meant that Lola would not receive a fair trial.

The judge, however, rejected this application. As the trial got under way there were early problems in the public gallery relating to Lola and Frankie's families, further exacerbated by the large number of other observers present. Frankie was the first witness to give evidence; Frankie's mother watched this from the public gallery, as did Lola's parents. When the court resumed for Jim to give evidence, the public gallery had filled up with two sets of students: one university and one school group. This created something of a hubbub amidst the already tense proceedings and the lack of room meant that Lola's parents had to stand for some of the afternoon.

In the course of Jim's cross-examination, it became apparent that the defence had received an accusation from Lola's parents that Jim had "compared notes" with Frankie's mother about Frankie's evidence during the preceding lunch break; a claim strenuously denied by Jim. A war of words ensued between the judge and the defence about the manner in which the defence was questioning Jim. This resulted in the judge sending the jury out for a short period; she also asked for the public gallery to be cleared on the grounds that "emotions may be running high". The gaggle of students was permitted to stay, but there was an angry outburst from Lola's father as he exited the courtroom. Lola's parents spent the remainder of the trial sitting quietly on a bench outside the courtroom.

The remaining witnesses gave evidence over the next three to four days and the process was relatively smooth. From time to time the judge dealt with other short hearings during natural pauses in proceedings – for example, just after the lunch break. A two minutes' silence on Remembrance Day was observed with much solemnity both inside and outside the courtroom. A significant delay was caused by the absence of one prosecution witness, Billy, who repeatedly claimed (by phone) to be on the way to court, but failed to materialise.

The missing forensic evidence relating to Lola's rape allegations, and the implications of this, was an issue to which the defence returned at many points over the course of the retrial. Another recurring theme was the use of Facebook both to support and to refute the claims of witnesses, even though it had not proved possible to obtain records showing the exact times that updates had been posted.

Verdict and sentencing

The jury retired at noon on the seventh day, and spent nine hours deliberating. During this period, the court dealt with various queries submitted in writing by jurors, and also with some other cases, including the initial stages of a new trial which soon became ineffective. Lola and her family remained in the corridor outside the court during deliberations, sometimes moving outside the building for a cigarette break. A majority direction was issued to the jury by the judge after a day of deliberations. The jury returned a majority verdict of guilty two hours later. Additional security staff were present as the verdict was delivered, presumably as a precaution in case of unrest in the public gallery; however, the court was by now much less busy than it had been previously.

After the guilty verdict was delivered, Lola was remanded in custody and a sentencing hearing was arranged for two-and-a-half weeks later, but this was adjourned for reasons that were not clear. At the rearranged sentencing hearing, Lola was not 'produced' at court from prison. The judge, visibly angry, said, "Something's gone badly wrong ... It's intolerable" and demanded an explanation from the prison service within 24 hours. The sentencing was rescheduled to take place two days later, and this time went ahead. Lola's parents were permitted back into the public gallery to watch the sentencing; a security officer sat alongside them. As Lola sat in the dock, her mother blew her a kiss. Lola was sentenced to two years' custody.

Notes

[1] A target of £300 million savings was set for HM Courts and Tribunals Service (HMCTS) for the years 2010/11 to 2014/15 and, according to the service's Business Plan 2013–14, this is due to be met, with savings being found on an ongoing basis through reductions to overhead and HQ costs and closure of under-used court buildings (HMCTS, 2013).

[2] http://open.justice.gov.uk/courts/criminal-cases (accessed 7 June 2014).

[3] In addition to following any directions given by the Lord Chief Justice, the Head of Criminal Justice, the Senior Presiding Judge and the Presiding judges.

[4] See 'Cut jury trials, says victims' champion Louise Casey', *BBC News*, 3 November 2010, www.bbc.co.uk/news/uk-11680382 (accessed 29 May 2014).

[5] A recent report by the House of Commons Committee of Public Accounts (2014) stated that a quarter of trials are cancelled or rescheduled due to late decisions by prosecutors or court manager; while the Ministry of Justice (2012b, p 49) noted that the main reason for ineffective trials (accounting for 23% of them in 2011) was 'court administration problems'.

[6] Efforts are being made to make these hearings more efficient by conducting an increasing number via video-link from prisons or police stations so that the defendant's actual presence in the courtroom is not required. See, for example: www.gov.uk/government/news/how-video-hearings-are-speeding-up-court-cases (accessed 11 December 2013).

[7] Carlen (1976a, p 25) provides a similar depiction of the 'precarious' nature of proceedings at the magistrates' courts; 'continuous inroads on the putative sanctity of the courtroom are made by the daily wear and tear of judicial proceedings which may involve the consecutive appearances of twenty or thirty defendants at one court

session. A series of brief but complex scenes have to be welded into a fast-moving but judicially satisfying documentary.'

[8] It was announced in June 2013, by Justice Minister Damian Green, that 'courtrooms will be fully digital by 2016 ending the court service's "outdated" reliance on paper' (www.gov.uk/government/news/damian-green-digital-courtrooms-to-be-rolled-out-nationally (accessed 1 February 2013)).

SIX

Reluctant conformity: court users' compliance with the court process

There is much about the court process that victims, witnesses and defendants alike find difficult. Appearing in court can be terrifying, humiliating, frustrating, or any combination of these. Various aspects of the experience can also be hard to understand. Cross-examination poses particular challenges for victims and witnesses, many of whom find it deeply troubling that they are seemingly 'not believed'. Those defendants who are habitual attendees in court, in contrast, frequently adopt a resigned or even entirely passive stance towards proceedings. But what characterises the response of the vast majority of lay participants is a *reluctant conformity*: they comply with the expectations and social rules of the process, and rarely do they actively disrupt it – notwithstanding the extreme circumstances and hostilities that are at the heart of most court cases.

> 'I believe in justice in court systems and stuff. I was anxious but I knew it was something I had to do, regardless of how I felt.'
> [Donna; witness]

In this chapter, we will consider some of the most problematic aspects of attending court for court users – and, particularly, the anxieties experienced, the inconveniences, the pressures of cross-examination, and difficulties of understanding – before going on to demonstrate that almost all court users, nevertheless, 'follow the rules' of the courtroom and judicial process.

The anxieties, uncertainty and inconveniences of appearing at court

Anxiety

Almost without exception, the victims and witnesses we interviewed were nervous about the prospect of going to court. For some, their court attendance was linked to a particularly difficult or traumatic event in their lives. But they were also anxious because the court was an unknown environment and their expectations were often formed with reference to court-based dramas on television and film rather than any direct experiences of the Crown Court. (Five of the victims and witnesses had had prior experience of the Crown Court as a defendant or witness.) In describing how they felt about going to court, "worried", being "a nervous wreck" or "feeling sick to the stomach" were among the emotions mentioned. We have shown in previous chapters how the formality and ceremony associated with the courts can be intimidating, and victims and witnesses also face the daunting prospect of public speaking in a room full of strangers. However, perhaps they worried most of all about coming face-to-face with the defendant or defendant's supporters, and possible reprisals for giving evidence.

The Crown Court is where the most serious criminal offences are dealt with. Trials concerning physical and sexual violence are their daily business, but for many victims and witnesses this world is both unfamiliar and disturbing. Dan, for example, gave evidence regarding an unprovoked attack in a local bar in which he was drinking. The defendant had 'glassed' another young man for speaking to his girlfriend. Dan was involved in calling the police and an ambulance and helping to stem the blood flow from the injured man's face. He felt he had done his bit and was initially unhappy when the police informed him that he would have to attend court as a witness when the case came to trial. He was worried about meeting the defendant unexpectedly at some point in the future:

> 'I said, "Actually, I'm not going to get involved. I've done what I've got to do and I don't want to get involved any further." ... My problem was [that] my wife had not long had our child. You get a bit protective. I don't want to be stood in court with a guy who can glass someone in a split second, who I've got to see in town in three years' time when he's out of prison.'

Some witnesses faced the particularly painful prospect of coming face-to-face with a once close family member now facing trial for intra-familial sexual abuse. Elaine attended court to give evidence against her son, who had been charged with the sexual assault of her daughter. Inevitably, the court case had had huge repercussions for the extended family, and while Elaine's daughter was to receive 'special measures' to help her give evidence, Elaine was worried about chance meetings with her son outside the strictures of the court room. As she arrived at the courthouse, she said, "I'm thinking: Oh my God, he smokes – he's going to be standing out on those steps … Oh my God, we've got to walk up these steps – he'll be there. We've got to walk past him." In fact, unintended encounters between defendants and witnesses in the public areas of the Crown Court – in the entrance hall, the canteen and in the smoking areas outside the court building – were commonplace and often caused considerable distress to victims and witnesses.

Elaine's description of how she felt on arriving at the court on the first day of the trial is perhaps an extreme example but it does give a vivid sense of how distressing this process can be for some witnesses who are, in effect, dealing with harrowing personal matters in a very public forum:

> 'They [other family members] had to help me out of the car … I could hardly stand; I wanted to die; it was just awful. I threw up when we got out the car and my whole body was shaking. I was sweating; they had to give me a fan. … Not just mentally, I thought I was going to die. My whole body was sweating. It was just awful. It was the worst of the worst of the worst things that anyone would ever want to do.'

Yet what is striking is that in the face of these very real fears and anxieties, most victims and witnesses attended court voluntarily (41 of 44 of those we interviewed) and did not need to be compelled through a witness summons. Their motivations for so doing were variously reported to be a sense of duty to protect others from becoming victims or their desire to secure justice for themselves or for others. For example Grace, who was a witness in a case concerning a care worker charged with stealing money from one of her clients, did not relish the prospect of appearing in court but "would *not* have *not* gone because the lady in question needed to be stopped"; and Amanda perceived there to be a "clear-cut" obligation for her to act as a witness in a case concerning the alleged sexual abuse of her sister:

> 'For myself, it was pretty clear-cut, do you know what I mean? It was, we've got three children and that's what should be done … But obviously, I appreciate the fact of how difficult it was for everybody in the family to bring the case forward to start with.'

The criminal justice professionals we interviewed, including judges and lawyers, understood, without exception, that attending court is anxiety-provoking for most victims and witnesses. They noted the concerns that had been mentioned by our respondents, including their lack of familiarity with the court environment or procedure, the personal nature of some trials and a dread of public speaking. In the colourful words of one barrister: "[Witnesses] would say it's a complete fucking nightmare. I hope that's the answer you've had because that's the truth. It's an absolutely horrible experience."

In talking about defendants' feelings on attending court, the criminal justice professionals tended to make a distinction between the more 'seasoned visitor' who appears to know court procedure backwards and the 'first timer'. This was typified by the following words of one barrister:

> 'Well, clearly it would depend on the defendant. There is a wealth of difference between a middle class man who's accused of causing death by dangerous driving, who's likely never to have been in court before and is unlikely to be in court thereafter, whether he's acquitted or convicted. The experience for that person, who's educated, who's confident, but for whom this is a novel experience, will be very different to the response that you will receive from somebody who has regularly appeared at the youth court and has advanced up a criminal ladder within a family, to whom appearing in court is no great surprise; who understands the ropes; who may have seen the judges more often than the counsel representing them.'

Our interviews with defendants supported this view. Those who had never been to court before articulated many of the same fears and concerns as those expressed by the witnesses – with the obvious additional anxiety about the sentence (and associated loss of freedom) they potentially faced and, in some cases, about the possibility of press coverage of the trial and their identification in the media. Those who had been to court on previous occasions seemed to be much more resigned to the process – like Ray, who told us that he had been to the court so many times "it was just like déjà vu". This resigned stance of many defendants will be discussed further in the chapter that follows.

Support for victims and witnesses

We have seen above that victims and witnesses are frequently highly anxious when attending court. There would seem to be little doubt, however, that the introduction of a range of provision for supporting victims and witnesses through the criminal justice process – and particularly at court – has helped to lessen some of the strains associated with giving evidence. The view of many of the professionals we interviewed was that the way in which victims and witnesses are treated by the courts has improved markedly over time thanks to the various measures introduced to support them. The Witness Service, for example, was regularly mentioned as a positive development, as were the options for 'special measures' afforded to vulnerable and intimidated witnesses.

On the basis of our interview findings, it would seem that many victims and witnesses are themselves appreciative of the available supportive provision at court. They tended to speak in highly positive terms about the Witness Service, including the pre-trial familiarisation visits offered by the service; its provision of waiting rooms that allow for some privacy and quiet for witnesses, away from the defendant and his or her family and friends; and the moral and emotional support offered by the Witness Service staff and volunteers who were frequently described as "amazing", "caring" and "kind".[1] Some respondents commented that they were surprised and impressed with the fact that volunteers should be providing such a valuable and important service. These findings provide support for Burton et al's (2006) suggestion that greater use should be made of the Witness Service, specifically in relation to their role in provision of 'special measures'.

'Special measures', as discussed in previous chapters, are intended to help vulnerable or intimidated witnesses to give evidence in court; the most common measures put in place are screens for the witness stand, and provision to give evidence to the court via live video-link from another room in the court building. However, some of our respondents reported that the criteria for entitlement to 'special measures', or even who had the authority to make this decision, had not been made clear to them; and some did not know until the very last minute if they were to be granted the measures. This added to distress and anxiety in some instances. Graham, for example, had been very keen to know if he was to be allowed to give evidence from behind a screen in the trial of his brother, who had been charged with sexually assaulting Graham's daughter:

'I didn't want to look at him, I didn't know how I would react, whether I'd sort of have a breakdown or get angry, I didn't know. I just wanted to get in there, give the evidence and get out. But I didn't know until literally the morning [of the trial] whether or not the judge had authorised it [the use of screens], because there was some wrangling, saying, "Well, he's a grown man."'

Chloe, similarly, had been given the impression by the police that she was eligible for 'special measures', but received no definitive answer to her request until the first day of the trial:

'It wasn't that easy to get [special measures]. I understand that's it's not really down to the police, but it was really unsure as to whether we'd get it and nobody really told us, definitively, until the actual day that we were in court that we'd be getting them [screens].'

In total, nine of the victims and witnesses we interviewed received 'special measures', including being permitted to give their evidence from behind a screen and via a live video-link. These measures were welcomed by those who received them and were seen as crucial to their capacity to give evidence, as expressed in the following comments:

'The screen is a big, big help, in the sense that it is quite daunting, the wigs, the procedure; the formal procedure of a judge and a jury. It's a formal procedure, and it helps focus you, not having the defendant or family or his friends staring at you when you're trying to give evidence, or trying to intimidate you. You can actually focus on the evidence which I think is a very important thing.'
   [Ron; witness]

'I'm glad I did it that way [via video-link]. I think I would have passed out if I'd have gone down there [into the courtroom] because I felt really bad; I thought I was going to pass out. I felt sick. I was frightened, shaking.'
   [Nikki; victim]

Waiting and other inconveniences

As discussed in Chapter Five, waiting is an integral part of the court experience for victims, witnesses and defendants: there is waiting, first, for the case to come to court, then waiting at court to give evidence, further waiting for verdict and, in many cases, for sentencing. The impact of the waiting and the frequent delays to the court process cannot be over-estimated; from the victim and witness perspective, these are hugely frustrating and often add to the anxiety they experience. The changing of trial dates and short-notice cancellations of trials were commonplace and had many practical as well as emotional ramifications for those involved – including for example, in relation to childcare arrangements, health appointments or work.

Officially,[2] witnesses are advised to give their employers as much advance notice as possible of their need to attend court, but that was not always possible within the court scheduling systems. Employers in turn are not legally required to allow their employee time off work to attend court but a 'witness summons' places a legal onus on the witness, making it more difficult for an employer to refuse. Furthermore, employers do not have to pay for an employee's time off work to appear as a witness although some payment for loss of earnings and travel and other expenses can be claimed by witnesses from the court. This is not substantial and at time of writing included a per day payment of £33.50 for up to four hours lost earnings or a total of £67 for more; the equivalent for the self-employed was £42.95 or a total of £89.90; £67 for childcare; the cost of a standard class travel fare or 25p per mile for drivers; and £2.25 for refreshments for up to five hours or £4.50 for over five hours in court.

Various strategies were reported by witnesses to make up for their 'lost time' at work. Dan had to attend court on two consecutive days as the case ran over time on the first day of trial. He described working in the evening to make up for the work time he missed during the day and taking annual leave on the second day so as to limit the disruption for his colleagues:

> 'I just had to say to work: "I'm off." The problem with my job is that like now, if I spend an hour with you, I'm doing an hour tonight. So if I spend half a day in [court] ... I've still got to get my work done in five and a half days.'

Graham had to ask for time off work on three separate occasions to attend court as a witness, and describes how initial support and sympathy from his employer and manager dissipated over time as the inconvenience of covering Graham's absence from work increased:

> 'The first time I said we are going to court, you know the manager was like, "Okay, yes, we will support you with all this that and the other," and I thought: "Great, thank you very much." The second time I went back in and said that we are having a retrial, and I gave him the date, and his first answer was ... "Head Office will have to sort something out." And then they said I had to take it as unpaid and it would go against me and everything else ... Literally, I think it was on the day that I went to court, the manager came up to me and he said, "Oh, I managed to sort it out for you." ... And then on the third time ... my anxiety levels were going through the roof.'

There were also emotional repercussions for victims and witnesses resulting from delays and cancellations of trials. Freya, a victim of serious sexual assaults committed by her ex-partner, had to wait a year for the case to go to trial; it had been postponed on more than one occasion due to, amongst other matters, the defendant sacking his barrister:

> 'I was really nervous. It felt like my life was on hold. ... In that time obviously you've got some holidays. I wanted to study and I was going to college and wanted to get a new job. And it was like all put on hold because I kept having to take off time giving interviews to the police and waiting for the court and then them changing dates. And it was like my life was on hold basically. I was really nervous.'

Carlen, nearly four decades ago, described the magistrates' court experience for the majority of defendants as 'characterised by long periods of waiting, unpunctured by any official explanations about the cause of the delays ... this uncertainty is not diminished by the dearth of information available to them' (1976a, p 27). Certainly, the effects of delays were not insignificant for the defendants in our own study, many of whom referred to the stress of not knowing their fate or spoke of wanting to get on with whatever punishment might be meted out to them. There are clear commonalities to the experiences of victims, witnesses and defendants in terms of wanting the timely completion of a trial (Doak, 2008).

Kevin, for example, had pleaded guilty at the first opportunity to a charge of sexual activity with a minor and downloading indecent images of children, but it took a further seven months before he was sentenced:

> 'I'd pleaded guilty at the police station. I'd pleaded guilty at magistrates' court. I'd pleaded guilty the first day I was in Crown Court. And from there, in my opinion, it should have taken no longer than a week to sort of say, "Right, well this is what needs to be done, we've got a guilty plea, all we need to do is sentence." For that to be hanging on and getting adjourned six times in six months and then finally getting the sentence – once the sentence was passed there was a lot of relief because it was over and done with. And I knew what I was facing and how long I'd have to stay in prison and things like that.'

Defendants can spend lengthy periods of time on remand awaiting trial. If a defendant is subsequently found guilty and sentenced to custody, this will count towards the total custodial sentence to be served. However, for those who are acquitted at trial, or receive a non-custodial sentence, the story is somewhat different. Andy, for example, was tried for the importation of a class A drug. He was remanded upon charge and waited nine months for his case to come to court. The jury were unable to deliver a verdict at the first trial and he was remanded again and waited a further two months for a decision to be made as to whether there would be a re-trial. At the re-trial, some six months after the first, he was found not guilty. "They could speed things up", he said, bitterly.

The pressures of cross-examination

As previously described, in the adversarial trial the burden of proof is on the prosecution, which means that a guilty verdict should be forthcoming only where the prosecution has proved guilt ('beyond reasonable doubt'). The defendant is not required to prove innocence and it is the defendant's right to have the evidence against him or her *vigorously* tested by the defence counsel. This means that the cross-examination of prosecution witnesses, including the alleged victim, can be gruelling.

Several recent, high profile cases have placed the spotlight on the process of cross-examination and reignited debates about the emotional and psychological costs of a fair trial to victims and witnesses. The trial of Levi Bellfield in 2011, for the murder of 13-year-old Milly Dowler, is one such example. Punishing cross-examination of both of Milly Dowler's parents by Bellfield's barrister – her father, for example, was questioned in depth about his sexual proclivities – caused consternation among victims' charities and prompted the then Commissioner for Victims and Witnesses, Louise Casey, to describe the Dowler family's experience of the legal process as 'quite appalling'.[3] In a statement after the trial, Milly Dowler's father, Bob, said that the experience had been "mentally scarring", and that "the questioning of my wife was particularly cruel and inhuman, resulting in her collapsing after leaving the stand".[4]

An ongoing public concern relates to current methods of cross-examination of alleged victims of sexual offences. Frances Andrade, for example, killed herself in 2012 after giving evidence against a former music teacher who was eventually found guilty of five counts of indecent assault. Amelia Gentleman, writing in *The Guardian* newspaper,[5] cited comments Andrade had made to family and friends after her court appearance about 'feeling raped all over again' by a cross-examination which included accusations that she was telling a 'complete pack of lies' and 'indulging in the realms of fantasy'. The four-month trial (ending in May 2013) against a group of men from Oxford accused of the sexual exploitation of young girls was condemned by the children's charity Barnardos for the way in which victims had to endure cross-examination by multiple barristers but also for the language used by defence counsel which, it was argued, showed 'a profound misunderstanding of how sexual exploitation is perpetrated'. This included describing the young witnesses as 'naughty girls' who had brought 'it' upon themselves.[6]

The revised Victims' Code (Ministry of Justice, 2013a), is intended to address some of these perceived weaknesses in how victims are treated by the criminal justice system. From our own interviews with victims and other witnesses, it is clear that cross-examination can be a harrowing and undermining experience. As discussed in Chapter Four, and by Fielding (2006), common reactions reported by victims and witnesses include the feeling that they are prevented, by the structure of the questioning process and the rules relating to admissibility of evidence, from telling their side of the story as they see it. The formal or technical legal language used by lawyers was also a cause of confusion or anxiety for some, and there was irritation at defence counsel's focus on minor inconsistencies between statements taken many months before and their verbal testimony in court. We have also seen that the lack of victims' and witnesses' own representation is a cause of some frustration and this can produce a sense of being marginalised or powerless within the court setting. Cumulatively, this can lead to a questioning of their decision to report an offence in the first place, as voiced in the interview extracts below:

> '... The way it was – we were feeling like *we* have done an offence. And because of that, we are ended up in this box ... Because when the person is not aware or not been in the witness box at any time in their life, and on the first day when you go in the witness box ... you feel nervous. And at the end of the day, the way they keep on asking you the same question repeatedly in different manner ... So that 40 minutes, when I was in the witness box and when I left the court – oh my God. It was literally draining me out. And I was just thinking, "Why should I have reported this?"'
> [Masood; victim]

> 'I was very nervous. You think "I'm going to say this, I'm going to say that." But you start to forget things. You forget dates and things. Because the nerves kick in and you feel like you're being on trial even though you're not.'
> [Julia; witness]

As in both the above comments, the feeling that they are themselves 'on trial' is something of which victims and witnesses commonly complain. This sense can emerge even before they come to court, if they feel bombarded into giving evidence by the police and/or Witness Care Unit, and sometimes threatened with being served a witness summons if they fail to attend. But it is during cross-examination that this feeling comes most to the fore. This was highlighted by a recent Crown Court case which has received widespread coverage in the British media: that involving the trial for fraud of two personal assistants of TV chef Nigella Lawson. The defendants were accused of large-scale fraudulent spending on credit cards of Nigella Lawson and her then husband Charles Saatchi, and Lawson appeared as a key prosecution witness – facing what some described as 'a more hostile cross-examination' than the defendants.[7] In a public statement made at the end of the court case, which resulted in the defendants' acquittal, Nigella Lawson complained that she had found the experience of giving evidence 'deeply disturbing', particularly because she had been closely questioned by the defence counsel about the defendants' claims that she was a habitual drug user. She commented, 'I did my civic duty, only to be maliciously vilified without the right to respond. I can only hope that my experience will highlight the need for a reform that will give witnesses some rights to rebut false claims made against them.'[8]

In a world far away from that of the famous and immensely wealthy Nigella Lawson and Charles Saatchi, a couple interviewed for this study had had their own experience of a cross-examination in which the 'bad character' of the victim came to the fore.[9] Anthony and Tracey had given evidence in the trial of two teenage boys accused of stabbing Anthony, after he had confronted them for throwing bottles at their house. Tracey was particularly disturbed that Anthony, under cross-examination, had been questioned about his own prior convictions for serious violence:

> 'The defence kept bringing up Anthony's past … I don't understand why they would. He's not the one that was on trial. I think that's *completely* wrong. Totally wrong. What he done in his past is his past. He did the time for it. He's paid the price. And he's got on with his life. I think it's very wrong. If you're the guilty person – then, yes. But if you're the innocent person, then I don't think that should come up at all. … I just thought that was completely unfair. Cause it made him look like a big Neanderthal thug.'

Cross-examination is especially difficult for victims as it is the *raison d'etre* of the process to discredit the evidence and raise doubts about any or all aspects of what is being said. This can include questioning an individual's state of mind or raising possibilities of some underlying motive for the accusation against the defendant. For example Nikki, a victim of sexual assault, had not expected to be questioned about her childhood and mental and physical health, even though she understood that this was being done to dispute the validity of her story about what had happened: "I wasn't prepared for being taken back to when I was five and six years old. … They were going for mental health; they were going for me to be unstable, that I was forgetful, because I kept forgetting things."

Among our court user respondents, there was a popular assessment of counsel as people who were out to get you, to verbally 'trip you up' and to outwit you – and given that many saw lawyers as considerably more educated or even intellectually superior to themselves, the cross-examination was largely experienced as an ill-matched fight, with witness as obvious underdog.

In a trial that we partially observed, the young female witness had accused the defendant, her college lecturer, of sexual assault. While examining the student, the defence counsel maintained a sneering tone, insisting that she had a poor academic record and as a result faced the threat of being thrown off her college course – which was in fact, he argued, the reason for her making the allegations against her lecturer. In response, she insisted vehemently that her academic record was "fine", but eventually conceded, under repeated questioning about her exam grades, "I'm not the brightest." The defence counsel pounced upon this phrase with delight, and in the rest of the cross-examination reminded her several times that she herself had admitted that *"you're not the brightest"*, as a method of undermining her testimony.

It was often galling for witnesses to have to go through these indignities in the public forum of the courtroom, as described by Chloe, who had been the victim of armed robbery:

> 'I felt a little bit like he was sort of badgering me and trying to catch me out. Trying to make out that I wasn't a valid witness. Sort of trying to muddle up things that I'd said to discredit the information that I was giving. Which, because I haven't got a great memory anyway, is probably [*laughs*] … quite easy to do. But under those circumstances, because it's a strange environment and, obviously, you've got an audience of the jury, it's sort of really intimidating anyway. And then he was just really aggressive and kept twisting my words.'

The above discussion of the pressures of cross-examination has focused on the experiences of victims and witnesses, largely because many of our defendant respondents had not had recent experience of being cross-examined themselves (having pleaded guilty at their latest appearance at court, or having appeared in trials without giving evidence themselves). However, in Case 1 we observed an interesting cross-examination of the defendant in which the obvious educational and intellectual disparity between prosecution counsel and defendant was ultimately used to good effect by the defence. The discomfort of the 21-year-old defendant, accused of physically assaulting his ex-girlfriend's two-year-old daughter, in the witness stand was evident. He stumbled over the oath, missing part of it out, and was made to repeat it. He had difficulty comprehending some of the questioning at a number of points in the cross-examination. He asked the prosecution barrister to slow down "cause I'm not very good with big words". He referred to having felt under pressure when he was interviewed by the police, saying that the proof for this was that the officer conducting the interview had used a "posh word"; the word in question was "inaudible" but the defendant pronounced it as "inadible" and apparently thought it meant "out of order". He appeared agitated during the cross-examination, frequently speaking over the prosecution counsel and gesticulating. He often repeated the language used by the barrister in a sarcastic manner and as the cross-examination progressed, he leaned over the witness box to make his points. The prosecution counsel sought to use this angry and frustrated demeanour to the advantage of the prosecution case; arguing that here was an obviously aggressive young man with a "short fuse".

However the defence counsel also referred back to the defendant's agitation in her closing speech to the jury. She presented the defendant as himself a victim of a complex and daunting court process that necessarily disadvantaged someone with limited education and evident learning difficulties:

> 'So put yourself in his shoes ... Having to defend yourself in words, where words are not your strong point ... Having to stand in a public courtroom and deal with clever questions from an experienced barrister ... How would you do? ... He's not a polished performer. He's not an actor. He's not a politician.'

The jury eventually delivered a not guilty verdict on all counts.

As neutral arbiters of courtroom exchanges, judges have a role to play ensuring that the rigour of cross-examination (on either side) does not veer into overly hostile, repetitive or aggressive questioning. Judicial interventions to lower the heat of cross-examination were much welcomed by some of our victim and witness respondents, such as Sarah, a witness:

> 'I could feel my hackles going up because [the defence counsel] keeps saying, "I put it to you that that is *not* what happened." And, "I put it to you that this *is* what happened." And when you know that that is not what happened, how many times can you say that to him? ... Even the judge did have a go at him in the end.'

Judges, too, stressed their role in keeping in check the advocates' zeal:

'Well, there are a number of situations when there's badgering ... Repetition of questions in relation to answers already been given. Putting the defendant's case over and over and over again, when it's already been adequately covered. Discourteous questions or with the sort of body language that can be used to convey discourtesy or contempt, which is not part of the process. He's just the mouthpiece for the defendant; he's not a campaigner for the defendant.'

Questions of understanding

In order to be actively engaged with the judicial process, court users must understand what is going on in court. Victims and witnesses who have problems understanding are likely to feel all the more marginalised from, or powerless within, the process. A defendant's understanding of the court process is generally considered a central criterion in determining his or her fitness to plead and to stand trial; in practice, however, a defendant whose level of understanding is deemed unproblematic may still struggle to comprehend certain aspects of court proceedings. The issue of understanding concerns not only court users' comprehension of the specific comments and questions addressed to them as they give evidence and are cross-examined, but also their wider understanding of court procedures and concepts; of the legal language used by the various professionals throughout the court process; and, ultimately, of any sentence handed down by the judge.

What we know of the socio-economic backgrounds of those in the legal profession would suggest they comprise a socially and educationally elite group. Judges, in particular, have often been caricatured as privately educated, Oxbridge types or as being part of 'an old-boys' network', and are frequently pilloried in the media for being out of touch with the rest of society. Research conducted by the Sutton Trust (2009) examined the educational background of 2,300 'leading figures in law, politics, medicine, journalism and business' between 2004 and 2008. It was found that seven in 10 judges and a similar proportion of barristers had been educated in the independent sector and, more commonly than in any other top profession, had attended Oxbridge universities (82% of barristers and 78% of judges). Darbyshire (2011), however, in her study of *The working lives of judges,* has sought to contest some of these stereotypes, arguing that while private schooling and Oxbridge degrees are prevalent amongst the senior judiciary, there is now more diversity among the judiciary as a whole. This she dates to the 1980s and the introduction of judicial training and more transparent methods of recruitment and appointment to the judiciary. A study of trainee barristers between 2004 and 2008[10] has found them to be a well-educated group. When compared to the university population more generally, pupil barristers had disproportionately attended the most prestigious universities and had much higher levels of attainment; for example they are much more likely to have obtained a first class degree (Zimdars and Souboorah, 2009).

Lay court users in the court process are, in the main, both socially and educationally 'poles apart' from the criminal justice professionals. While this is true of most victims and witnesses, it applies to a greater extent to defendants. Research on offenders consistently shows them to be a largely under-educated group, among whom many lack even basic numeracy and literacy skills. For example, HM Government's *Reducing Reoffending through skills and employment* (2005) has reported that over half (52%) of male prisoners and nearly three quarters (71%) of female prisoners have no qualifications whatsoever; half of prisoners have literacy skills at or below those expected of an 11 year old. Further data show that nearly half of male prisoners have had periods of exclusion from school (Social Exclusion Unit, 2002). The extract below from an interview with defendant Jerome, convicted of various driving offences, illustrates his own perception of the divide between legal professionals and defendants:

> 'They used very long, powerful words where if you're not well educated, if you didn't do well at school or didn't go to university or college or anything like that, because I didn't do any of that, it's very hard to take in and understand … If you are a bit common you are going to find it very hard to understand what they're saying.'

One of the judges we interviewed highlighted the various potential barriers to understanding and communication faced by defendants:

> 'Well, the language; not having English as a first language or having difficulties with language generally; literacy problems. They're sent papers. They don't get to spend, if they're on remand, hours and hours with their lawyers. If they can't read, that's a great difficulty. IQ; very often we're dealing with defendants who are on or below that magic number of 70. But even between 70 and 100 you're going to find some difficulty in communication. Then you have

the usual mixed bag of mental health problems, of difficult personality traits, of troubled histories, people who've been beaten, people who have abused drugs over a long period of time or alcohol. Yes, the usual collection of happiness that our criminal courts seem to attract.'

While there are defendant 'experts' whose routine involvement with the criminal justice system means that they are familiar with it and have at least a veneer of knowledgeability, others who have had little or no contact with the system are more likely to acknowledge confusion. Jenny, a defendant in a fraud and deception case, noted her ignorance of the legal terminology used throughout the process, from the point of her arrest:

> 'Yes, I don't know how it all – from being arrested, even down to the word "bail" and "charged" because I had never dealt with these sorts of circles or had any involvement. I didn't really understand what even any of those terms meant. So when I was told I had a bail date until October that didn't really mean anything to me. And I didn't really understand – I mean I did eventually but I didn't understand why we had to go to the magistrates' court, to the Crown Court and why it took so long. Like there was no kind of explanation … I didn't even know really what the difference between a solicitor and a barrister. At the time it just was a complete new world.'

The language of the courtroom is often complex and includes legal terminology that will likely exclude most lay participants. This is accepted by legal professionals who often see it as part of the role of the advocate and the judge to explain legal concepts to court users:

> 'I think a lot of them find legal argument very difficult but then that's to be expected. I mean, any lay person sitting there hearing barristers discussing "hearsay" and "abuse of process" is going to find it difficult. But it's up to us to explain it to them properly. And also to the judge as well to explain what's going on.'
> [Defence lawyer]

Not only does their abundant use of technical language or 'legalese', and their range of vocabulary and the conventions of speech, differentiate the judges and lawyers from the court users, but also their diction or enunciation is typically that of the most highly-educated and socially elite in our society. Indeed, we found during our observations that accent and styles of speech frequently distinguished the lawyers and judges from other players within the courtroom, such as police officers and court clerks and ushers, as well as from the lay court users.

If court users sometimes struggle to understand the language used by the legal professionals in court, this does not simply reflect the gulf in levels of education between the two groups, or the complexities of legal jargon and concepts. In questioning and cross-examining witnesses, lawyers may deliberately use language in such a way as to hide or obscure what is being said. Fielding (2006, p 136) has highlighted a barrister 'custom' of wording or phrasing questions in a certain way in order to get the answer they want which can often leave witnesses 'baffled'. The use of complex sentence structures, often including double negatives, is a technique that advocates frequently use to this end; although, as we have seen with the example from Case 1 cited above, a witness or defendant who is evidently confused in the face of cross-examination by an eloquent and demanding lawyer can elicit sympathy from the jury.

In Case 5, nine-year-old Letitia was cross-examined via video-link concerning her allegation of sexual assault by Jamal. Despite her very young age, Letitia proved herself a match for the convoluted questioning in which the defence counsel engaged (whether or not the lawyer in this case was deliberately over-complicating the wording of his questions was difficult to ascertain). She was being probed as to her certainty that the defendant in the courtroom was the same man who had assaulted her. This was important to the case because her assailant had been wearing a hooded top which may have obscured his face; and, shortly after the incident, a witness who had observed the assault had attacked the presumed assailant and identified him to the police – in Letitia's view. There was no question that the man punched and identified by the witness was Jamal, the defendant now standing trial; but the question was whether Jamal had in fact been Letitia's assailant, as both the witness (referred to by the defence counsel as "the Turkish man") and victim claimed.

This complicated scenario was reflected in the defence counsel's questioning of Letitia: "That's the man who the Turkish man identified and later assaulted, isn't it? But you can't say if it was the same man who touched you earlier, can you?" She asked the defence barrister to repeat the question, which he did, but she still did not answer. The judge then intervened, asking her if she needed the question to be repeated once more. She said she did, and the judge told the advocate to repeat his question "with fewer negatives, if possible". The barrister continued to focus on this point for several minutes, eventually saying: "The man who you identified, who was the man who was pointed out, was not the man who assaulted you?" To this Letitia responded, in a somewhat weary but pointed tone: "Is that a question?" The lawyer reformulated his question yet again, and Letitia, undaunted, firmly asserted that Jamal was indeed the man who had assaulted her.

In our partial observation of a trial of a young man accused of rape, we saw the prosecution counsel's use of elaborate language produce simple incomprehension on the part of the defendant. The defendant had said that he had known the alleged victim for some weeks prior to the night on which they had had sex; his cross-examination included discussion of how he had first met her. He said that he began talking to her on a bus, and the counsel suggested that he had initiated this chat for one reason only:

Prosecution counsel:	It was as a prelude to sexual activity?
Defendant:	What?
Prosecution counsel:	It was as a prelude to sexual activity?
Defendant:	I don't understand.
Prosecution counsel [*snaps*]:	*You spoke to her because you wanted to have sex with her!*
Defendant:	No.

In court, a victim or witness with learning difficulties or needs may be assigned a witness intermediary to facilitate communication, under 'special measures' provisions. A witness intermediary interviewed for this study described the reluctance of some barristers to adapt their language to meet the needs of the witness, when advised to do so by an intermediary, as they can see this as 'taking away the tools of their trade'; it is their role after all, to challenge, to question, to confuse and thereby to undermine witness testimony, and language is key to achieving this.[11] The intermediary commented that the vocabulary, phrasing and very structure of the language used by counsel will be "nothing [witnesses] would come into contact with normally". Another intermediary, stressed that witnesses' lack of understanding is often hidden because they "don't ask for help [and] they don't necessarily *know* that they haven't understood it. If they say 'I don't know' a lot, they lose confidence."

A barrister echoed this point when discussing how he seeks to reassure witnesses:

'Well, I always speak to [them] and try and make sure that they do know what's going on, and always try to ask if they've got particular questions. ... I suppose there's an implied question of, do they know what question to ask, do they know what it is they're not understanding? And often they don't until they actually go through the experience of giving evidence themselves, I think.'

During our interview with this respondent, he was called back into court: he was defending in a case of dangerous driving. The jury had been unable to reach a unanimous verdict and was being instructed by the judge to reach a majority verdict on "the two counts". After the judge and jury had left the courtroom (and we were waiting to resume our interview), the defendant called over the barrister and asked him to explain what were "the two counts". This question came after two days of trial and provides a clear example of a defendant's limited comprehension of a fundamental aspect of the case – that is, the precise charges he was facing – notwithstanding the barrister's stated commitment to easing court users' problems of understanding.

Another example of lack of understanding of the fundamentals of a case was provided by Mila, a victim in an assault case. She had arrived in the UK two years previously from Iraq and had required an interpreter in court. During the research interview she was asked if she had noticed the jury whilst giving evidence. Her response highlights starkly her lack of understanding of the process in which she was a main participant:

Interviewer:	Did you notice the jury, who would have been watching – the 12 people ...?
Mila:	Yes. But I don't know what they do, I just know the judge and the barrister and – yes. I don't know really what job they're doing.
Interviewer:	Okay. The jury, they listen to all the evidence and then they decide whether they think [the defendant] is guilty or not guilty. So because she'd said she hadn't done it, the jury watch all that happens, like you giving evidence –
Mila:	Yes, but I was thinking the judge says who was guilty or not.

Following the rules

We have noted above the fears, anxieties, general inconveniences and problems of understanding endured by victims, witnesses and defendants during the court process. The process poses many challenges, and yet few fail to comply with it. Victims and witnesses (almost invariably) attend court when told to do so; they rearrange their work and other commitments and they do so on more than one occasion if required. They wait for long periods to give their evidence, and sometimes it emerges after a lengthy wait that they are not even needed. Victims and witnesses often cite their belief in the law and in what is right and wrong, and their wish to help prevent further crime, as their motivation for attending court. Defendants, of course, attend court under compulsion; but here, too, it is notable that those who are not on remand make the necessary effort to turn up at court to face their fate when told to do so (albeit sometimes late), and hardly ever challenge social rules and etiquette of the courtroom once they are there. Carlen, in her study of magistrates' courts, similarly observed that defendants tend to be highly compliant, even while they struggle to understand much of the process in which they are involved:

> Most defendants cause no trouble in the courtroom. After a long wait in the corridors or waiting-room, many of them make an initial attempt to hear and follow the proceedings and then visibly give up the pretence of understanding and stare restlessly around the courtroom until the policeman, touching them on the arm, indicates that the formalities are over. (1976a, p 32)

There is no doubt that although most of our victim and witness respondents appreciated the various forms of support made available to them, such as the option for pre-trial visits, Witness Service facilities, and 'special measures' to help with giving evidence, many are unprepared both for the restrictions on what they can say in court and for the tone and rigour of cross-examination. Yet while nervousness and tears are common in the witness stand, there are few serious disruptions to procedure. This compliance is illustrated by Samantha's account of giving evidence. She was witness to an unprovoked and violent assault on her boyfriend by two young men. She described being extremely nervous about giving evidence and had to endure questioning from two defence lawyers. She got so upset at their line of questioning that she ran from the witness stand and out of the courtroom. However, swift reassurance from the prosecution counsel helped her to calm down, to the point that she felt able to return to the witness stand to be dismissed by the judge according to correct procedure, and hence the discipline of the courtroom was rapidly re-established.

> 'I didn't cry but I just ran out of the courtroom. I just had to. I just put my hands up to the judge, said "sorry" and ran outside. Then I started thinking – oh no, am I in trouble now? Because I'd left the courtroom without being asked to leave. ... The judge sort of said, "Look, you've asked her enough questions." My man [the prosecution counsel] came over and comforted me and got me a glass of water and said, "Look, I'll give you a 15 minute break." ... And then he came back and said, "Look, just go back in. The judge is now going to say that it's all over, end it officially. And then you can go." So I ... walked in there, stood there, and then he said this thing and I left.'

Fielding (2006, pp 6–7), whose Crown Court study entailed observation of 55 trials concerning allegations of violence, found that *not one participant* in these cases 'refused to accept the authority of the courts'. As a group, court users were compliant: 'Defendants mostly accept the process, victims do not expect over-much, and witnesses want to be seen as playing the role expected of them.' As Rock also has observed (1993), the emphasis on protocol is paramount in maintaining order within the courtroom, and serves to underpin or strengthen the authority of the courts.

In the often emotionally charged courtroom atmosphere, in which serious conflicts and tensions are being played out, compliance with the authority of the courts is nevertheless the norm in the public gallery. It is here that family members and friends of both defendant and victim often share the seating space and sit in close proximity throughout proceedings with minimal official supervision. In Case 3, for example, the mother and father of the 21-year-old defendant, Lola, were seated in the public gallery in the row above the mother and a friend of one of the young men she had accused of rape (in relation to which she was standing trial for perverting the course of justice, on the grounds that it was a false allegation). This was a retrial and both families had been dealing with the courts for nearly two years. For the most part they pointedly ignored each other, but on the second day of trial, the judge asked the usher to clear the public gallery until further notice as "emotions may be running high". Those in the public gallery who were linked to either the prosecution or defence were asked to leave. As Lola's father went out he shouted: "Arseholes, fucking arseholes!" and thereafter was told he could not observe proceedings from the gallery. For the next five days of the trial, and as the guilty verdict was delivered on day eight, he and his wife sat in quiet and subdued fashion on a bench outside the courtroom; Lola sat with them, equally subdued, before she entered the dock at the beginning of each day and during breaks in proceedings. Some weeks later, when the sentence was passed, Lola's father was permitted back into the public gallery to hear the sentencing. Both parents sat quietly looking on as their daughter was sentenced to two years' custody and described by the judge as "a manipulative young woman".

In Case 2, the extended family of the defendant, Emmanuel, charged with inflicting grievous bodily harm in the course of a brawl during a Sunday morning football match, sat through four days of trial, the verdict and sentencing. While visibly anxious and upset, particularly as a custodial sentence was handed down, they remained quiet and deferential throughout the proceedings: for example, always bowing to the judge as they entered and left the public gallery. Tina described to us the experience of observing the cross-examination of her daughter, who was the victim of a sexual assault. Tina spoke of her feelings of turmoil and powerlessness at the sight of the defence counsel's seeming attack on her daughter's character, and her effort to keep her emotions in check:

> 'Oh, I felt like slapping him straight in the face, to be honest with you. … You know, he tried to make my daughter sound like she was a drunken old slut … I tried not to react in any way at all. I just wanted to say something, but for fear of being held in contempt of court, I didn't say anything at all. I wanted to say to this bloke that he'd got it wrong … In my opinion, he had a free ticket to stand there and slag my kid off. And I couldn't do nothing about it.'

Even in instances where emotions and disorder erupt, order is restored quickly and efficiently. In the course of observed Case 4, an aborted trial of two defendants for armed robbery, a fight broke out between the defendants' respective families immediately after the judge had announced that the case would not proceed. As the court staff were dealing with some outstanding administrative matters inside the courtroom, a barrister rushed in to ask the usher to call security as there was "a kerfuffle outside". Swearing and shouting could be heard coming from the lobby area outside the courtroom, and a woman screamed, "Get the police! Get the police." Several security guards appeared from both higher and lower floors of the court building, as barristers and court staff collected in the courtroom entrance, watching the drama. A few minutes later all was quiet again as the two warring groups were separated and ushered out of the building.

Somewhat chaotic scenes also accompanied, but did not derail, the sentencing of four teenagers for robbery (of mobile phones), all of whom had various family members in the public gallery. Three of the teenagers were sentenced to custody and were taken down by the security officer; one of them waved at his family, at which point his mother started to sob loudly and appeared to have a panic attack. She was comforted by her husband and daughter (who was in a wheelchair) and the usher got her a glass of water, although this did not abate her tears. The judge began to sentence the fourth defendant but struggled to make himself heard and told the mother to leave the court. The woman's husband, daughter and the usher tried to calm her down but failed to persuade her to move. The fourth defendant received a 12-month suspended sentence and was released from the dock, while attempts were still being made to get the sobbing mother out of the court. She was eventually moved by her husband and the usher; however, her daughter was now crying and unable to manoeuvre her wheelchair through the door, until she was helped by a family member of one of the other defendants.

Like the moment when the judge passes sentence, a jury's pronouncement of the verdict is a point of high tension; and yet, whichever side is favoured by the verdict, rarely does the order of the courtroom come under serious threat. The setting, the ritualised procedures that must be followed, and the formality of the official dress and language of the court are largely successful at containing hostilities and emotion, and this, in the view of one resident judge we interviewed, demonstrates a general acceptance of the authority of the court process:

> 'And I think, what I would say is that actually given that we are dealing with people who are in stressful situations by definition, either because they are in the dock or because they are witnesses giving evidence, or indeed because they are juries having to make very important decisions about people's lives – given that we are dealing with people under stress in those ways, it is remarkable how the system works and caters for those stresses. You very, very rarely get a

very unpleasant incident happening in the courtroom. It does happen, it can happen, but it's quite rare. It's quite rare that anyone either actually gets out of the witness box and assaults counsel or that a defendant tries to escape. ... Or even that the defendant starts shouting abuse when sentenced. ... So, I think what I draw from that is that there is a general acceptance that the system is working.'

One judge interviewed as part of Darbyshire's study of the judiciary commented on the high levels of compliance among defendants who often turn up at court with their bags packed in readiness to be sent to prison, 'like turkeys voting for Christmas' (2011, p 199). In fact, so rare is any contravention of court etiquette that it tends to make news headlines when it happens, as in the case reported in the national press in June 2013 of a man in Ipswich jailed for 18 months for contempt of court because he had jumped from the public gallery and attacked the judge, knocking his wig off, after his brother had been sentenced to 30 months' custody.[12]

Concluding remarks

This chapter has examined the emotions, including feelings of tension, anxiety and distress, experienced by those attending court as victims, witnesses or defendants. We have shown how aspects of the court environment, including the formality of its procedures and processes and the very public arena in which the 'action' takes place, can be both intimidating and alienating, especially for those for whom this is a novel and, usually, most unwelcome experience. We have highlighted how legal language and aggressive cross-examination can upset and confuse and have noted the appreciation, reported by many victims and witnesses, of the support provided by the Witness Service and, for those permitted to have them, the 'special measures' afforded by the court, which can make giving evidence a little less daunting. As the title of this chapter underlines, despite the emotional strains and difficulties associated with attending court, and the inconveniences and discomfort caused by delays and adjournments to hearings, victims, witnesses and defendants alike show a strong tendency to attend court as required, perform the roles expected of them, and comply with the rules and etiquette of the courtroom.

Notes

[1] Similarly positive comments about the Witness Service were also forthcoming from victim respondents in the WAVES qualitative research (Commissioner for Victims and Witnesses, 2011).

[2] www.gov.uk/going-to-court-victim-witness (accessed 27 May 2014).

[3] 'Milly Dowler Family: "Too high a price for Bellfield conviction"', www.justice.gov.uk/news/press-releases/victims-com/vcnewsrelease240611c (accessed 1 February 2014).

[4] www.bbc.co.uk/news/uk-england-13908358 (accessed 3 January 2014).

[5] Amelia Gentlemen, 'Prosecuting sexual assault: "Raped all over again"', *The Guardian*, 13 April 2013.

[6] Jamie Doward, 'Grooming victims in danger of "reliving abuse" by giving evidence in court', *The Observer*, 19 May 2013.

[7] Geoffrey Robertson, 'The vilification of Nigella Lawson: this is no way to treat a witness', *The Guardian*, 20 December 2013.

[8] Cited in Robert Booth, 'Nigella Lawson bites back over "ridiculous sideshow" of drug use claims', *The Guardian*, 20 December 2013.

[9] Evidence on the 'bad character' of non-defendant witnesses is admissible in certain prescribed circumstances under Section 100 of the Criminal Justice Act 2003.

[10] Based on four consecutive years of the 'Pupillage Survey' (2004/5–2007/8) currently administered by the Bar Standards Board. The Survey is enclosed with the mailing for the annual pupillage registration forms and has a response rate of over 90%, making it the most authoritative source of information on pupil barristers.

[11] An Advocacy Training Council report on the handling of vulnerable people at court considers what kinds of communication and questioning methods are appropriate for vulnerable defendants and witnesses and notes that, for example, 'Leading questions are a mainstay of the cross-examining advocate's technique' and can be especially problematic for children. It is suggested that 'a change of culture' is required if advocates are to move away from this traditional approach to cross-examination (Advocacy Training Council, 2011, p 37).

[12] Press Association, 'Attack on judge lands man in jail', *The Guardian*, 4 June 2013.

SEVEN

Legitimacy: court users' perceived obligation to obey, and what this is based on

In the preceding chapter, we have described the conformity of victims, witnesses and defendants at court as 'reluctant'. Clearly, most have no desire to come to court: defendants are there because they have no choice in the matter, and there is also a degree of compulsion for witnesses, who can potentially be summonsed if they refuse to attend. We would contend, however, that court users' conformity within the court process is at least partially voluntary rather than being entirely coerced: we are, in other words, distinguishing 'voluntary acceptance from simple compliance ("I did what I was told to do.")' (Tyler, 2009, p 320).

On the basis of how court users described their experiences of court to us, and our own observations of behaviour in court, we are of the view that court users' conformity is, in part, based on a belief in the legitimacy of the court process: that is, they obey the rules because they *perceive an obligation* to do so (Hough et al, 2010; 2013b). Our findings echo those of Fielding that, 'Whether attentive and distressed, or disdainful and ostentatiously at ease, one thing lay participants rarely do is reject the legitimacy of the proceedings' (2006, p 53) – albeit the sense of legitimacy is implicit rather than explicitly articulated. Similarly, Bottoms and McClean noted that defendants do not 'struggle' against the authorities in court (1976, p 227); and Ball has observed:

> Participants in judicial proceedings ... bring with them a willing suspension of disbelief. It is manifested in their willingness to observe the rules and forms of the proceedings, their willingness to abide by the outcome of the proceedings, and their willingness not to dismiss the legitimacy of the legal system, characterized though it may be by curious formulae, arcane rites and untoward results (1975, pp 108–9).

This final substantive chapter of the book will explore the various dimensions to the perceived legitimacy of the court process. We have discussed at length, above, the many and profound incongruities – and the degree of chaos – that often characterise court proceedings, and we have made it clear that attending court can be terrifying, humiliating, upsetting and frustrating. Why is it that, despite all this, court users largely accept the legitimacy of what goes on in court? This is a compelling question, with significant implications for how the public perceive and experience the criminal justice system more widely.

As discussed in the introduction to this volume, procedural justice theorists are particularly concerned with identifying the mechanisms which secure and sustain the legitimacy of criminal justice institutions. Broadly, they argue that individuals' sense of the legitimacy of the justice system tends to reflect their direct interactions with it, and that the perceived fairness or otherwise of the *outcomes* of these interactions generally have less impact on overall views of the system and its legitimacy than the perceived fairness or otherwise of the *processes* in which individuals have been involved. Much of the work of procedural justice theorists has emphasised that there are two key dimensions of *fair procedure*: first, *fair decision-making* by the authorities; secondly, *respectful treatment* of members of the public by the authorities (Tyler, 2001, 2003, 2009; Fagan, 2008; Bottoms and Tankebe, 2012).

Our own research findings, to be elaborated below, support this contention of procedural justice theorists that fair decision-making and respectful treatment are important factors in shaping victims', witnesses' and defendants' sense of the legitimacy of the court process. However, it also became apparent from our study that, in the stark setting of the courtroom, the outcome of a case – in terms of whether or not the defendant is found guilty and, following a conviction, the type of sentence passed – is a crucial determinant of court users' perceptions of legitimacy.

Beyond the three factors of fair decision-making, respectful treatment and positive outcome, we would argue that there is a further important dimension of legitimacy for court users. This can be described as 'moral alignment'. Here we are, again, drawing on the procedural justice literature, within which the 'moral' dimension of legitimacy is a key theme. Legitimacy is seen as that which 'instantiates within the individual the moral and social norms of law' (Fagan, 2008, p 139). Tyler (2006c, p 314) discusses the relationship between legitimacy and personal morality, both of which he defines as 'social values' which are internalised and help to regulate behaviour independently of concerns about the risk of being sanctioned for wrongdoing. The public's sense of the legitimacy of legal authorities is reinforced to the extent that the authorities' actions are seen as consistent with their own moral or ethical code. Such consistency thus enables the authorities 'to activate the motivation force of morality'. Following David Beetham, Hough et al (2013b, p 246) argue that there are three dimensions to legitimacy: namely, 'obligation to obey', 'legality' and '"moral alignment" between power-holder and the governed, reflected in shared moral values'.

Finally, for defendants (if not for victims and witnesses) there is a fifth factor related to the above four dimensions of legitimacy: namely, a passive acceptance of the court system. This is similar to what Bottoms and Tankebe (2012, p 165) have characterised as 'pragmatic acquiescence' or 'dull compulsion', whereby an individual's perceived obligation to obey the law is based on the sense that 'I have to do this' rather than a sense of moral duty. For Bottoms and Tankebe, this (at best) morally neutral aspect of 'dull compulsion' thus distinguishes it from 'true legitimacy'. However, it is our view that defendants' passive acceptance extends beyond pure resignation to varying degrees of belief in the internal logic and coherence of the vast machinery of the criminal courts. In other words, it is the conception that the court system is as it is because *this is how it has to be*, even if there is no clearly or explicitly normative aspect to this belief. In these terms, passive acceptance can be said to contribute to a weak sense of the legitimacy of the court process – where the individual's compliance is not entirely coerced but is based on a sense of obligation to obey, if not necessarily a sense of *moral* obligation.

In short, then, we have identified five, inter-related dimensions of legitimacy, each of which will be considered in turn over the remainder of this chapter:

a. moral alignment;
b. positive outcomes;
c. fair decision-making;
d. respectful treatment;
e. passive acceptance.

In considering court users' responses to the court experience in terms of the above dimensions of legitimacy, the diversity of those responses becomes immediately apparent. If, as noted above, an overarching theme is that most court users largely accept the legitimacy of the court process, the specific factors that make it legitimate vary from individual to individual. And while it is, therefore, difficult to generalise, there would appear to be some broad differences between type of court user: with 'passive acceptance' prominent among defendants but not others, and a concern with 'respectful treatment' more evident among victims and witnesses than defendants.

Crucially, three of the dimensions of legitimacy are related to specific court experiences: namely, 'positive outcomes', 'fair decision-making' and 'respectful treatment'. Any or all of these three factors can be present or absent in any given individual's experiences (or any individual's interpretation of those experiences, since they are largely subjective) and hence can, variously, support or undermine the individual's sense of legitimacy. What became clear from our interviews, however, is that *negative* experiences and attitudes relating to outcomes, decision-making or treatment were often outweighed by the presence of other (positive) legitimating factors. In other words, our respondents' overarching sense of the legitimacy of the court process tended to reside in differing combinations of the five factors listed above, but very rarely, if ever, in all of them simultaneously.

Moral alignment

For most of the witnesses and victims we interviewed, there appeared to be a taken-for-granted sense of moral alignment with the work of the courts: they had witnessed, or had themselves experienced, a wrong, and the court process was a matter of bringing the wrongdoer to justice:

> 'I feel strong about justice and I want things to be right. If you've done something you have to answer for it. So if I would witness something, some crime, I would go again of course. It doesn't matter if I wouldn't like it, or it would be something more serious or less serious, whatever. It's just I believe that there must be justice done.'
> [Helga; witness]

The securing of justice in their own respective cases was seen, by the victim and witness respondents, as something that should quite straightforwardly contribute to the wider public good, as it would help to prevent others suffering what the initial victim had been through. The act of giving evidence was thus couched in moral terms – as, for example, in the case of Elaine, who said that in considering whether to give evidence against her son, charged with the sexual assault of her daughter (his half-sister), she had to ask herself: "What do you do as a *person* – not just as a mother, but as a person?"

Attached to this, individuals also sometimes expressed a sense of personal achievement or some pride at having overcome their anxieties about giving evidence. Rhona had acted as a witness in a sexual assault case, and described being called afterwards by a women from the Witness Care Unit: "She rang us and said, 'Thanks for all your help.' She was grateful. I thought: I've done my bit as well." Maggie said of having acted as a witness that it was "just one of those situations that you've got to go in and face and do it". She described her feelings about giving evidence as follows:

> '[I was] nervous, very nervous, very hot, because I was nervous, I suppose. But other than being really nervous, I was there to do what I had to do for [the victim], and I knew that I was doing the right thing, so ... I was nervous, but knew I was there for the right reasons.'

For many victim and witness respondents, their sense of moral alignment with the criminal justice process was shaken by aspects of their experience in court: what they perceived to be poor outcomes, decision-making or treatment undermined rather than reinforced their general and pre-existing belief in the legitimacy of the process. Usually, however, this did not result in a complete breakdown of the criminal justice system's legitimacy in their eyes: they tended to express their continuing, if qualified, support for a system which had disappointed but not entirely alienated them. This was most apparent in what they said about the prospect of giving evidence in court again, should they ever witness another crime. Tracey, who had witnessed the stabbing of her partner and had been very upset by the not guilty verdict in the trial at which she gave evidence, said that she would report another crime and would be willing to appear in court again, "but I would just be a little less optimistic next time". Debbie, who had witnessed a non-residential burglary to which the defendant pleaded guilty on the day of trial, said that she would be willing to act as a witness again only in a case involving a more serious crime, and that she would do so "with a bit of a heavy heart knowing how much hassle it was going to come to, that I would have to go through". Ryan had been the victim of a serious assault and was dissatisfied with a court process that had eventually resulted in a conviction, but had been stressful and long drawn out. Nevertheless, he insisted that he maintained some trust in the system:

> 'I think in the end I would end up [giving evidence] again. I would do it again because if you don't, they don't get nothing; where if you give it a try, at least you've given it a

go, haven't you? That is the only way to look at it. I know it was poor this time – might be better next time.'

Ryan's girlfriend Samantha had witnessed the assault on Ryan, and had found giving evidence to be an ordeal – to the extent that, as described in the previous chapter, she had fled the courtroom in tears. Nevertheless, when interviewed (separately to Ryan) about the experience, she also insisted that she would be prepared to act as a witness again; and clearly felt there was a moral imperative to do so:

> 'But I will [give evidence again] anyway, because I think people shouldn't get away with it. There's nice people out there: like I've never committed a crime in my life. And I don't think it's right that it's people like us that get attacked, assaulted, robbed, everything else. So these people need to get done; otherwise they'll keep doing it. So I will put myself through it again. I will probably cry again … because I don't think I am getting used to it. And hopefully I won't have to do it again. But yes, I would still do it.'

Elaine, as we have seen, had believed that acting as a witness was the right thing to do, "as a person". But she was perhaps the only one of our victim and witness respondents whose prior faith in the criminal justice system had been entirely shattered by her personal experiences of it. We noted in Chapter Three that she had come to the conclusion that the system was "all trickery". She was adamant that if she was ever called on to give evidence again, she would "never, never" do so; that she would "walk away" if she were to witness another crime.

Moral alignment of defendants

One might assume that most defendants who have been convicted at the Crown Court will not have straightforward feelings of moral alignment with the court process and wider criminal justice system. Nevertheless, we have argued above that for most of the defendants we interviewed, as for the victims and witnesses, there is a broad (albeit implicit) acceptance of the legitimacy of the court process; and it would seem that a sense of moral alignment does play some part in this.

This can be expressed in different ways – including as summed up in the comment, "You do the crime; you do the time". This is undoubtedly a hackneyed phrase, but the variants of it which were uttered by a few of the defendant respondents do seem to imply, at the very least, some belief that the courts are justified in setting out the punishments for those who break society's laws, even when they themselves are the recipients of punishment. However, such a perspective can readily merge with the passive and resigned stance that was commonplace among the defendants (and will be discussed under the sub-heading 'Passive acceptance', below). "As the old saying goes", said Jack, who had received a sentence for burglary, "I committed a crime – had to be punished for it." Leon, who had recently been sentenced for a violent offence and had a number of prior convictions, described the experience of going to court in the following terms:

> 'If it's like a minor offence, it's not that bad, cause you get fines – but then again, if you do a serious crime, then you have to pay – you do the time, you do the crime. It's just the waiting procedure [that I hate about going to court] and – that's it. And not knowing where your life's gonna end. That's it.'

Calvin, who had also been convicted of a violent offence, appeared to accept the court's rightful authority to pass sentence on him, while also distancing himself from what he sees as *true* criminality:

> 'The thing is if you do a crime which is – my one is a bit petty – but you do the crime, you have to face the facts so I don't have any qualms about that really. I'm too old to commit any more crime. I'm not a thief; I'm a working man; I'm 51 years old.'

A more fundamental sense of alignment with the endeavour to punish wrongdoing was expressed in comments from some defendants about the failure of the criminal courts to be *tough enough* with the most serious offenders (in whatever way 'serious offending' is defined). Here, defendants are not questioning the overarching legitimacy of the judicial process, but are criticising how the courts go about their business of delivering justice. These criticisms, moreover, are no different from the criticisms voiced in a great deal of public and political debate on sentencing. As criminologist Shadd Maruna (2007), drawing on the work of Jock Young, has made clear, it is a mistake to assume that convicted offenders inhabit a moral universe that is somehow divorced from that of others. Maruna observes of long-term offenders with whom he has worked, that

... their lives were also eerily similar to our own: watching rubbish television, talking about how much they hate paedophiles, and reading little more than celebrity gossip. As Young argues, they appeared not to suffer so much from exclusion as from over-inclusion into a wider culture stuck in a rut. ... [Young's] is not a subcultural analysis that says that people who commit crime come from communities or families that are morally bankrupt. Far from it, to Young and others in this tradition, criminal subcultures are simply funhouse mirror reflections of wider society and our own cultural values.

In the following two interview extracts, defendants explicitly linked their views on the practices of the courts with accounts in the media:

'Like I said previously, some of the sentences that are given out, they're too lenient. That's the worst thing. I listen, like everyone else, to the media, and what's happening, i.e. with children being killed, and it's atrocious. Tougher and stiffer sentences should be handed out.'
  [Rodney; defendant (convicted of burglary)]

'Well, you watch the news don't you? ...They don't get enough – some people don't get good enough sentence for the things they do.'
  [Stacey; defendant (convicted of perverting the course of justice)]

Positive outcomes

'I believe I was asked whether I wanted to go to the Crown or magistrates'. I decided to go to the Crown Court because I felt that possibly I'd get away with it, if you like.'[1] [*Laughs*]
  [Rodney; defendant]

We are in broad agreement with procedural justice theorists who argue that procedural aspects of the experience of the criminal courts are often important determinants of overall perceptions of the courts and the wider criminal justice process. Where we depart from some of the procedural justice research is in our assertion that, for many court users, outcomes matter decidedly more than process – although most of our respondents did not make their focus on outcome quite as explicit as the defendant Rodney, quoted above. In this context, we understand 'outcome' to mean the guilty or not guilty verdict in a contested trial, and the type and severity of sentence passed following a guilty verdict or guilty plea.

Verdict

In most of the cases in which our witness and victim respondents were involved, the defendants were found guilty on all or at least some of the counts with which they had been charged, or changed their pleas to guilty as the trial was about to start. For the most part, the guilty verdicts produced a general feeling of satisfaction with the court process and supported perceptions of its legitimacy:

> 'That 40 minutes [in the witness box] was painful. But at least the outcome is good and I am happy ... [The best thing about the courts is that they are] fair and honest. Fair and honest decision.'
> [Masood; victim]

> 'I guess justice worked.'
> [James; witness]

In contrast, 10 of our interviewees appeared in court for cases in which there was ultimately a not guilty verdict on all counts. As we have already seen with respect to Elaine, this outcome could be devastating. Others whose confidence in the justice process was rocked by a not guilty verdict included Michelle. She had acted as a prosecution witness in a rape case, of which she said: "You have got the jury and you have got the judge and the barristers and, in our case, we laid everything on the line; everything we said was the truth – [just] to get it thrown back [at us]." Maggie, who had given evidence against a woman accused of seriously assaulting Maggie's elderly and infirm neighbour, explicitly drew a distinction between certain (positive) procedural aspects of the case and the (negative) outcome:[2]

| Maggie: | Everybody [at court] was very good, very kind, helpful. Yes, no problems with that at all. I just think the verdict was rubbish. |
| Interviewer: | To the best of your knowledge, do you think the defendant was treated fairly in court? |

Maggie: Well, she'll think she was treated fairly because
                                 she got off.

For most of the defendants interviewed, their most recent appearance
of the Crown Court had been for sentencing only rather than trial; but
just under half had *ever* had experience of a Crown Court trial. Among
those with experience of a trial, the jury's delivery of the verdict was
not usually spoken of as a defining moment of their court experience.
Some appeared to have regarded the verdict with resignation more than
anything else. Others voiced to us their anger about having been found
guilty, and in doing so tended to focus on what they perceived to be
elements of bias and flaws in the court process and decision-making,
thus seeming to support the claims of procedural justice theorists about
the dominance of process over outcome. But when we examine the
defendants' comments more closely, it becomes immediately apparent
that it is often not possible, even for analytic purposes, to disentangle
their feelings about outcome from their feelings about process.

> 'I have never had a result from court, never. And I have been
> there a lot. ... My whole court experience is just horrible;
> I have never had a result, so that just tells you everything.'
>   [Jonathan; defendant]

> 'You know, I've never been found not guilty in a court.
> Never. And I can tell you – because I have got a few
> convictions – at least 50%, *at least 50%*, of the things I've
> been in court for, that I've been accused of [and convicted
> of], was never the case. ... So don't think that ain't biased.
> If it looks like a duck, it quacks, it walks like a duck – it's
> a duck. Period.
>   [Steve; defendant]

What is also apparent is that the outcome that was at the forefront of
many of the defendants' minds was the sentence they received; and it
is the topic of sentencing to which we now turn. Discussion of how
defendants and others viewed the decision-making *process* will follow.

Sentence

As could only be expected, our respondents' views on the
appropriateness or otherwise of the sentence passed in their respective
cases varied widely. Some of the victims and witnesses complained

that the sentences passed in 'their' cases were not harsh enough and, as with a not guilty verdict, this potentially undermined their sense of the legitimacy of the entire process. Tina, the mother of a victim of a sexual assault, was of the view that "they put these victims – genuine victims – through an awful lot for very little prison time, to be honest". Others, however, were satisfied with the sentences passed; and evident in some of their comments was a nuanced reflection on the purposes of sentencing. Some appeared more concerned with instrumental matters than punishment; such as Francesca, a victim of domestic violence, who stated that "the judge has given me my life back", because her ex-husband was not just given a prison sentence, but also a restraining order. Freya, who had been sexually assaulted by her former boyfriend, was disappointed with the length of the prison sentence, but delighted that the offender was due to be deported on release from custody as she felt that he no longer posed a threat to her.[3]

Masood had been subjected to racist abuse from a customer at the shop where he worked. He said that he reported the crime to the police because he wanted to prevent the abuse happening again, and clearly felt ambivalent when the case came to the point of sentencing and he realised that the defendant possibly faced a prison sentence (which in the event was suspended):

'The things is, when I heard that he is going in the prison … I was thinking about his family. That he might have got family. And that's because I'm too much emotional and I'm too much sensitive. So sometimes I think the things like, "Oh, who is going to look after the family? Or he's a main bread earner. He'll be in prison for 12 months."'

Masood was not alone in expressing this kind of ambivalence about sentencing. A number of our victim and witness respondents appeared to worry about the punitive nature of the sentence:

'I get upset [on hearing of the sentence] because I don't want anyone, because of me, going to prison or something.' [Mila; victim]

'I was surprised that the defendant was sentenced to 20 months; of course I was glad. It's good that the police take robbery so seriously, but it's a shame for that kid who has

wasted 20 months of his life and has a criminal record ...
His parents were actually in court crying.'
   [Faris; victim]

'It's very difficult [hearing of the sentence]. If it's someone
you really dislike I think it would be a lot easier.'
   [Grace; witness]

Among many of the defendants, the perceived severity of the sentence
they had received was an important determinant of their overall view
of the court process. Rodney, who had been sentenced for burglary,
was particularly clear about that. When asked what he thought of the
court process he replied: "I believe I was treated very fairly. I could've
gone to prison." Matthew, convicted of supplying class A drugs, had
a similar attitude:

Interviewer:	Can you think of any good things about the courts and how they deal with crime?'
Matthew:	'Sometimes they give you fair sentences. ... Like I went to court recently, and instead of sending me back to prison they gave me a tag. Just things like that: sometimes they do the right [thing].

The defendants were evenly divided between those who, like Rodney
and Matthew, felt their sentence was fair and those who did not;
and their notions of fairness in sentencing tended to revolve around
whether they had received a harsher or more lenient sentence than
they had expected, or relative to others. Jerome, for example, received
a community sentence and driving ban for various driving offences, in
relation to which he commented: "For the offences I've done, it went
really well. I was expecting imprisonment of at least two years." Ali also
spoke of feeling pleased when his pessimistic expectations of sentence
were not met; unusually, he also demonstrated some awareness of the
decision-making process in which judges engage:

'Obviously depending on the nature of the crime, you
can expect to receive the sentence. So what I done, I just
researched it in *Archbold* – you know, you've got the *Archbold*
book of law?[4] That's what the judges use as guidelines, so I
just followed that ... I just expect the worst and then when
I get lower I feel a bit better, innit.'

Among those who were unhappy with sentencing were Gerry and Paul, sentenced for a sexual assault and violent disorder respectively:

> 'I was gutted. I knew I was going to go to prison, obviously, but I was thinking, "Eight years, eight years? That's a long time. How long am I going to live? What percentage of my life is it?"'

> 'I've got more sentence than most of the people in the [August 2011] riots and I wasn't even involved in the riots and I thought the riots was an example to teach these people a lesson.'

For the most part, then, defendants did not appear to reflect, in a more abstract way, on whether the severity of their sentence reflected the seriousness of the crime – although Charlie, who was convicted of a serious robbery (his first offence, at the age of 34) was an exception to this. Charlie had no criticisms of what went on in court, "because what I have done was bad", and said that the five-year prison sentence he received "is fair for the crime that was committed: yes, I would say". In this comment we also see, again, some indication of a sense of moral alignment with the work of the courts.

Fair decision-making

As we have observed above, it is often impossible to disentangle defendants' perceptions of outcome from their perceptions of the decision-making process. This is true also of much of what was said by the victims and witnesses. Nevertheless, some comments by victims, witnesses and defendants alike did focus explicitly on the nature of decision-making and, where this was seen as an intrinsically fair process, this fed into positive evaluations of the court and wider criminal justice system. Conversely, negative perceptions of the decision-making process undermined confidence in the system.

Jury decision-making

In a Crown Court trial, it is the jury that has the ultimate responsibility for decision-making on verdict. Attitudinal surveys in various common law jurisdictions 'repeatedly suggest that the public strongly support the concept of the jury' (Roberts and Hough, 2009, p i), and, in England and Wales, tentative steps towards restricting the right to trial by jury have met general resistance.[5] Our research findings provide mixed evidence as to whether the broad public support for the jury system is reflected among those who have direct experience of it.

Among our victim and witness respondents, more spoke in broadly positive than in negative terms about how they perceived the jury in their respective cases. Only two, however, voiced a *principled* approval of the jury system. Ryan, the victim of an assault, responded to a question about what he considered the best aspects of the Crown Court by saying: "I think definitely the fact that there is a jury. That does make it fair. There's more than obviously one person." And Ernie, another assault victim, described the jury in the following terms:

> 'It seemed a complete range of people, particularly in ages. There were one or two younger people … as well as one or two more adult, mature people as well. By clothing they were of a range of social strata, shall we say. So, yes, I thought that was quite useful because obviously there were older heads there with some wisdom and younger people with newer, modern views, maybe. But they obviously were all in complete unison about the ABH [actual bodily harm] and the fact that every single one of them came along on that third day for the sentencing.'

Other positive comments about the jury by victims and witnesses tended to focus on what was perceived to be the jurors' attentiveness: two respondents spoke approvingly of jurors taking notes; and others spoke of them listening carefully. Faris, a victim of robbery, said that he thought the jurors were "empathising" with him "because they were all looking at me with sad faces while I was talking". On the other hand, there were also a few complaints from victims and witnesses about jurors who appeared uninterested or inattentive. In two cases where a not guilty verdict caused particular anguish, the very nature of the jury system was regarded as partly or largely to blame:

> 'You go up there, you expose yourself, whatever happened, all the evidence you give, all the stress you go through, everything from the incident up until then … You have got these 12 people looking at you that don't know you from Adam and you just think, "I can say anything I want, but you haven't listened."'
> [Michelle; witness]

Ian: 'You know, you realise what it had taken
              everybody to get to that point [the trial].
              Then to feel that the jury, the 12 people of
              our – peers, supposed to be. Yes, and you
              looked and you thought: "Where did you
              come from?"'

Amanda: 'Which sounds really harsh; but, yes, you get
              that impression: was you just picked off the
              corner of the street: "Just come and listen to
              this and see what you think?" It didn't feel
              like there was any interest in there. ... [The
              not guilty verdict] made you want to go find
              the jury and say: "*What didn't you get? What
              did you not understand?*"'
              [Witnesses]

We have already seen, in Chapter Four, that there was some considerable degree of mistrust towards juries among defendants. A few defendants, however, expressed a belief in the intrinsic fairness of the jury system. Among them was Sidney, who had been acquitted of assault at his last Crown Court appearance, but had several previous convictions. He expressed his belief that jurors are less likely to be harsh than a judge because they come to each case afresh: "Judges are there all day, every day ... I have heard judges say before, they are sick of seeing people like me. Juries don't have that opinion – only judges do."

Impartiality

Looking beyond the issue of the jury system to broader decision-making within the Crown Court, we can see that some victims and witnesses felt that those processes were appropriately impartial or neutral, and thereby in accordance with basic principles of justice. Julia, who had given evidence in the trial of the man convicted of sexually assaulting her daughter, Freya, was one of the respondents who emphasised this point: "The whole process seemed quite fair; for both sides it seemed to be. And the whole thing you could tell was a tried and tested process and everyone seemed to know what they were doing. Everyone was treated equally." For her part, Freya expressed her disappointment at the failure of the court to convict her attacker on all the charges he faced, but also explained that she had understood why this outcome had come about:

'It's not what I wanted and he deserved what he deserves. He was guilty. He did do those things so he deserves to be found guilty. But I can understand why maybe he wasn't [found guilty on all counts], because of evidence or because there wasn't enough evidence, because it was historic, because it's my word against his on a lot of the charges.'

Other victims and witnesses spoke approvingly of the legal rights afforded to the defendant but, at the same time, said that they had found the defendant's exercise of these rights painful or wearisome to observe. Tina, who had observed the trial of the man accused (and ultimately convicted) of sexually assaulting her daughter, said that she had felt like "slapping" the defence lawyer who tried to make her daughter "sound like she was a drunken old slut", while acknowledging that the defendant "deserves to be defended; that's the way our system works. Nobody is guilty until proven." Janice was called to give evidence in an appeal against conviction for a racially aggravated public order offence. She stated that she felt "quite positive about the law process and that defendants are given the best opportunity to defend their position"; but that she also found it "galling" to see what she perceived as the "abuse of the system" by a defendant who had managed to drag out the court process over an extended period of time and cause much inconvenience to the various parties:

'I think it's a phenomenal amount of money is spent on the process. Someone like him can use it to his advantage and spend tax payers' money, because he gets legal aid, on defending the indefensible, really. You know, I'm a tax payer. How dare he spend my taxes like that?'

Another respondent who expressed ambivalence was Ron – the victim of a serious assault in the pub of which he was a landlord. He felt let down by a system which had permitted what he perceived to be a very partial account of the assault to be told in court, and was deeply disappointed by the not guilty verdict which resulted. And yet he regarded the court process as essentially fair: "Well, if you ask me, the court case was obviously fair. It was obviously proper justice – you go to a Crown Court and there's a judge and jury. You know, it *seems* fair. You can't say it's *not* fair."

The defendants we interviewed did not speak, in general terms, about impartiality of decision-making or the balancing of different legal rights. A sizeable proportion did, however, speak approvingly of judges' capacity to maintain a neutral stance in court proceedings. In fact, the theme of judicial fairness and neutrality emerged as a significant one across our interview sample, as many of the victim and witness respondents also spoke in these terms:

> 'The judge had figured out that [the victim] had lied about parts of his statements and stuff. No one else picked up on that. So that was pretty impressive for me to see that he wasn't just biased towards that; that he was independent. So they sort of sit there as a neutral and view both sides.'
> [Sam; defendant]

> '[The judge was] fair ... He turned around to my defence and said, "You tell me why this man shouldn't go to prison", and then listened to what my man said.'
> [Jack; defendant]

> '[The process was] fair in that the judge seemed to treat everybody the same. You could see he wasn't favouring anybody. ... The way the prosecution and the defence were questioning was equal.'
> [Francesca; victim]

> '[The judge was] impartial and informative. He wouldn't take no shit in his court.'
> [Nikki; victim]

Dexter, who had received an 18-month prison sentence for burglary (a sentence he deemed to be fair) had been impressed by another aspect of decision-making. The fact that his lawyer and the judge had consulted "a whole load of books" in court appeared to reassure him that sentencing was systematic and considered, rather than an arbitrary process:

> 'The solicitor I had, he was a Muslim fellow. He was very good ... He had a whole load of books, and the judge referred to such and such, such and such. You know those books? ... The solicitor referred to his books, that's why I like the way he did it. He was just carrying a whole load of books when he went in the courtroom, put them down, and started saying, "Can Your Honour refer to this?" I was

like, "Whoa –". Then Your Honour's getting *her* book and saying, "Yes, yes," looking at me.'

Perceptions of bias

But while many of our respondents regarded the decision-making of the court as essentially impartial and therefore fair, others perceived there to be an intrinsic bias in the process. As has been discussed elsewhere in this volume at some length, a number of the victims and witnesses were resentful of a process which, in their eyes, marginalised them and denied them a voice, and seemed to be structured in such a way as to favour the defendant overall. They spoke, for example, of the lack of their own representation in court, of not being permitted to tell the "full story" of what had happened, and of feeling like they themselves had been "on trial" when they were cross-examined.

Bias was a prominent theme in interviews with some defendants, who argued that they had faced prejudice and discrimination in the courts or within the wider criminal justice system relating to the type of offence with which they had been charged, their history of criminal convictions, or their class or ethnicity. We have already seen, for example, that some of the defendants felt they had little or no chance of a fair hearing from jurors who, in Patrice's words, "ain't the same class as me. Not in my circle." More broadly, Patrice maintained the view – based not so much on his own experiences of the courts, where he has been convicted of violent and various other offences, but on the experiences of others – that the justice system favours certain social groups:

> 'Even though I ain't really had a problem with the sentence I've received, but I've seen in the media and talked to friends that's been sentenced. There's a lot of mistakes, where they shouldn't have got so much bird [prison], or they shouldn't've got the sentence they got, and the people then who do certain things – they get a light sentence because they're Masons or Illuminati or whatever! [*Laughs*] … So it all depends on your class, and your background, and where you come from. So it's still a – what's it called? [*Mimes a pair of weighing scales with his hands*] The weights don't go right.'

While a larger proportion of defendants (as observed above) described judges as impartial and fair, some others echoed Patrice in complaining of bias in the way the judicial role was played. Steve, who had been found guilty at trial for arson, was one of a few defendants who felt that prior convictions inevitably counted against any defendant in court: "Obviously [a criminal record] is going to taint the way [the judge] looks at you. So straight away you're handicapped – you're hamstrung." And Louise, whose partner had been convicted of robbery, said of the Crown Court: "Where they send you, there's serious crimes like terrorism and rape and they're so used to dealing with the bad crime that you get treated the same."

In the comment that follows, from our interview with Gerry, we see a profound cynicism expressed about the sentencing process; cynicism which then extends to the wider justice system and, indeed, society as a whole – and doubtless reflects what could be seen as the ultimate 'outsider' status of an individual who has pleaded guilty to a sexual assault on a child (for which he had received an eight-year prison sentence):

> 'Why is [the judge] working to guidelines anyway? Is he not capable of making up his own mind? Who has made up these? Were they made up five hundred years ago along with the rest of it? Was it in the Bible? They are all these questions that I've asked myself since; how fair is the judicial system? And I'd have to say, "It's not fair." And especially nowadays with the way the press have been influencing everything. Who is running the press? Who is running the country? Who is making the rules? Who is making the laws? Are they level-headed people or are they privileged people from privileged classes? I don't really know, but I certainly don't think it's people like me; I don't really have very much say in anything.'

Overall, however, is it notable that complaints of serious bias or other lack of fairness in decision-making were relatively rare among the comments from the defendants. This finding echoes that of Hood et al (2003, p 133) who noted, with respect to their interviews with almost eight hundred defendants (mostly from black and minority ethnic backgrounds) who had appeared at Crown and magistrates' courts:

> We recognised that one could hardly expect to find, amongst people who had just been punished by the criminal justice system, especially with imprisonment, that *no one* felt unfairly treated. ... What can be said is that the findings from this study, based on interviews mostly with convicted

defendants immediately after they had been sentenced (what may have been a 'worst case scenario'), have revealed that a far smaller proportion than has been hitherto supposed said that their treatment had been unfair.

Respectful treatment

In the victim and witness interviews conducted for this study, multiple examples of good interpersonal treatment by the authorities in court were recounted. Respondents spoke of being treated with humanity, kindness, consideration and respect; and, in line with one of the central tenets of procedural justice theory, it would seem that this experience often contributed to a positive overall evaluation of the justice system and belief in its legitimacy. Among defendants, less weight as a whole appeared to be accorded to the quality of treatment they received – although this is by no means to suggest that treatment was always insignificant for this group.

Victims' and witnesses' experiences of respectful treatment

Donna had acted as a witness in a serious assault case, and had been very disappointed with the not guilty verdict which resulted. In the following quotation, she explicitly contrasts the two main dimensions of procedure: decision-making (which she experienced as poor) and treatment (experienced as good):

> 'I don't think it's always the same for defence and prosecution, by the sounds of what happened that day. The prosecution have to put on a whole case, don't they, with all the witnesses, and apparently the defence witnesses do the same but it's not as stringent as it is with prosecutors. But as to *how they dealt with us as people*, they were really helpful. Like the way they brought us in the back way and they didn't want us around the other guys, and looked after us all day, because it's a long old day.' [Emphasis added.]

Many judges were praised not only for their apparent impartiality in the courtroom, but also for the considerate or kindly way in which they treated witnesses. Often, relatively small reassuring gestures by judges had made a significant impact on anxious or distressed victims and witnesses, particularly at the point when they were about to start giving evidence. This was true of Anna, a witness, who said that the judge had told her, after she was sworn in, "that if I at any point wanted to sit down I was welcome to and I could have a drink of water if I wanted to, and I could take my time and whatever". Another witness, Tracey, described the judge as "very polite". It was clear that his words to her, as she took the stand, had made quite an impression on her, because she quoted them to us: "He said: 'There's no need to be nervous; speak loudly and clearly, if there's anything you don't understand, ask me and I'll explain it to you.'"

Michelle's disappointment in the jury's not guilty verdict in the rape case at which she gave evidence did not taint her view of the judge. She not only saw him as a commendably neutral arbiter in the courtroom, but also felt he demonstrated interpersonal skills:

> 'When he didn't understand a question that the barrister had asked me or didn't see the point in it he was quick to the mark and said: "I don't actually think that is a relevant question." To me, he was very patient; when things did get a bit emotional he stopped everything.'

As observed in previous chapters, the Witness Service came in for particular praise for the support it offered – for example, through the provision of pre-court visits and separate waiting areas in court – and, crucially, for the *way* in which that support was provided. The sympathy, kindness and consideration shown by Witness Service volunteers were frequently noted. Occasional criticisms that were made of the service tended to focus on what were said to be cramped or otherwise inadequate facilities. Court staff – that is, ushers, clerks and (to a lesser extent) security officers – were often described as especially "helpful" and "friendly". This general view of court staff came as little surprise to us because, during our observations in court, we found that the habitual cheeriness and chattiness of most clerks and ushers tended to stand out against the backdrop of sordid and often immeasurably sad court business.

The victims' and witnesses' views on how they were treated by the lawyers in court were more mixed. Many, of course, felt that defence lawyers conducted their cross-examinations with more aggression or in a more under-handed manner than was necessary (for justice to be served) or appropriate. For the most part, however, they understood that it was the defence lawyer's role to challenge them, and that this could not be a pleasant experience. As we have already seen, the very nature of the prosecution counsel's role in court was the source of some confusion (among those who thought that this was 'their' lawyer, and failed to understand why he or she did not quite act accordingly) and some unhappiness (among those who felt that they *should* have their own lawyer, and perceived their lack of representation as unfair). Nevertheless, a number of respondents were impressed with individual prosecution barristers who took the time and effort to explain what was happening in court, and took witnesses' feelings into account in so doing.

The potentially critical importance of an empathetic approach was highlighted by Janice, who was called as a witness in an appeal against conviction for a racially aggravated public order offence. She and her fellow-witnesses – two parents who had been the victims of the offence – had arrived at court first thing in the morning, but various delays to the hearing meant that by mid-afternoon they had not yet given evidence. The victims, by now, were angry and frustrated (all the more so because the original conviction which was being appealed had been a very protracted process), but Janice was highly impressed with how the prosecution counsel responded to this:

> 'Basically, at about three o'clock, the Dad lost it and was threatening to leave [the court]. The barrister was called to try and persuade him to stay that little bit longer. The Dad and the Mum were like: "Look, we've got to pick up the kids from school. This is unacceptable – we've been here all day. ..." The barrister was very good calming them down. [He] said: "Right: you can leave now and I will get the case adjourned until tomorrow. But please return tomorrow because you mustn't let him win." ... So the Dad did dutifully turn up the following morning ... [I had] nothing but admiration for the way the barrister dealt with him and persuaded him to stay.'

We have seen, in preceding chapters, that delays to court proceedings are commonplace, and have a wide variety of causes: witnesses, defendants and others fail to turn up when they are supposed to; equipment breaks down; paperwork goes missing or contains mistakes; and legal arguments interrupt all stages of proceedings. Hitches and hiccups of these and other kinds often cannot be avoided; but where advocates and court staff recognise the toll they can take on anxious victims and witnesses, and make efforts to explain and reassure – as the prosecution counsel did in Janice's case – this can clearly go a considerable way towards mitigating the harms caused.[6]

Police treatment of victims and witnesses

While many victims and witnesses praised judges, the Witness Service staff and volunteers, court staff and (to a lesser extent) some lawyers for their sensitive and respectful approach in court, much of the strongest praise was reserved for police officers. Several of the respondents had been highly impressed with the support and care offered by individual officers – particularly the main 'officer in the case' – in the lead-up to and during court proceedings. They spoke about officers who, from the initial investigation through to the conclusion of the case, went out of their way to provide information, explain developments and answer questions. Some respondents made it clear that the assistance, encouragement and reassurance provided by officers had helped sustain them through the lengthy and often fraught prosecution process. Most of all, the warmth of relations with particular police officers – variously described as "compassionate", "helpful", "very easy to talk to", "charming", "lovely" and "kind" – had a big impact on many of the victims and witnesses we spoke to.

Within some of the procedural justice literature, there is a concern with what has been described as an essential 'asymmetry' in the effects of the public's experiences of the police. As elaborated by Skogan (2006), quantitative studies of police-public contact have tended to find that public confidence in the police is impacted much more by negative than by positive encounters (see also Bradford et al, 2009). Our own – much smaller-scale, qualitative – findings suggest that, in fact, the asymmetry can work in the other direction: that *positive* experiences of treatment by the police can have a disproportionate effect, at least where individuals are highly distressed or anxious as a consequence of victimisation. In such circumstances of vulnerability, it would seem that kind words and empathetic treatment can take on a much greater significance than they might otherwise have. This echoes our finding that relatively small but supportive gestures by a judge, in the tense and frightening atmosphere of the courtroom, can make a profound impression on a victim or witness; and, likewise, that a high value is accorded to the "friendly" demeanour of Witness Service volunteers. But of all criminal justice practitioners, police officers are likely to have the most intimate and sustained involvement with victims and witnesses over the course of the prosecution process; and, as such, their skills (or lack thereof) in handling these court users may carry particular weight. It may also be that, to some extent, police officers are more inclined than others within the criminal justice system to convey a sense of being 'on the side of' the victim or witness.

Among our respondents who had especially painful experiences of victimisation, and were most vocal in their praise of the police officers with whom they dealt, was Ernie. At the age of 72, he had been subjected to an unprovoked, violent assault by another man while out walking his dog. The support of the officer in the case, he said, was what "gave us the courage really to go ahead with this right from the outset"; and he added that "we can't speak highly enough" of the police. Elaine told us that she had sent flowers as a "thank you" to the female officer who had investigated the sexual assault of her young daughter, and said of her: "If this had been someone else, a police*man*, I wouldn't have coped. It was only her personality and strength to help me and [my daughter] and the family." Nikki, in contrast, said that she had been glad that a male rather than female officer had led the investigation into her sexual assault, because she felt that a woman would have been more judgemental of her own behaviour. She said that the officer:

> '... talked to me about anything and everything. He'd phone me up, see how I'm doing. I'd phone him up if I had any questions ...The littlest thing, he'd be there, no matter what. And if I left a message, he'd always phone me back. ... He kept supporting me ... He goes: "I really want you to go to court." He goes: "This is going to happen. This will work. We will get a conviction," he said "but you've got to go to court."'

Freya, another sexual assault victim, described the police as "fantastic". Like others, she felt that her very strength in going to court and giving evidence had depended on them: "I think if it wasn't because of them I wouldn't have been able to get through it. They were just so amazing." Freya's mother, Julia, had been equally impressed by the "absolutely brilliant" police officers, whom – as she repeatedly told us in interview – she "can't thank enough".

While we heard a great many very positive accounts of victims' and witnesses' dealings with the police, some harsh criticisms were also voiced by respondents. For the most part, those who were critical did not primarily focus on interactions with individual police officers, but tended to talk in more general terms about their case being poorly handled by the police and/or by the Crown Prosecution Service over the course of the prosecution process. Inefficiencies and administrative incompetence were at the heart of many of the problems; with the negative effects sometimes compounded by the failure of officials not only to correct mistakes being made but also to recognise their impact on the individuals involved. Thus, for example, delays in the prosecution process were most problematic when they were not explained, or when no account was taken of their implications for victims and witnesses in terms of both practical inconvenience and stress. Other problems referred to by respondents included limited provision of information about case progression or outcomes; or the provision of inconsistent information about the case, about what was expected of witnesses, or about the availability of special measures. In such instances, poor procedural practice and poor or off-hand treatment at an interpersonal level combined to cause distress and, at times, undermined confidence in the process as a whole.

Defendants' perceptions of their treatment

Overall, the defendants interviewed for this study appeared to be less concerned than the victims and witnesses about the quality of the treatment they received within the criminal justice system. This may reflect, in part, defendants' lower expectations of treatment; and related to this also would seem to be a general apathy that pervaded many of their responses to the court process (as will be discussed below). A few defendants were quite explicit that displays of politeness by judges, lawyers and others meant little or nothing to them. Steve – a defendant with a long criminal record, and most recently sentenced for arson – was the most expressive on this topic.

> 'Listen. They put on this facade that they're very civil, and you know – [*in affected tone*] "*Hello!*" – but deep down you know that's just a game. The judge – because he knows what I've been done for in the past, and my character's, my copybook's been blotted already anyway, he's aware of that. So all this cuts no ice with me. I'm not that naive. [*Laughs*] … Oh – it's all lovely, and everything's nice, you know – so polite, and very civil. But deep down – you know.'

Steve's dismissal of the judge's sentencing remarks was particularly stark: "Listen: I don't care how you cut it, or how pretty you dress it – what he said would be irrelevant to me."

Most defendants spoke in neutral or mildly positive terms about the behaviour of court staff towards them, although there were also occasional complaints about some who were said to be "rude". They usually understood that the barrister for the prosecution was in court for the purpose of putting the case against them, and most expected little of their treatment by this individual, and perhaps cared even less. "The prosecution? Their job is to be the worst of the worst, so there aren't any niceties from them," said Jonathan, bluntly. Jerome said of the prosecution counsel: "What's the person called – the person who don't like me, saying all the things about me?"

Defence counsel were generally evaluated in terms of the service they had provided rather than their 'treatment' of defendants per se. Positive comments about defence lawyers tended to focus on good outcomes achieved: as Sidney said, for example, "Like I say, I have got a good barrister and he has never been beaten." Conversely, negative comments were mostly about unhappy outcomes and, related to this, what was often perceived to be a rushed or distracted approach by the professional.

We noted above that many defendants spoke approvingly of the seeming impartiality of judges in the Crown Court. On the more specific question of how the judge addressed them, some were positive ("the judge was quite polite"; "you didn't feel that you'd been belittled in any way"); some negative (one judge was said to be "not the most pleasant"; another to have "no compassion"); but more were neutral. It was evident that some judges had endeavoured to make some kind of connection with the defendant before them, although with mixed results. Alfie had liked the judge who, in passing sentence on him for drugs offences, "weren't like talking down to me – he was talking on a level to me". Patrice, on the other hand, felt that the judge was "fair" but disliked the way he spoke to him: "The way he summed up and said certain things – I felt like I was getting told off by me dad and that [*laughs*] – God rest his soul!" Two respondents complained of the way the judge "looked over his glasses" when he addressed them. Ali clearly remembered the sentencing remarks made by a judge whom he described as "cool" but, in the end, had little regard for:

> 'Basically, in layman's terms he said to me I'm a naughty boy, innit, and he's going to give me a sentence and he hopes that I learn from it and he doesn't want to see me in his courts again. And he found out that my children have been taken by social services because of this and all that, and he said I should use my time constructively to better myself and not let myself get down and all of that. To not always think so negative, innit. He was cool actually, you know that? He was cool but like – I don't care what he says anyway.'

Only one of the defendants had had experience of appearing in court as prosecution witness; and three of our victim and witness respondents said that they had been to court (magistrates' or Crown) as defendants. One of the latter (Nikki) gave a vivid account of the difference in treatment she had experienced as a victim of sexual assault, compared to her experience as a defendant in a drink driving case:

> 'I've been a victim now and I've been a perpetrator: there is a difference. For me, I found it quite clear cut. [As a defendant] you will sit in a cell. You will poo with a door open. If the door wasn't open then the camera was on you; you will do that. But when you've been sexually assaulted or you're the victim, completely different; complete respect. Everything's all nice, you know: kid gloves, cotton wool. They do the best they can of a bad situation.'

Passive acceptance

Among the defendants we interviewed – as also among the victims and witnesses – views of the court process were diverse, reflecting differing expectations and experiences of the process and differing interpretations of those experiences. However, there was a common thread in much of what the defendants said to us, and this was their display of what can be called a 'passive acceptance' of the court process. By this we mean that, as defendants, they tended to see themselves as tiny parts in a vast criminal justice machine that operates by its own unstoppable and inevitable logic. Others who have researched the criminal courts have described broadly the same phenomenon, including Bottoms and McClean (1976) who constructed an eight-fold typology of defendants' approaches to court, and identified 'passive respondents' as making up the largest category within this. Blumberg described a substantial proportion of male defendants whom he interviewed as 'basically fatalistic'; inclined to:

> ... perceive the total court process as being caught up in a monstrous organizational apparatus, in which the defendant role expectancies were not clearly defined. Reluctant to offend anyone in authority, fearful that clear-cut statements on their part as to their guilt or innocence would be negatively construed, they adopted a stance of passivity, resignation and acceptance. (1969, p 234)

Among the defendant respondents in our study, there were many manifestations of what we are grouping together under the broad heading of passive acceptance. One was a sense of disengagement from the court process, as illustrated by the following interview extracts:

Interviewer:	And how did you feel when you were giving evidence?
Jonathan:	How would anyone feel, really?
Interviewer:	Can you remember what your Defence Counsel said in mitigation ...?
Jonathan:	Not really.
Interviewer:	And can you remember what the judge said when they passed the sentence?
Jonathan:	No; I just remember what sentence he gave me.
Interviewer:	What do you think were the worst things about going to Crown Court?'
Jerome:	... Bad thing about going to Crown Court is knowing that you may not walk out. That's all I can say on that one.
Interviewer:	Is there anything you think that could have been done to make your experience in the Crown Court better?
Jerome:	I could've done with a drink of water halfway through it.
Interviewer:	They didn't offer you water?
Jerome:	No. I could have done with a drink of water, but that's about it.

Another manifestation of passive acceptance was a largely apathetic response to being in court. Dexter said of being sentenced for an offensive weapons offence: "I've got issues anyway, so I didn't really – not to say I didn't care, but I didn't have any feeling in it, because I've got other things on my mind as well." (This was notwithstanding his satisfaction, noted earlier, with the way his lawyer and the judge consulted "a whole load of books" during the sentencing hearing.) Apathy sometimes appeared to combine with a reluctance or inability to reflect on their court experiences, and can also be described as a kind of 'court deafness' (Carlen, 1976a, p 66). Some respondents have made little appearance on these pages precisely because, when interviewed for this study, they had little to say about what it was like to go to court (in contrast to others, it is important to acknowledge, who were articulate and expressive in interview). The quieter and less articulate individuals were by no means hostile when interviewed, but appeared genuinely to struggle to remember and describe their experiences.[7] One such individual was Latif, who had pleaded guilty in the Crown Court to the serious offence of wounding:

Interviewer:	At sentencing, can you remember what the prosecution said about the offence?
Latif:	They were just talking about my criminal background.
Interviewer:	Did you think what the prosecution said was fair?
Latif:	Well ... I knew I was going to get done so there wasn't really a point in arguing.
Interviewer:	Can you remember what your defence said in mitigation?
Latif:	Can't remember.
Interviewer:	That's all right. And so how did you feel when the judge passed the sentence that he gave you?
Latif:	I felt all right.
Interviewer:	And did you understand it? Was it explained to you?
Latif:	Yes, Miss.
Interviewer:	Did he say why he had chosen the sentence that he chose, the length?
Latif:	I think he did, but I can't remember.
Interviewer:	... Did you have any family or friends in the public gallery while you were being sentenced?
Latif:	Yes, a few.
Interviewer:	Did you find that helpful? How did you find that?
Latif:	I wasn't really bothered, Miss.
Interviewer:	Did you notice anyone else in the public gallery other than the people that you knew?
Latif:	There was weird people there, I think it was in the newspapers so –
Interviewer:	Newspapers. How did you feel about them being there?
Latif:	I didn't really care, Miss.

Interviewer:	'Okay. Was there anything you didn't understand about the sentencing process?
Latif:	No, it was clear, Miss.
Interviewer:	Did you think the sentence that the judge gave you was fair?
Latif:	It was all right, Miss.

Perhaps the claims of some defendants to have been entirely apathetic in the face of sentencing were an expression of bravado (in the context of the research interview) more than a genuine lack of concern about their fate. Steve told us that when he received his custodial sentence for arson: "It could've been 6 months or 60 years – it made no difference to me. None. Same old same old. I've been down that road already." Ali, for his part, claimed that not only did he "not care" about his sentence for drugs offences, but he informed the judge of this: "I had to tell the judge, like, 'Listen mate, I don't care. Do your thing innit, whatever.'"

A number of defendants indicated that their main feeling about being at court was a desire to get the experience over with. Christian described having been sentenced to a four-year custodial sentence for violent disorder, and being urged by his lawyer to appeal the sentence because it was harsh. He had been, he said, reluctant to appeal because he wanted to "just get on with it; just get on with my time and stuff like that … [The case] was going on for months and months. Just get it out of the way." (In the event, his girlfriend "kept going on about it" and persuaded him to go ahead with the appeal; this was successful and resulted in a substantial reduction of his sentence from four to two-and-a-half years.) When asked how he had reacted to being sentenced for drugs offences, Alfie replied:

> 'Ummm – dunno – I was just: get on with it – it's all I could do, you know. No one wants to go to prison. But it happens. Just gotta deal with it, innit. … Like – I don't really take notice – I'm just there to get my sentence and get my punishment and get out. … Like I said – I just go there to get my sentence – not there to meet and greet. … Get in and get out.'

A certain fatalism – "it happens" – as well as a wish to "get on with it" was expressed in the above comment by Alfie. Leon, who had recently served a prison sentence for an assault on his partner, was similarly fatalistic (or, in Blumberg's words, displayed 'stoic submission' (1969, p 234)) about a new sentencing hearing that he was awaiting at the time of the interview: "I don't know if I could be getting locked up or not, so it's a thing where you just have to wait and pray that I don't get locked up. But if I do, I get locked up – that's life. Just have to deal with it."

A small minority of the defendants we interviewed had very little or no prior experience of attending court and, unsurprisingly, were much less inclined than their more seasoned counterparts to speak in apathetic or resigned terms about what it was like to go to the Crown Court; and much more inclined to talk of it being "frightening" or "nerve-wracking". Some of this group also described the profound sense of unreality and numbness they experienced when in court; as Gerry said about being sentenced for a sexual offence: "Well there's nothing that can prepare you for it … it's just unreal. You just go on to some sort of different plane." Charlie said of being sentenced for robbery: "I can't remember to be honest. I was in a bit of a daze. I was just wondering about what I was going to get sentenced to, I weren't listening to the talking. Actually when the judge actually sentenced me I still didn't hear what he said fully." Trish described the experience of attending court in support of her partner as follows: "Your mind is kind of blank; it is such a surreal experience … It is like a kind of dream. You know, where you are waiting to be woken."

A recurring, but implicit, theme in defendants' comments about their feelings when attending court was their lack of 'voice' within the court process. (Our victim and witness respondents, we have seen, also experienced a lack of 'voice', but were better able to articulate this state and their accompanying frustration, and hence it could be said that their voicelessness is less complete.) In interview, defendants gave the strong impression – which was borne out also in our observations, as reported elsewhere in this book – that they had not been actively engaged in the judicial process but, rather, had spent their time in court as mere observers of their own fate: or, in Carlen's words (1976a), as the 'dummy player' in the 'game' of courtroom proceedings. Doubtless there are aspects of the court process itself that have the (unintended) effect of silencing defendants: these include the ritual and formality of the courtroom; the intimidating and complex language used; the exclusionary chumminess of the lawyers; even their very location in the glass-screened dock – 'a separate enclosure at the margins of the courtroom' (Mulcahy, 2013, p 1140). But for many defendants, their disengagement from the court process is also likely to be rooted in their wider disaffection or alienation from the social order, which itself may have numerous causes, and may be intimately bound up with their offending.

In this chapter, we have described many facets of a phenomenon we term 'passive acceptance'. It is, however, important not to overstate the extent to which the defendants were passive and accepting. Many expressed anger and cynicism about the court process as well as, or alongside, apathy, resignation, fatalism or detachment. We have seen this in the complaints some made about apparent bias in decision-making, or about rude or dismissive treatment by certain professionals or staff. But defendants' expressions of anger were often infused with a profound sense of their own powerlessness. Perhaps none provides a more vivid illustration of this than Dexter: a 37-year-old with a string of convictions for (serious) violent offences behind him. We have observed, above, that he described himself as having "no feeling in it" when he was most recently sentenced. But what emerged most strongly from our interview with Dexter was a picture of a hugely disturbed and angry individual, who had the habit of expressing his anger in a manner that was – as he himself fully acknowledged – self-destructive and entirely futile. When held in the cells during his last appearance at the Crown Court, he said:

> 'I was causing a lot of trouble, kicking doors and all kind of stupidness; banging, punching the doors, making noise and shouting. Stupid behaviour; stupid, stupid behaviour. I was upset. At the time you don't know. You say, "I should have handled, conducted myself differently", but you're not thinking that at the time; you're in that moment of the anger, fresh. Afterwards, you look and think, "I shouldn't have carried on like that; that was stupid." I've been very silly at times, very, very silly. Even over there, that court there, very stupid; very, very stupid ...'
>
> ... It's like me, when I went to the police station, I had a thing with the custody sergeants. I just started kicking up the place like a mad lunatic, kicking it and messing up my legs again, both legs. ... It was about an hour and a half of kicking and pure noise. ... The only reason why I calmed down was because I injured myself. I couldn't be kicking the doors and doing all that; it started to really hurt. When you kick those doors, they're solid; they hurt. They hurt a lot, and the harder you kick them, and the more you kick, the more damage you do to yourself. It's very silly, but I can understand why.'

'Doing their job'

We will close this discussion of 'passive acceptance' with a brief discussion of a particular phrase which appeared – in several variants – with striking frequency in defendants' comments about their experiences of court. This phrase was one used in talking about the professionals in court: "They were doing their job."

This seems to have various shades of meaning or implication: that the professionals were doing what they should do; that they were simply following the rules (however good or bad) of the court process; that they were doing what they did because they were being paid to do so; that they were doing the *minimum* required of them. But all these meanings could be said to signal the speaker's acceptance that the courts are a world in themselves, on which outsiders have little impact. The following are just a few examples of the many appearances of the phrase:

> 'People are there to do the job and – me personally – you feel they do it to the best of their ability ... I find the Crown Court all right.'
> [Jack]

> 'They don't care. They're just doing their job, and getting paid loads of money. They don't care who comes in front of them. They're just doing their job, basically.'
> [Leon]

> '[The judge was] doing his job. [The prosecution] done what he had to do.'
> [Mosi]

> 'There was nobody that was rude in court, everyone was just doing their job. Yes, everyone was just doing their job. I don't know them, they don't know me, so everyone was just doing their job.'
> [Faraji]

> 'Well that's just how I presume it works: the prosecution try to find people guilty and the defence try to prove they are innocent and they were just trying to do their job.'
> [Jodie]

Interviewer: And did you think the plea in mitigation was helpful?

Ray: Well, I would never say no because they're just doing a job aren't they? I mean if I was a barrister and I was defending myself I'd probably do it slightly better.

It is interesting to note that the phrase "doing their job" (and variants thereof) was also regularly deployed in the victim and witness interviews. Indeed, this marks it out as having many more occurrences across the entire set of research interviews than any other phrase. However, those victims and witnesses who utilised the term generally did so in a narrower context than the defendants – in acknowledging that defence lawyers who had cross-examined them in a seemingly unpleasant manner were, in fact, simply "doing their job".

'He just had a bit of a smarmy smile on his face all the time. I didn't really like him very much. But I know he's only doing his job.'
[Julia; witness]

'They did their job: they were picking holes in what I was saying.'
[Eva; witness]

Interviewer: And how did you feel overall about talking to the defence barrister?

Nikki: Fucking bastard. Good at your job. Good at your job. Because I met him before, actually. He goes 'This isn't me. This is my job.' ... My barrister goes 'This is my colleague; he's for the defence,' or whatever it is. 'I'm the prosecutor and he's the defence.' And he said 'Pleased to meet you. Just remember this is not me; this is my job.'
 ... Very professional, and then at the end he said: 'Well done. Thank you.' I was like: 'No, thank you. Done your job.' He ripped me apart but my barrister said he would.
[Nikki; victim]

The last word on "doing their job" can go to Tamwar. He had been acquitted, following a trial, of an extremely serious violent offence, but convicted of a lesser one. He described the prosecution counsel in the following terms:

> 'For him – it's just a formality; it's just a case. He was [name] … and the reason they got him is because – the way his mannerisms are and that, he's very good in court. Very kind and very nice. That's why, my barrister told me, that's why they got him. The jury liked it. A really *nice* guy. … Such a *nice* guy, the prosecutor. But … one of my solicitors asked: "Why are you prosecuting these kids?" He goes: "It's just a job." … It's just a job – to give somebody a life sentence? What a wretched job.'

Concluding remarks

This chapter has sought to explain the 'reluctant conformity' observed in most court users, and has done so with reference to the concept of legitimacy. We have argued that most court users perceive the court process as, broadly, legitimate – meaning that they obey the rules of the process not because (or not solely because) they are forced to do so, but because they feel *obliged* to do so. We have identified five constituent parts of court users' perceptions of the legitimacy of the court process, which co-exist in differing combinations for different individuals. These five constituent parts of perceived legitimacy are: a sense of *moral alignment* with the work of the courts and the wider criminal justice system; experiences of *positive outcomes* (however defined) of the court process; experiences of *fair decision-making* (again, however defined) within the court process; experiences of *respectful treatment* by the professionals and practitioners with whom the court users have interpersonal contact at court; and – on the part of many defendants – a certain *passive acceptance* of what goes on in court and its consequences for them.

Notes

[1] Ashworth and Redmayne (2010) note that the incentives for selecting a Crown Court over a magistrates' court trial are mixed for defendants in 'either-way' cases: on the one hand, there is a higher acquittal rate at Crown Court; on the other hand, pre-trial delays are longer at the Crown Court, and sentences tend to be higher for equivalent offences.

[2] This reflects the finding of qualitative research with victim respondents to the WAVES survey, who 'could clearly distinguish between their views on their treatment by the CJS and their views on the outcome' (Commissioner for Victims and Witnesses, 2011, p 11).

[3] Similarly, the qualitative research with WAVES victim respondents found that victims did not necessarily want the most severe sentence possible, but 'had more nuanced views on the appropriateness of sentencing' and wanted tangible, properly enforced sanctions that were appropriate the offence, its circumstances and the harms caused (Commissioner for Victims and Witnesses in England and Wales, 2011, p 32).

[4] *Archbold Criminal Pleading, Evidence and Practice* (Sweet & Maxwell), usually referred to simply as *Archbold*, is published annually and sets out the practices and procedures of the criminal courts for practitioners.

[5] For example, the 1993 (Runciman) Royal Commission on Criminal Justice included a proposal for reducing the range of defendants entitled to a jury trial, which was not implemented. In 2001, the Auld Report proposed that complex fraud cases be tried alone by a judge (Auld, 2001), but the House of Lords blocked the resultant Fraud (Trials without a Jury) Bill in 2007. Sections 44 and 46 of the Criminal Justice Act 2003 (which came into force in 2007) allow a Crown Court trial to be heard without a jury where there is a clear danger of jury tampering. Under these provisions, the case of *Twomey and others* in 2010 was the first Crown Court criminal trial to take place without a jury for over 350 years.

[6] Among the factors found to have the greatest impact on court users' overall satisfaction with their court experiences, according to the Ministry of Justice Court User Survey, were 'being treated fairly and sensitively by court staff, staff being able to respond promptly to queries, and staff keeping users informed of reasons for delays' (Ministry of Justice, 2010, p 4).

[7] Similarly, among the 'passive respondents' identified by Bottoms and McClean were those further characterised as 'dissociative defendants' who 'passively dissociated themselves from courtroom processes, and reacted with inertia and boredom to the whole tedious official ritual of "dealing with" their behaviour in court'; members of this group of defendants were also monosyllabic and evidently bored during the research interviews (1976, p 66).

EIGHT

Conclusion

Within the criminal justice system of England and Wales, the Crown Court is the arena in which the most serious criminal offences are prosecuted and sentenced. Over the course of this book, we have looked at what it is like to attend the Crown Court as a victim, a witness or a defendant; and it is clear that, for many, this is an immensely daunting experience. A victim coming to court to give evidence faces the prospect of reliving the offence in a public and alien setting. Recounting to the court the details – including, potentially, harrowing and intimate details – of what allegedly happened can leave a victim feeling exposed and vulnerable; feelings that are likely to be heightened when, during cross-examination, the victim's account is robustly challenged and undermined, and when the jury's verdict is awaited. Other (non-victim) witnesses may also be fearful or distressed when attending Crown Court: they may, for example, find it difficult to express themselves and to make themselves heard in the unfamiliar and highly formal environment of the courtroom; they may feel intimidated by the lawyers; and they may be scared of encountering the defendant and about possible repercussions of giving evidence. But it is defendants, very often, who have the most at stake when they come to the Crown Court: their reputation, their livelihood and, ultimately, their liberty may turn on a jury's verdict or a judge's decision about sentence.

The nature of Crown Court proceedings

Proceedings in the Crown Court, and much of the interaction and language of the courtroom, are elaborate, ritualised and, in many respects, archaic. Not least, the wigs and gowns worn by the legal professionals in court help to create a sense of other-worldliness, even while most of the day-to-day substantive business of the court is centred on grim, sordid and often violent happenings within a world that is all too real. The deployment of formality and ritual can be seen as, in part, a deliberate strategy to sustain the Crown Court's aura of authority for those who work in court and, especially, those who enter this space as outsiders – that is, the victims, witnesses and defendants, and their friends and family members who come to support them.

However, while Crown Court hearings, and particularly trials, are elaborate and formal affairs, they are also chaotic. Many trials have a large cast of characters, including one or more defendants, witnesses for the defence and prosecution (potentially both experts and laypeople), 12 jurors, lawyers, court staff and, overseeing it all, the judge. Bringing these people together in the courtroom over the requisite period of time – along with the necessary documentation and evidence in the form of video or audio recordings and physical artefacts – is a challenging task which can, and often does, go wrong, with the result that delays and interruptions to proceedings are commonplace. Delays, adjournments and scheduling problems cause considerable frustration, anxiety and inconvenience to victims, witnesses and defendants eager for the case to progress and be done with. Other types of Crown Court hearings (for sentence, for example, and pre-trial and pre-sentence hearings) tend to be much simpler affairs than trials, involving far fewer participants, and are typically conducted in quick-fire fashion, one after another, in busy and congested courtrooms; this also gives rise to mishaps and a level of chaos. Nevertheless, court hearings of all kinds almost always – eventually – proceed in accordance with the preordained rules and legal conventions, and reach some kind of conclusion; this is why we have characterised the court process as a process of *structured* mayhem.

The observation that the adversarial criminal trial is a kind of theatre has been made a great many times. What is, perhaps, somewhat less obvious is that the undoubted drama of the Crown Court trial is one in which those who might be presumed to be lead players – the victims, witnesses and defendants – are in fact side-lined and tend to play only minor, walk-on parts. Victims and witnesses are often frustrated that they have little 'voice' within the courtroom: even when it is their moment to take the witness stand, what they say is heavily circumscribed by the legal rules of evidence. They also discover that their own viewpoint is not represented in the courtroom by any lawyer, as the prosecution case is presented not on their behalf, but on behalf of the Crown. They are usually quickly ushered off the 'stage' after giving evidence and have no direct impact on proceedings thereafter. Defendants, in contrast, are always present, almost always represented (other than on rare occasions of self-representation), and they are necessarily the focus of proceedings which, by definition, concern whether they did or did not commit certain acts and the nature of those acts. Nevertheless, defendants frequently adopt a silent and passive stance in the courtroom through all or most of the trial process and also, if they are convicted, at sentencing. At most, they play a peripheral role; often, they are mere observers as their fate is decided.

The starring roles in a trial and throughout the court process are played by the judge and, particularly, the prosecution and defence counsel. In presenting their respective cases to the court, and drawing out the weaknesses in witness testimony and other evidence offered by the opposing side, counsel seek to outdo each other with displays of eloquence, quick-wittedness and legal knowledge; albeit some with more vigour than others. There are many aspects of these lawyerly performances, aimed primarily at judge and jury, which serve to underline the marginalised, outsider position shared by victim, witness and defendant in the courtroom. In particular, much of the language used and concepts deployed by counsel, and the frames of reference within which they operate, can be difficult to understand and disconcerting; and aggressive or disparaging questioning during cross-examination can further alienate the individual on the witness stand. When opposing counsel spar directly with each other, the interactions are frequently overlaid with an overt and obvious joviality or, at the very least, a mutual recognition of status, indicating that the most significant divide in court is not that between prosecution and defence, or between victim and defendant, but that between the legal professionals and the lay court users.

Compliance and legitimacy

In short, our study has revealed many distressing, stressful and perplexing aspects of the Crown Court experience for victims, witnesses and defendants alike. And yet we have also found, like other court researchers, that notwithstanding these inherent and often immense difficulties of the court experience, the vast majority of court users are highly compliant: they turn up where they are told to (even if sometimes late); they sit or stand as instructed; they answer the questions posed to them and, largely, in the required manner; and they generally conduct themselves in line with the social rules of the courtroom. This is true of defendants as much as it is for victims and witnesses. Likewise, friends and family supporters of court users rarely challenge or resist courtroom etiquette when observing proceedings from the public gallery. And while court users' compliance is at least partially coerced, the nature and extent of compliance strongly suggests that there is a voluntary element to it, reflecting an implicit belief in the legitimacy of the court process: that is, they obey the rules not simply because they have to, but because they feel *obliged* to do so.

In the final empirical chapter of the book (Chapter Seven), we have considered what victims', witnesses' and defendants' sense of the legitimacy of the court process, or sense of obligation to obey, is based upon. Drawing on insights provided by procedural justice theorists such as Tom Tyler and others, we have concluded that there are five inter-related dimensions to court users' perceptions of the legitimacy of the Crown Court. The first of these dimensions is a sense of *moral alignment* with the judicial process, whereby it is accepted that, as a general rule, the criminal courts contribute to the public good by holding to account those individuals who have wronged others or society at large. This is, in other words, a generalised attachment to the principles of justice and the institutions responsible for administering it.

Contrasting with moral alignment are three dimensions of legitimacy which reflect victims', witnesses' and defendants' direct experiences of the court process: namely, a *positive outcome* of the case in which they are involved; the perception of *fair decision-making* in the case; and experiences of *respectful treatment* during the court process. For a victim or prosecution witness, a positive outcome is likely to be a guilty verdict in a contested trial and/or a sentence perceived to be appropriate to the offence (whether appropriateness is defined in punitive, instrumental or other terms). Conversely, from a defendant's perspective, only a 'not guilty' verdict or a sentence that is relatively lenient may be regarded as a positive outcome. Court users' perceptions of fair decision-making within the court tend to be associated with impartiality, attentiveness and rule-following on the part of the decision-makers – that is, the jurors in a trial, and the judge at sentencing. Respectful treatment encompasses treatment by police, lawyers, judges, court staff and Witness Service volunteers that is considerate, humane and empathetic; this can, and often does, have a substantial positive impact on how court users feel about their involvement in the court process.

Finally, there is a fifth dimension of legitimacy: namely, a *passive acceptance* of the court process on the part of many defendants, particularly those who are frequent visitors to the criminal courts. (It does not appear to be a typical feature of victims' and witnesses' experiences.) Defendants' passive acceptance implies, at best, a morally neutral sense of obligation to obey the court authorities and hence can be described as contributing to legitimacy only in a weak sense.

While we have identified five dimensions, or components, of legitimacy, we are by no means suggesting that court users' overall sense of legitimacy tends to reside in all five simultaneously. Rather, we would contend that these constituent parts co-exist in various combinations, and that where some are absent or have a negative charge, the effects of this are usually outweighed by other (positive) legitimating factors. Hence, for example, negative experiences in relation to outcome, decision-making or treatment might severely dent an individual's perceptions of the legitimacy of the court process; but a strong sense of moral alignment could nevertheless prevail. Or good treatment could limit the damaging impact on perceived legitimacy of a deeply disappointing outcome, and vice versa. Or a defendant's passive acceptance might ultimately hold more sway than his or her deep cynicism or disgust concerning court outcomes or decision-making. Thus the main thrust of our argument about legitimacy is that the large majority of court users perceive the court process as broadly legitimate – despite its pressures, strains and manifold incongruities – and that this sense of legitimacy is manifest in a variety of ways.

Implications for policy and practice?

This book has not set out to consider whether and how policies and practices within the Crown Court could be changed so as to make victims', witnesses' and defendants' experiences more positive.[1] We have sought, rather, to identify and analyse some of the essential features of those experiences. Nevertheless, by way of bringing the book to a close, we would like to touch on the question of how the treatment of court users might be improved throughout the judicial process.

With respect to victims and witnesses, there is no doubt that the way they are treated before and while at court has substantially changed for the better over the past two decades. The movement for victims' rights in England and Wales, of which there have been parallels in other jurisdictions, has unquestionably had a profound impact on both policy and practice. The introduction of 'special measures' to help vulnerable and intimidated witnesses give evidence has been one of the most concrete and significant developments, while the provision of Witness Service waiting facilities and support within the criminal courts has also done much to ease some of the anxiety and stress experienced by victims and witnesses. Nevertheless, despite the change for the better, there remain various aspects of judicial proceedings that make the experience of attending court as a victim or witness – admittedly, never likely to be in any way an easy or happy occasion – more troubling and distressing than it needs to be.

The findings of our study suggest that, among victims and witnesses, the aspects of the court process which tend to cause most concern – beyond the substantive issues at the heart of their respective cases – include encounters with defendants or defendants' supporters in the public areas of the court; inefficiencies and disorganisation, and the resultant delays to proceedings; the sense of being marginalised and denied a proper 'voice' at court, which is a source of frustration in itself and is also sometimes seen as negatively impacting case outcomes; and the overly hostile nature of some cross-examination. These are not isolated concerns: public disquiet about these and related matters has been fuelled by a number of recent high profile cases in which victims and witnesses appear to have been subjected to unnecessary trauma and stress.

Determining how best to address the enduring concerns about the victim and witness experience at court is by no means straightforward. There is a need for improved case management procedures which would reduce levels of inefficiency, disorganisation and delay,[2] while changes to court routines and the management of space in court buildings could help to address the problems of inadvertent meetings between victims or witnesses and defendants at court. Whether these improvements can be achieved in the context of cuts to funding of court administrative services is a moot question; it also needs to be recognised that the great complexity of pulling together the range of people and information required for any case to proceed through the courts makes it almost inevitable that most cases will encounter some practical and procedural hitches. However, the impact of practical problems, delay and disruption can be reduced if explanations are offered wherever possible to the individuals involved, and if the emotional and practical costs are appreciated and acknowledged.

It is more difficult to address victims' and witnesses' feelings of marginalisation throughout the court process, and of being treated with aggression or contempt on the witness stand. These issues raise questions far beyond the scope of this book about the extent to which it is possible further to protect victims' and witnesses' sensibilities and to increase their procedural rights within a justice system that is adversarial in nature. But it is important to note that many of the changes that have already been made in terms of victim and witness provision at court – particularly help with giving evidence for those who are vulnerable – might once have been seen as far exceeding what was lawful or reasonable within an adversarial system. Further real changes in this general direction are feasible, given sufficient political and judicial will, even if they have to be pursued incrementally and cautiously. Beyond this, the work of procedural justice theorists teaches us (as also supported by our own findings) that victims' and witnesses' direct experiences of just procedure within the courts – meaning, in essence, that decision-making is seen to operate in a fair and principled manner and that they receive respectful treatment – substantially boosts positive perceptions of the court process as a whole and a sense of its legitimacy. Enhancing procedural justice within the courts does not demand extensive additional investment of resources or significant change to practice; it is more a matter of a cultural shift towards a justice system which more actively and effectively engages with its lay participants, and which recognises that treating people in a bullying, arrogant or condescending manner is simply unacceptable.

It seems, then, that the position of victims and witnesses at court has considerably improved over the past two decades, but could yet be improved much further. What of the position of defendants? In general, changes in court-based provision for defendants have been less marked and obvious in recent times than the changes in victim and witness provision. There has been no comparable movement to the victims' rights movement. In fact, some campaigners and politicians, in making the case for greater victims' (and witnesses') rights within the justice process, have predicated their arguments on the assumption that defendants' rights are already adequately addressed or should even be curtailed in order that there can be a 'rebalancing' with victims' rights. The weight carried by this viewpoint is illustrated, for example, by the explicit exclusion of defendants from the 'special measures' provisions for vulnerable victims and witnesses introduced by the Youth Justice and Criminal Evidence Act 1999. Even so, recent years have seen moves towards greater support for defendants at court. This includes some provision for vulnerable defendants that is similar – if not identical – to that made available to vulnerable victims and witnesses, in the form of practical assistance with giving evidence and measures to make the court environment less intimidating.

Notwithstanding the available provision for defendants, many appear to feel, during the court process, a sense of marginalisation which is not entirely dissimilar to that of which many victims and witnesses complain. Defendants, we have noted above, are in the paradoxical position of being central to and yet, at the same time, at the periphery of the court proceedings that concern them. Many feel belittled by aspects of the process, certainly excluded and often confused by much of the language used in the courtroom, and sometimes frustrated by the apparent grandstanding, game-playing and chumminess of the lawyers. Arguably, those who are more inclined to display 'passive acceptance' of the court process than actively to complain about it are the ones who are most thoroughly excluded and silenced, because they simply take for granted, or are barely aware of, their highly peripheral role within the court. The marginalisation of defendants and particularly their 'passive acceptance' have troubling implications for defendants' capacity to exercise fully their right to a fair trial – as enshrined in Article 6 of the European Convention on Human Rights. It is an established principle in law that in order to exercise this right, a defendant must be able to participate effectively in the court process: but it appears that 'effective participation' in a meaningful sense is a standard that a great many defendants at the Crown Court do not attain.

In light of concerns about defendants' marginalisation, a procedural justice perspective on court processes and interactions may, again, show a way forward. A procedural justice approach, furthermore, encourages a move away from simplistic notions of a zero-sum relationship between victims' and defendants' rights: if the intention is to enhance the (demonstrable) fairness of decision-making and the quality of courtroom interactions between court users and professionals, there is no logical reason why the benefits of this should be exclusive to one group of court users and at the expense of another. Other developments within the courts and wider justice system also offer scope for tackling defendants' passivity and building their capacity for participation. These include greater involvement of sentencers in the active supervision of certain types of sentence, and the establishment of 'problem-solving courts', within which there is a focus on the problems underlying offending behaviour – such as substance misuse – as an integral part of the judicial process.[3] Together, such initiatives may have the potential to produce 'courts which concentrate on people as well as cases' (Bowen and Whitehead, 2013, p 6). Restorative justice – which entails bringing victims and offenders together to address the harms caused by offending – is an approach which strongly promotes active engagement on the part of offenders who are expected to take responsibility for their harmful actions; the other core feature of this approach is that victims, too, are given much more of a 'voice' than is permitted in traditional criminal justice proceedings. The past few years have seen increasing efforts by government to incorporate restorative justice initiatives as both formal and informal components of the justice process, partly on the grounds that they offer a means of meeting victims' needs.[4]

The greatest challenge, however, lies in the fact that defendants' marginalisation and passive acceptance are likely to have roots much deeper than the way the criminal justice system operates. Criminal justice initiatives aimed at supporting defendants' engagement with the justice process may have limited impact if they do not at least recognise that there are usually underlying problems – for whatever myriad reasons – of social exclusion and disaffection, lack of a sense of agency, and limited capacity to reflect on oneself and what is going on around one. Only to the extent that these broader issues are considered is there likely to be significant success in efforts to translate defendants' 'passive acceptance' into active participation, and weak into true legitimacy.

Notes

[1] Other publications based on our findings, however, have a focus on policy and practice: namely, a report on provision for victims and witnesses (Hunter et al, 2013), and two briefings aimed at supporting fair and respectful treatment of witnesses and supporting effective participation of defendants (Jacobson et al 2014a, 2014b).

[2] For discussion of criminal case management see Garland and McEwan (2012) and Darbyshire (2014).

[3] See, for example, Woolf, 2007; Policy Exchange, 2009; Plotnikoff and Woolfson, 2005. Problem-solving (or what are sometimes termed 'community justice' courts) have their origins in the United States, and since the mid-2000s have fallen in and then out of favour in England and Wales. Insights provided by advocates of therapeutic jurisprudence, which 'strives to accomplish harmonious functioning of the law by observing court proceedings and outcomes with an eye directed towards increasing therapeutic value for participants' (Erez et al, 2011, p x), are also relevant here. See also, for example, Wexler (2008); Winick and Wexler (2003); Stolle et al (2000).

[4] See, for example, Ministry of Justice (2012a, 2012d).

Details on court user respondents and outline of observed cases

Table A1: Details on prosecution respondents and their most recent experience of the Crown Court

Name	Socio-demographic characteristics			Most recent Crown Court experience				Prior experience of criminal courts
	Age	Ethnicity	Occupation	Offence	Role	Verdict	Sentence	
Anthony	50	Black	Unemployed	Assault	Victim	Not guilty	-	Several appearances as defendant in magistrates' and Crown courts
Tracey	47	White	Unemployed		Witness and partner of victim (Anthony)			None
Abdul	44	Asian	Unemployed	Robbery and assault	Witness; did not give evidence	Guilty plea on day of trial	Custody	None
Adam	23	White	Care worker	Theft (from workplace)	Witness	Guilty	Custody	None
Anna	22	White	Student	Sexual offences involving a child	Witness	Guilty	Awaiting sentence	None
Barbara	66	White	Social worker	Theft (from workplace)	Witness and daughter of victim	Guilty	Suspended custody	None
Grace	60	White	Housing manager		Witness			Witness in magistrates' court
Chloe	30	White	Personnel manager	Robbery and firearms offence ('carjacking')	Victim	Guilty	Custody	None
Natasha	26	White	Local authority officer		Victim			None
Eva	28	White	Events organiser		Witness (and friend of victims)			Witness in magistrates' court

211

Table A1: continued

Name	Socio-demographic characteristics			Most recent Crown Court experience				Prior experience of criminal courts
	Age	Ethnicity	Occupation	Offence	Role	Verdict	Sentence	
Dan	35	White	Pub manager	Assault	Witness	Guilty	Custody	None
Debbie	38	White	Student	Non-domestic burglary	Witness	Guilty plea on day of trial	Unknown	Witness in Crown Court
Denise	46	Black	Unemployed	Assault (domestic violence)	Victim	Guilty plea on day of trial	Custody	None
Elaine	58	White	Care worker	Sexual offences involving a child	Witness and mother of victim	Not guilty	—	None
Amanda	36	White	Student		Witness and sister of victim			None
Ian	42	White	Long-term sick leave		Witness and brother-in-law of victim			None
Elsie	79	White	Retired	Criminal damage – appeal against conviction	Witness	Guilty	Fine	None
Ernie	74	White	Retired	Assault	Victim	Guilty	Suspended custody	None
Faris	22	Asian	Student	Robbery	Victim	Guilty	Custody	None
Francesca	48	White	IT consultant	Assault (domestic violence)	Victim	Guilty	Custody	One appearance as defendant and several as victim (domestic violence) in Crown and magistrates' courts
Freya	20	Mixed ethnicity	Care worker	Sexual and violent offences (by Freya's ex-boyfriend)	Victim	Guilty on most counts	Custody	None
Julia	55	White	Care worker		Witness and mother of victim (Freya)			None
Ilan	27	Mixed ethnicity	Self-employed		Witness and brother of victim (Freya)			None

Table A1: continued

Name	Socio-demographic characteristics			Most recent Crown Court experience					Prior experience of criminal courts
	Age	Ethnicity	Occupation	Offence	Role	Verdict	Sentence		
Graham	44	White	Leisure industry	Sexual offences involving a child	Witness and father of victim	Guilty on some counts	Community		None
Karen	43	White	Leisure industry		Witness and mother of victim				None
Ibrahim	19	Black	Unemployed	Assault	Victim	Guilty	Custody		None
James	20	White	Apprentice	Attempted robbery	Witness	Guilty	Community		None
Janice	49	White	Council worker	Public order offence (racially aggravated) – appeal against conviction	Witness	Guilty	Fine and ASBO		None
Linda	36	White	Sales worker	Sexual offences involving a child	Witness	Not guilty	—		Witness in Crown Court
Maggie	61	White	Retired	Assault	Witness	Not guilty	—		Witness in Crown Court
Masood	47	Asian	Post office worker	Public order offence (racially aggravated)	Victim	Guilty	Suspended custody		None
Helga	31	White	Post office worker		Witness and colleague of victim (Masood)				None
Michelle	20	White	PA	Rape	Witness	Not guilty	—		None
Mila	26	Asian	Unemployed	Assault	Victim	Guilty plea on day of trial (second trial); custody			None
Olga	25	White	Student		Witness and friend of victim (Mila)				None
Nikki	38	White	Youth worker	Sexual assault	Victim	Guilty	Custody		Defendant in magistrates' court
Rhona	38	White	Social worker		Witness and friend of victim (Nikki)				None

Table A1: continued

Name	Socio-demographic characteristics			Most recent Crown Court experience				Prior experience of criminal courts
	Age	Ethnicity	Occupation	Offence	Role	Verdict	Sentence	
Ron	54	White	Pub landlord	Assault	Victim	Not guilty	—	None
Donna	29	White	Barmaid		Witness and colleague of victim (Ron)			None
Ryan	24	White	Mechanic	Assault and criminal damage	Victim	Guilty plea on day of trial (second trial)	Suspended custody	None
Sarah	57	White	Secretary		Witness and mother of victim (Ryan)			None
Samantha	19	White	Witness		Witness and girlfriend of victim (Ryan)			Witness in magistrates' court
Stella	54	White	Librarian	Possession of offensive weapon	Witness	Guilty plea on day of trial	Suspended custody	Witness in magistrates' court
Tina	47	White	Unemployed	Sexual assault	Observer in court; mother of victim	Guilty	Custody	Defendant in magistrates' court
Tom	33	White	Chemist	Non-domestic burglary	Witness	Guilty plea on day of trial	Unknown	None

Table A2: Details on defence respondents and their most recent experience of the Crown Court

Name	Socio-demographic characteristics				Most recent Crown Court experience					Prior experience of criminal courts
	Age	Ethnicity	Occupation		Offence	Type of hearing	Verdict	Sentence		
Alex	20	White	Unemployed		Drug offences (supply)	Sentencing	–	Custody		Two appearances as defendant in youth court
Alfie	30	White	Unemployed		Drug offences (supply)	Sentencing	—	Custody		Several appearances as defendant in magistrates' courts
Ali	28	Asian	Unemployed		Drug offences (supply)	Sentencing	–	Custody		Many appearances as defendant in magistrates' and Crown courts for drug and violent offences
Alistair	38	White	Unemployed		Sex offences involving a child	Sentencing	–	Custody		One appearance as a defendant in the Crown Court
Andy	52	White	Lorry driver		Drug offences (importation)	Trial	Not guilty	–		None
Calvin	53	Black	Builder		Assault (domestic violence)	Sentencing	–	Suspended custody		One appearance as defendant in magistrates' court
Charlie	34	White	Scaffolder		Robbery	Sentencing	–	Custody		None
Christian	20	White	Unemployed		Violent disorder	Trial	Guilty	Custody		Several appearances as defendant in magistrates' courts
Damien	33	White	Artist		Theft	Sentencing	–	Custody		Many appearances as defendant in magistrates' and Crown courts for acquisitive and drug offences
Danny	32	Black	Unemployed		Robbery	Sentencing	–	Suspended custody		Several appearances as defendant in magistrates' and Crown courts
Derek	62	White	Volunteering		Murder	Sentencing	–	Custody		Several appearances as defendant in magistrates' and Crown courts

Table A2: continued

Name	Socio-demographic characteristics			Most recent Crown Court experience				Prior experience of criminal courts
	Age	Ethnicity	Occupation	Offence	Type of hearing	Verdict	Sentence	
Dexter	37	Black	Unemployed	Violent and sexual offences	Sentencing	—	Custody	Several appearances as defendant in magistrates' and Crown courts
Dominic	33	Black	Engineer	Possession of an offensive weapon	Trial	Case dismissed	—	Juror
Faraji	30	Black	Unemployed	Robbery	Sentencing	—	Custody	Several appearances as defendant in magistrates' and Crown courts
Gerry	59	White	Unemployed	Sex offences involving a child	Sentencing	—	Custody	One appearance as defendant in juvenile court
Jack	55	White	Long-term sick	Burglary	Sentencing	—	Community	Numerous appearances as defendant in magistrates' and Crown courts, mostly for acquisitive crimes
Jenny	29	White	Wedding planner	Fraud	Pre-trial	Case dismissed	—	None
Jerome	22	Mixed ethnicity	Engineer	Theft and driving offences	Sentencing	—	Suspended custody	Several appearances as defendant in magistrates' courts
Jonathan	40	Black	Hairdresser	Possession of offensive weapon	Sentencing	—	Suspended custody	Several appearances as defendant in magistrates' and Crown courts
Kevin	34	Mixed ethnicity	Unemployed	Indecent exposure	Sentencing	—	Community	None
Kwame	27	Black	Construction manager	Attempted murder and assault	Trial	Not guilty of attempted murder; guilty of assault	Custody	Several appearances as defendant in magistrates' and Crown courts

Appendix

Table A2: continued

Name	Socio-demographic characteristics			Most recent Crown Court experience				Prior experience of criminal courts
	Age	Ethnicity	Occupation	Offence	Type of hearing	Verdict	Sentence	
Latif	23	Black	Unemployed	Assault	Sentencing	—	Custody	Several appearances as defendant in magistrates' and Crown courts
Leon	29	Black	Unemployed	Assault (domestic violence)	Trial	Guilty	Community	Several appearances as defendant in magistrates' courts
Matthew	18	White	Unemployed	Drug offences (supply)	Sentencing	—	Custody	Two appearances as defendant in youth court
Maurice	52	White	Long-term sick	Indecent exposure	Sentencing	—	Community	None
Michael	57	White	Unemployed	Sex offences	Sentencing	—	Community	None
Mosi	22	Black	Unemployed	Robbery	Trial	Guilty	Custody	None
Nathan	32	White	Unemployed	Assault	Sentencing	—	Custody	Many appearances as defendant in magistrates' and Crown courts for violence
Patrice	42	Black	Lorry driver	Assault	Sentencing	—	Suspended custody	Many appearances as defendant in magistrates' and Crown courts, mostly for violence
Peter	30	White	Accountant	Indecent images of children	Sentencing	—	Suspended custody	One appearance as defendant and one as a witness in Crown Court
Paul	29	Black	Self-employed	Violent disorder and criminal damage	Sentencing	—	Custody	Several appearances as defendant in magistrates' and Crown courts
Ray	55	White	Unemployed	Sex offences against children	Sentencing	—	Custody	Many appearances as defendant in magistrates' courts, including for sex offences; acted as juror
Rodney	55	Black	Shop worker	Burglary	Sentencing	—	Suspended custody	Three appearances at magistrates' courts

Table A2: continued

Name	Socio-demographic characteristics			Most recent Crown Court experience				Prior experience of criminal courts
	Age	Ethnicity	Occupation	Offence	Type of hearing	Verdict	Sentence	
Sam	27	White	Unemployed	Burglary	Sentencing	—	Custody	Many appearances as defendant in magistrates' and Crown courts, predominantly for burglary
Sidney	33	White	Unemployed	Assault	Trial	Not guilty	—	Many appearances as defendant in magistrates' and Crown courts for violence and other offences
Sizwe	46	Black	Unemployed	Deception	Sentencing	—	Suspended custody	Several appearances as defendant in magistrates' and Crown courts
Stacey	21	White	Unemployed	Perverting the course of justice	Sentencing	—	Community	None
Steve	52	Mixed ethnicity	Unemployed	Arson	Trial	Guilty	Custody	Many appearances as defendant in magistrates' and Crown courts for various offences
Tamwar	27	Asian	Student	Various violent offences	Trial	Not guilty of most serious charge; guilty of others	Custody	Two appearances as defendant in youth court
Vikram	21	Asian	Unemployed	Fraud	Sentencing	—	Custody	A few appearances as defendant in magistrates' courts
William	22	White	Unemployed	Indecent images of children	Sentencing	—	Community	None

Appendix

Table A2: continued

Name	Socio-demographic characteristics			Most recent Crown Court experience				Prior experience of criminal courts
	Age	Ethnicity	Occupation	Offence	Type of hearing	Verdict	Sentence	

Defendant family members

Name (relation to defendant)	Socio-demographic characteristics			Family member's most recent experience of Crown Court				Prior court experience (own)
	Age	Ethnicity	Occupation	Offence	Type of hearing	Verdict	Sentence	
Jodie (partner)	36	White	Carer	Drug offences (supply)	Trial	Guilty	Custody	One appearance as defendant in magistrates' court
Louise (mother)	44	White	Unknown	Robbery	Trial	Guilty	Custody	Attended previous trials of her son
Shona (partner)	29	White	Trainee beautician	Drug offences (supply)	Sentencing	—	Custody	None
Trish (partner)	35	White	Carer	Assault	Trial	Guilty	Custody	None

Table A3: Outline of observed cases

Case 1: Assault occasioning actual bodily harm

Defendant: Mark Littlewood
Chief prosecution witness: Vicky Simons; mother of Millie
Alleged offences: Mark was charged with two counts of assault occasioning actual bodily harm on his girlfriend's two-year-old daughter, Millie. The assaults were said to have caused bruising to Millie's legs and back. He was also charged with additional counts of assault by beating on Vicky and damaging property (Vicky's mobile phone).
Outcome: Not guilty verdict.
The case had been listed for trial twice previously without having gone ahead; on at least one of these prior occasions this was because an important prosecution witness failed to attend.

Case 2: Inflicting grievous bodily harm

Defendant: Emmanuel Robinson
Chief prosecution witness: Spencer Wright
Alleged offence: Emmanuel was charged with inflicting grievous bodily harm on Spencer in the course of a Sunday morning football match. Emmanuel and Spencer were players on opposing sides; the injury – a badly broken cheekbone – had been sustained in the course of a fight involving a number of players from the both teams.
Outcome: Guilty verdict; sentence of nine months' custody.

Case 3: Perverting the course of justice

Defendant: Lola Smith
Chief prosecution witnesses: Frankie Nicholls and Jim Lewis
Alleged offence: Lola was charged with perverting the course of justice on the grounds of having made a false allegation to the police that she had been raped by Frankie (her ex-boyfriend) and Jim (Frankie's friend).
Outcome: Guilty verdict; sentence of two years' custody.
This was a retrial; at the first trial, the jury had failed to reach a verdict.

Case 4: Armed robbery

Defendants: Jayden Safar and Ike Johnson
Chief prosecution witness: Joe Owen
Alleged offence: Jayden and Ike were charged with conspiracy to commit robbery (of a substantial sum of cash) against Joe; Jayden was also charged with two firearms offences related to the robbery.
Outcome: The trial was stopped after three days, when Ike was charged with perverting the course of justice following alleged contact with a witness.
This was a retrial; at the initial trial, Jayden had been convicted of several drugs and firearms offences but the jury had failed to reach a verdict on the robbery and other firearms offences. A second retrial took place some months later after the observed case; at this third hearing, the jury found Jayden guilty of all charges and failed to reach a verdict on Ike (who had, in the meantime, pleaded guilty to perverting the course of justice).

Case 5: Sexual assault and abduction of a child

Defendant: Jamal Taban
Chief prosecution witness: Letitia Norman
Alleged offence: Jamal was charged with sexually assaulting nine-year-old Letitia by way of having 'intentionally touched' her in a sexual manner while she was on her way to the corner shop to buy some sweets. He was also charged with abduction of Letitia on the grounds that he 'had detained her so as to remove her from the lawful control of her father'.
Outcome: Guilty verdict on the assault charge; sentence of suspended custody. Not guilty of abduction.
This was a retrial; the jury in the first trial had failed to reach a verdict.

Case 6: Robbery

Defendant: Dionne Mackie
Chief prosecution witnesses: Oliver Jackson and Josh Melton
Alleged offence: Dionne was charged with having robbed Oliver of his mobile phone, while he was returning home from a night out with his friend, Josh. She had already pleaded guilty to a charge of assault occasioning actual bodily harm against Josh.
Outcome: Guilty verdict; sentence of suspended custody.

Case 7: Dangerous driving

Defendant: Ahmed Feroz
Chief prosecution witness: Athena Georgiou
Alleged offence: Ahmed was accused of dangerous driving following an argument with Athena, who was in another car. Ahmed faced a second count of assault by beating against Athena.
Outcome: Not guilty verdict on both counts.

References

Advocacy Training Council (2011) *Raising the Bar: The handling of vulnerable witnesses, victims and defendants in court*, London: The Advocacy Training Council.

Advocate's Gateway (2013a) *Effective participation of young defendants: Toolkit 8*, London: The Advocacy Training Council.

Advocate's Gateway (2013b) *General principles from research – Planning to question a vulnerable person or someone with communication needs: Toolkit 2(a)*, London: The Advocacy Training Council.

Ainsworth, P.B. (1998) *Psychology, law and eyewitness testimony*, Chichester: John Wiley and Sons.

Alge, D. (2013) 'Negotiated plea agreements in cases of serious and complex fraud in England and Wales: A new conceptualisation of plea bargaining?', *Web Journal of Current Legal Issues*, vol 19, no 1.

Ashworth, A. (2010) *Sentencing and criminal justice* (5th edn), Cambridge: Cambridge University Press.

Ashworth A. and Redmayne, M. (2010) *The criminal process* (4th edn), Oxford: Oxford University Press.

Ashworth, A. and Roberts, J.V. (2012) 'Sentencing. theory, policy, and practice', in R. Morgan, M. Maguire and R. Reiner (eds) *Oxford Handbook of Criminology* (5th edn), Oxford: Oxford University Press: 866–94.

Astor, H. (1986) 'The unrepresented defendant revisited: A consideration of the role of the clerk in magistrates' courts', *Journal of Law and Society*, vol 13, no 2, pp 225–39.

Auld, Lord Justice (2001) *Review of the criminal courts of England and Wales*, London: Lord Chancellor's Department.

Baldwin, J. (2008) 'Research on the criminal courts', in R.D. King and E. Wincup, *Doing research on crime and justice*, Oxford: Oxford University Press, pp 375–98.

Baldwin, J. and McConville, M.J. (1977) *Negotiated justice*, London: Martin Robertson.

Ball, M. S. (1975) 'The play's the thing', *Stanford Law Review*, vol 28, no 1, pp 81–115.

Benesh, S.C. and Howell, S.E. (2001) 'Confidence in the courts: A comparison of users and non-users', *Behavioural Sciences and the Law*, 19, pp 199–214.

Blumberg, A.S. (1967) *Criminal justice*, Chicago: Quadrangle Books.

Blumberg, A.S. (1969) 'The practice of law as a confidence game: Organizational cooptation of a profession', in W.J. Chambliss (ed) *Crime and the Legal Process*, New York: McGraw-Hill, pp 220–37.

Bottoms, A.E. and McClean, J.D. (1976) *Defendants in the criminal process*, London: Routledge & Kegan Paul.

Bottoms, A. and Tankebe, J. (2012) 'Beyond Procedural Justice: A dialogic approach to legitimacy in criminal justice', *The Journal of Criminal Law and Criminology*, vol 102, no 1, pp 119–170.

Bowen, P. and Whitehead, S. (2013) *Better courts: Cutting crime through court innovation*, London: NEF, Centre for Justice Innovation.

Bradford, B., Jackson, J. and Stanko, E.A. (2009) 'Contact and confidence: revisiting the impact of public encounters with the police', *Policing and Society*, vol 19, no 1, pp 20–46.

Bradley, K. (2009) *The Bradley Report: Lord Bradley's review of people with mental health problems or learning disabilities in the criminal justice system*, London: Department of Health.

Brammer, A. and Cooper, P. (2011) 'Still waiting for a meeting of minds: Child witnesses in the criminal and family justice systems', *Criminal Law Review*, no 12, pp 925–942.

Brants, C. and Ringnalda, A. (2011) *Issues of convergence: Inquisitorial prosecution in England and Wales?*, Nijmegen: Woolf Legal Publishers.

Burton, M., Evans, R. and Sanders, A. (2006) *An evaluation of the use of special measures for vulnerable and intimidated witnesses*, London: Home Office Findings 270.

Carlen, P. (1976a) *Magistrates' justice*, London: Martin Robertson.

Carlen, P. (1976b) 'The staging of magistrates' justice', *British Journal of Criminology*, vol 16, no 1, pp 48–55.

Charles, C. (2012) *Special measures for vulnerable and intimidated witnesses: research exploring the decisions and actions taken by prosecutors in a sample of CPS case files*, London: CPS.

Commissioner for Victims and Witnesses (2010) *The poor relation – Victims in the criminal justice system*, London: Ministry of Justice.

Commissioner for Victims and Witnesses (2011) *Victims' views of court and sentencing: Qualitative research with WAVES victims*, London: Ministry of Justice.

Crawford, A. and Hucklesby, A. (eds) (2013) *Legitimacy and compliance in criminal justice*, Abingdon: Routledge.

Criminal Justice System (2004) *No Witness, No Justice*, London: Criminal Justice System.

Darbyshire, P. (2011) *Sitting in judgement: The working lives of judges*, Oxford: Hart Publishing.

Darbyshire, P. (2014) 'Judicial case management in ten crown courts', *Criminal Law Review*, no 1, pp 30–50.

Deffains, B. and Demougin, D. (2008) 'The inquisitorial and the adversarial procedure in a criminal court setting', *Journal of Institutional and Theoretical Economics*, vol 164, no 1, pp 31–43.

Devers, L. (2011) *Plea and charge bargaining: Research summary*, Bureau of Justice Assistance, United States.

Doak, J. (2008) *Victims' rights, human rights and criminal justice: Reconceiving the role of third parties*, Oxford: Hart Publishing.

Duff, A., Farmer, L., Marshall, S. and Tadros, V. (eds) (2007) *The trial on trial, Volume 3: Towards a normative theory of the criminal trial*, Oxford: Hart Publishing.

Duff, P. (2007) 'Disclosure in Scottish criminal procedure: Another step in an inquisitorial direction', *International Journal of Evidence and Proof*, vol 11, no 3, pp 153–80.

Emerson, R.M. (1969) *Judging delinquents: Context and process in juvenile court*, Chicago: Aldine.

Engelhardt, L. (1999) 'The problem with eyewitness testimony: a talk by Barbara Tversky, Professor of Psychology and George Fisher, Professor of Law', *Stanford Journal of Legal Studies*, vol 1, no 1, pp 25–9.

Erez, E., Kilchling, M. and Wemmers, J.-A. (2011) 'Therapeutic jurisprudence and victim participation in justice: An introduction', in E. Erez, M. Kilchling and J.-A. Wemmers (eds) *Therapeutic Jurisprudence and Victim Participation in Justice: International Perspectives*, Durham, NC: Carolina Academic Press, pp ix–xix.

Fagan, J. (2008) 'Legitimacy and criminal justice: Introduction', *Ohio State Journal of Criminal Law*, no 6, pp 123–40.

Feeley, M.M. (1992) *The process is the punishment: Handling cases in a lower criminal court*, New York: Russell Sage.

Fielding, N.G. (2006) *Courting violence: Offences against the person cases in court*, Oxford: Oxford University Press.

Findley, K.A. (2012) 'Adversarial inquisitions: Rethinking the search for the truth', *New York Law School Law Review*, no 56, pp 911–41.

Fisher, G. (2003) *Plea-bargaining's triumph: A history of plea bargaining in America*, Stanford: Stanford University Press.

Flood, J. and Hviid, M. (2013) *The cab rank rule: Its meaning and purpose in the new legal services market*, Report for the Legal Services Board.

Franklyn, R. (2012) *Satisfaction and willingness to engage with the criminal justice system: Findings from the Witness and Victim Experience Survey 2009–10*, London: Ministry of Justice.

Fulero, S.M. (2009) 'System and estimator variables in eyewitness identification: A review' in D. A. Krauss and J. D. Lieberman (eds) *Psychological Expertise in Court: Psychology in the Courtroom, Volume II*, Farnham: Ashgate, pp 57–78.

Garland, F. and McEwan, J. (2012) 'Embracing the overriding objective: difficulties and dilemmas in the new criminal climate', *International Journal of Evidence and Proof*, vol 16, no 3, pp 233–62.

Gibson, B. and Cavadino, P. (2008) *The criminal justice system: An introduction*, Hampshire: Waterside Press.

Hamlyn, B., Phelps, A., Turtle, J. and Sattar, G. (2004) *Are special measures working? Evidence from surveys of vulnerable and intimidated witnesses*, London: Home Office Research Study 283.

Henderson, E. (2014) 'All the proper protections – The Court of Appeal re-writes the rules for the cross-examination of vulnerable witnesses', *Criminal Law Review*, no 2, pp 93–108.

HM Courts and Tribunals Service (2013) *Business Plan 2013–14*, London: HMCTS.

HM Government (2005) *Reducing reoffending through skills and employment*, London: HMSO.

Home Office (1996) *The Victims' Charter: A statement of service standards for victims of crime*, London: Home Office.

Home Office (2001) *Victim Personal Statements*, Home Office Circular 35/2001, London: Home Office.

Home Office (2002) *Justice for All*, London: The Stationery Office.

Home Office (2005) *The Code of Practice for Victims of Crime*, London: Office for Criminal Justice Reform.

Home Office (2010) *The Stern Review: A report by Baroness Vivien Stern CBE of an Independent Review into how rape complainants are handled by public authorities in England and Wales*, London: Home Office.

Hood, R., Shute, S. and Seemungal, F. (2003) *Ethnic minorities in the criminal courts: Perceptions of fairness and equality of treatment*, London: Department for Constitutional Affairs.

Hough, M. (2012) 'Researching trust in the police and trust in justice: A UK perspective', *Policing and Society*, vol 22, no 3, pp 332–45.

Hough, M. and Sato, M. (eds) (2011) *Trust in justice: Why it is important for criminal policy, and how it can be measured: Final Report of the Euro-Justis project*, Helsinki: HEUNI.

Hough, M., Jackson, J. and Bradford, B. (2013a) 'Legitimacy, trust and compliance: an empirical test of procedural justice theory using the European Social Survey', in J. Tankebe and A. Liebling (eds) *Legitimacy and criminal justice: an international exploration*, Oxford: Oxford University Press, pp 326–52.

Hough, M., Jackson, J. and Bradford, B. (2013b) 'Trust in justice and the legitimacy of legal authorities: topline findings from a European comparative study', in S. Body-Gendrot, M. Hough, R. Levy, K. Kerezsi and S. Snacken (eds) *European Handbook of Criminology*, London: Routledge, pp 243–65.

Hough, M., Jackson, J., Bradford, B., Myhill, A. and Quinton, P. (2010) 'Procedural justice, trust and institutional legitimacy', *Policing*, vol 4, no 3, pp 203–10.

House of Commons Committee of Public Accounts (2014) *The Criminal Justice System: Fifty-ninth Report of Session 2013–14*, London: The Stationery Office.

Hoyle, C. (2012) 'Victims in the criminal process and restorative justice', in M. Maguire, R. Morgan and R. Reiner (eds.) *The Oxford Handbook of Criminology* (5th edn), Oxford: Oxford University Press, pp 398–425.

Hunter, G., Jacobson, J. and Kirby, A. (2013) *Out of the shadows: Victims' and witnesses' experiences of the Crown Court*, London: Victim Support.

Jackson, J.D. (2005) 'The effect of human rights on criminal evidentiary processes: Towards convergence, divergences or realignment?', *The Modern Law Review*, vol 68, no 5, pp 737–64.

Jackson, J., Bradford, B., Stanko, E.A., and Hohl, K. (2012) *Just authority? Trust in the police in England and Wales*, London: Routledge.

Jackson, J., Hough, M., Bradford, B. Pooler, T., Hohl, K. and Kuha, J. (2011a) *Trust in justice: Topline results from Round 5 of the European Social Survey*, London: City University.

Jackson, J., Bradford, B., Hough, M., Kuha, J., Stares, S. R., Widdop, S., Fitzgerald, R., Yordanova, M. and Galev, T. (2011b) 'Developing European Indicators of Trust in Justice', *European Journal of Criminology*, vol 8, no 4, pp 267–85.

Jacobson, J. and Hough, M. (2007) *Mitigation: The role of personal factors in sentencing*, London: Prison Reform Trust.

Jacobson, J. and Talbot, J. (2009) *Vulnerable defendants in the criminal courts: A review of provision for adults and children*, London: Prison Reform Trust.

Jacobson, J., Hunter, G. and Kirby, A. (2014a) *Supporting fair and effective treatment of witnesses: A research-based briefing from the Institute for Criminal Policy Research*, London: Institute for Criminal Policy Research.

Jacobson, J., Hunter, G. and Kirby, A. (2014b) *Supporting the effective participation of defendants in court proceedings: A research-based briefing from the Institute for Criminal Policy Research*, London: ICPR.

Judge, Lord (2013) 'The evidence of child victims: The next stage', *Bar Council Annual Law Reform Lecture*, 21 November 2013.

Judicial Studies Board (2009) *Reporting restrictions in the criminal courts*, London: Judicial Studies Board.

Judicial Studies Board (2010) *Crown Court Bench Book – Directing the jury*, London: Judicial Studies Board.

Keane, A. (2012) 'Towards a principled approach to the cross examination of vulnerable witnesses', *Criminal Law Review*, no 6, pp 407–20.

King, M. (1981) *The framework of criminal justice*, London: Croom Helm.

KM Research and Consultancy Ltd (2009) *Access to justice: A review of the existing evidence of the experiences of adults with mental health problems*, London: Ministry of Justice.

Krahenbuhl, S. (2011) 'Effective and appropriate communication with children in legal proceedings according to lawyers and intermediaries', *Child Abuse Review*, no 20, pp 407–20.

Kupchik, A. (2006) *Judging Juveniles: Prosecuting Adolescents in Adult and Juvenile Courts*, New York: New York University Press.

Lawrence, J., O'Kane, M., Rab, S. and Nakhwal, J. (2008) 'Hardcore bargains: what could plea bargaining offer in UK criminal cartel cases?' *Competition Law*, vol 7, no 1, pp 17–42.

Manikis, M. (2012) 'Navigating through an obstacle course: The complaints mechanism for victims of crime in England and Wales', *Criminology & Criminal Justice*, vol 12, no 2, pp 149–73.

Maruna, S. (2007) 'Why volunteerism "works" as prisoner reintegration: Rehabilitation for a "bulimic society"', the 18th Edith Kahn Memorial Lecture, 24 April 2007.

Mason, P., Hughes, N., with Hek, R., Spalek, B., Ward, N. and Norman, A. (2009) *Access to justice: A review of existing evidence of the experiences of minority groups based on ethnicity, identity and sexuality*, London: Ministry of Justice.

McConville, M. J., Hodgson, J., Bridges, L. and Pavlovic, A. (1994) *Standing accused: The organization and practices of criminal defence lawyers in Britain*, Oxford: Clarendon Press.

McEwan, J. (2013) 'Vulnerable defendants and the fairness of trials', *Criminal Law Review*, no 2, pp 100–13.

McIvor, G. (2009) 'Therapeutic jurisprudence and procedural justice in Scottish Drug Courts', *Criminology and Criminal Justice*, vol 9, no 1, pp 29–49.

McLeod, R., Philpin, C., Sweeting, A., Joyce, L. and Evans, R. (2010) *Court experience of adults with mental health conditions, learning disabilities and limited mental capacity*, London: Ministry of Justice Research Series 8/10.

Memon, A., Vrij, A. and Bull, R. (1998) *Psychology and law: Truthfulness, accuracy and credibility*, London: McGraw-Hill.

Mencap (2010) *Don't stand by: Ending disability hate crime together*, London: Mencap.

Miller, G. R. and Burgoon, J. K. (1982) 'Factors affecting assessments of witness credibility', in N. L. Kerr and R.M. Bray (eds) *The Psychology of the Courtroom*, New York: Academic Press, pp 169–94.

Ministry of Justice (2008) *The Witness Charter: Standards of care for witnesses in the criminal justice system*, London: Ministry of Justice.

Ministry of Justice (2010) *Her Majesty's Courts Service Court User Survey 2009–10*, London: Ministry of Justice.

Ministry of Justice (2011) *Achieving best evidence in criminal proceedings: Guidance on interviewing victims and witnesses and on using special measures*, London: Ministry of Justice.

Ministry of Justice (2012a) *Getting it right for victims and witnesses: The Government response*, Response to consultation CP3/2012 carried out by the Ministry of Justice, London: Ministry of Justice.

Ministry of Justice (2012b) *Judicial and Court Statistics 2011*, London: Ministry of Justice.

Ministry of Justice (2012c) *Swift and sure justice: The government's plans for reform of the criminal justice system*, London: Ministry of Justice.

Ministry of Justice (2012d) *Restorative justice action plan for the Criminal Justice System*, London: Ministry of Justice.

Ministry of Justice (2013a) *Code of Practice for Victims of Crime*, London: The Stationery Office.

Ministry of Justice (2013b) *Consolidated Criminal Practice Direction: Practice Direction III*, London: Ministry of Justice.

Ministry of Justice (2013c) *Making a Victim Personal Statement: A guide for all criminal justice practitioners*, London: Ministry of Justice.

Ministry of Justice (2013d) *The Witness Charter: Standards of care for witnesses in the criminal justice system*, London: Ministry of Justice.

Ministry of Justice (2014) *Criminal Justice Statistics 2013*, London: Ministry of Justice.

Mueller-Johnson, K., Dhami, M.K. and Lundrigan, S. (2013) *Effects of judicial instructions and juror characteristics on interpretations of beyond reasonable doubt*, Manuscript submitted for publication.

Mulcahy, L. (2011) *Legal architecture: Justice, due process and the place of law*, Abingdon: Routledge.

Mulcahy, L. (2013) 'Putting the defendant in their place: Why do we still use the dock in criminal proceedings?', *British Journal of Criminology*, vol 53, no 6, pp 1139–56.

National Audit Office (2009) *Her Majesty's Courts Service: Administration of the Crown Court. Report by the Comptroller and Auditor General.* London: The Stationery Office.

Padfield, N. (2008) *Text and materials on the criminal justice process*, Oxford: Oxford University Press.

Penrod, S., Loftus, E. and Winkler, J. (1982) 'The reliability of eyewitness testimony: A psychological perspective', in N. L. Kerr and R. M. Bray (eds) *The Psychology of the Courtroom*, New York: Academic Press, pp 119–68.

Peters, J.S. (2008) 'Legal performance good and bad', *Law, Culture and the Humanities*, no 4, pp 179–200.

Plotnikoff, J. and Woolfson, R. (2005) *Review of the effectiveness of specialist courts in other jurisdictions*, London: Department for Constitutional Affairs.

Plotnikoff, J. and Woolfson, R. (2009) *Measuring up? Evaluating implementation of Government commitments to young witnesses in criminal proceedings*, London: NSPCC.

Plotnikoff, J. and Woolfson, R (2014) 'Coming soon to a court room near you', *Law in Practice*, February, pp 11–12.

Policy Exchange (2009) *Lasting change or passing fad? Problem-solving justice in England and Wales*, London: Policy Exchange.

Rauxlho, R. (2012) *Plea bargaining in national and international law*, Abingdon: Routledge.

Reeves, H. and Dunn, P. (2010) 'The status of crime victims and witnesses in the twenty-first century', in A. Bottoms and J. V. Roberts (eds) *Hearing the victim: Adversarial justice, crime victims and the State*, Abingdon: Routledge, pp 46–71.

Resnik, J. (2008) 'Courts: In and out of sight, site and cite', Yale Law School Faculty Scholarship Series, Paper 680.

Roberts, J.V. and Hough, M. (2009) *Public opinion and the jury: an international literature review*, Ministry of Justice Research Series 1/09, London: Ministry of Justice.

Roberts, J.V. and Manikis, M. (2011) *Victim Personal Statements: A review of empirical research*, Oxford: Report for the Commission for Victims and Witnesses in England and Wales.

Roberts, J.V. and Manikis, M. (2013) 'Victim personal statements in England and Wales: Latest (and last) trends from the Witness and Victim Experience Survey', *Criminology & Criminal Justice*, vol 13, no 3, pp 245–61.

Rock, P. (1993) *The social world of an English Crown Court*, Oxford: Oxford University Press

Royal Commission on Criminal Justice (1993) *Report on the Royal Commission on Criminal Justice*, Chaired by Viscount Runciman, London: HMSO.

Sanchirico, C. W. (2001) 'Character evidence and the object of trial', *Columbia Law Review*, vol 101, no 6, pp 1227–311.

Scheffer, T. (2010) *Adversarial case-making: An ethnography of English Crown Court procedure*, Leiden: Brill.

Scheffer, T., Hannken-Illjes, K. and Kozin, A. (2010) *Criminal defence and procedure: Comparative ethnographies in the United Kingdom, Germany, and the United States*, Basingstoke: Palgrave Macmillan.

Scott, R.E. and Stuntz, W. J. (1992) 'Plea bargaining as contract', *Yale Law Journal*, vol 101, no 8, pp 1909–68.

Sentencing Council (2013) *Crown Court Sentencing Survey*, London: Sentencing Council.

Sentencing Guidelines Council (2007) *Reduction in sentence for a guilty plea: Definitive guideline, Revised 2007*, London: Sentencing Guidelines Council.

Shapland, J. and Hall, M. (2010) 'Victims at court: Necessary accessories or principal players at centre stage?', in A. Bottoms and J.V. Roberts (eds) *Hearing the victim: Adversarial justice, crime victims and the State*, Abingdon: Routledge, pp 163–99.

Shute, S., Hood, R. and Seemungal, F. (2005) *A fair hearing? Ethnic minorities in the criminal courts*, Cullompton: Willan.

Simon, J., Temple, N. and Tobe, R. (eds) (2013) *Architecture and justice: Judicial meanings in the public realm*, Farnham: Ashgate.

Sklansky, D.A. (2009) 'Anti-inquisitorialism', *Harvard Law Review*, vol 122, no 6, pp 1634–704.

Skogan, W.G. (2006) 'Asymmetry in the impact of encounters with police', *Policing and Society*, vol 16, no 2, pp 99–126.

Social Exclusion Unit (2002) *Reducing reoffending by ex-prisoners*, London: ODPM.

Stolle, D.P., Wexler, D.B. and Winick, B. J. (2000) *Practicing therapeutic jurisprudence law as a helping profession*, Durham, NC: Carolina Academic Press.

Sudnow, D. (1965) 'Normal crimes: Sociological features of the penal code in a public defender office', *Social Problems*, vol 12, no 3, pp 255–76.

Sunshine, J. and Tyler, T. (2003) 'The role of procedural justice and legitimacy in shaping public support for policing', *Law & Society Review*, vol 37, no 3, pp 513–48.

Sutton Trust (2009) *The educational backgrounds of leading lawyers, journalists, vice chancellors, politicians, medics and chief executives*, The Sutton Trust submission to the Milburn Commission on access to the professions.

Talbot, J. (2008) *Experiences of the criminal justice system by prisoners with learning disabilities and difficulties*, London: Prison Reform Trust.

Talbot, J. (2012) *Fair access to justice? Support for vulnerable defendants in the criminal courts*, London: Prison Reform Trust Briefing Paper.

Tonry, M. (2010) '"Rebalancing the Criminal Justice System in favour of the victim": the costly consequences of populist rhetoric', in A. Bottoms and J. V. Roberts (eds.) *Hearing the victim: Adversarial justice, crime victims*, Abingdon: Routledge, pp 72–103.

Tyler, T.R. (2001) 'Public trust and confidence in legal authorities: what do majority and minority group members want from the law and legal institutions?', *Behavioural Sciences and the Law*, no 19, pp 215–35.

Tyler, T.R. (2003) 'Procedural justice, legitimacy, and the effective rule of law', *Crime and Justice*, no 30, pp 283–357.

Tyler, T.R. (2006a) *Why people obey the law*, Princeton, NJ: Princeton University Press.

Tyler, T.R. (2006b) 'Psychological perspectives on legitimacy and legitimation', *Annual Review of Psychology*, no 57, pp 375–400.

Tyler, T. R. (2006c) 'Restorative justice and procedural justice: Dealing with rule breaking', *Journal of Social Issues*, vol 62, no 2, pp 307–26.

Tyler, T.R. (2008) 'Procedural justice and the courts', *Court Review*, no 44, pp 25–31.

Tyler T.R. (2009) 'Legitimacy and criminal justice: The benefits of self-regulation', *Ohio State Journal of Criminal Law*, no 7, pp 307–59.

Tyler, T.R. and Fagan, J. (2008) 'Legitimacy and cooperation: Why do people help the police fight crime in their communities?', *Ohio State Journal of Criminal Law*, no 6, pp 231–75.

Tyler, T. R. and Huo, Y. J. (2002) *Trust in the law: Encouraging public cooperation with the police and courts*, New York: Russell-Sage Foundation.

Victim Support (2011) *Left in the dark: Why victims of crime need to be kept informed*, London: Victim Support.

Victim Support (2013) *At risk, yet dismissed: The criminal victimisation of people with mental health problems*, London: Victim Support.

Walklate, S. (2012) 'Courting compassion: victims, policy, and the question of justice', *The Howard Journal of Criminal Justice*, vol 51, no 2, pp 109–21.

References

Wexler, D.B. (2007/8) 'Adding color to the White Paper: Time for a Robust Reciprocal Relationship Between Procedural Justice and Therapeutic Jurisprudence', *Court Review*, vol 44, nos 1/2, pp 78–81.

Wexler, D.B. (2008) *Rehabilitating lawyers: Principles of therapeutic jurisprudence for criminal law practice*, Durham, NC: Carolina Academic Press.

Winick, B.J. and Wexler, D.B. (eds) (2003) *Judging in a therapeutic key: Therapeutic jurisprudence and the courts*, Durham, NC: Carolina Academic Press.

Woolf, R.V. (2007) *Principles of problem-solving justice*, New York: Center for Court Innovation.

Zimdars, A. and Souboorah, J. (2009) *Some observations on meritocracy and the law: The profile of pupil barristers at the Bar of England and Wales 2004–2008*, London: Bar Council.

Index

Note: page numbers in italic type refer to Figures; those in bold type refer to Tables. Page numbers followed by 'n' and another number refer to Notes.

Index